Climate Governance and Urban Planning

Urban planning as a discipline is deeply integral to implementing a low-carbon future. This book fosters an understanding for how the rules-in-use that govern urban planning influence the ability to implement low-carbon development patterns. Drawing on the theoretical foundations of the climate governance and urban planning literatures, the book provides a context to understand plan implementation challenges and obstacles in metropolitan areas.

As metropolitan regions across the globe seek to reduce emissions from transportation, many levels of governments have developed ambitious climate action plans that make land use and transportation recommendations in order to reduce vehicle miles traveled. Many have recommended low-carbon development patterns which are characterized by intensified and diversified uses around rapid transit stations. However, the implementation of these recommendations is done within the context of different "rules-in-use" unique to the planning systems in each metropolitan region. The book examines the rules-in-use in three metropolitan regions of similar demographic size: the Metro Vancouver, Puget Sound, and the Stuttgart regions. By examining the implementation of low-carbon development patterns, the book focuses on growth management related questions about how to coordinate transit investments with land use decisions in metropolitan regions. The book finds that state legislation that deals with metropolitan planning and regional growth strategies can greatly aid in creating accountability among actors as well as provide a road map to navigate conflicts when implementing low-carbon development patterns.

By focusing on the rules-in-use, the book is of interest to policy-makers, planners, advocates, and researchers that wish to assess and improve the odds of implementing low-carbon development patterns in a metropolitan region.

Regions and Cities

In today's globalised, knowledge-driven and networked world, regions and cities have assumed heightened significance as the interconnected nodes of economic, social and cultural production, and as sites of new modes of economic and territorial governance and policy experimentation. This book series brings together incisive and critically engaged international and interdisciplinary research on this resurgence of regions and cities, and should be of interest to geographers, economists, sociologists, political scientists and cultural scholars, as well as to policy-makers involved in regional and urban development.

About the Regional Studies Association (RSA)

The Regions and Cities Book Series is a series of the Regional Studies Association (RSA). The RSA is a global and interdisciplinary network for regional and urban research, policy and development. The RSA is a registered not-for-profit organisation, a learned society and membership body that aims to advance regional studies and science. The RSA's publishing portfolio includes five academic journals, two book series, a Blog and an online magazine. For more information on the Regional Studies Association, visit www.regionalstudies.org

There is a **30% discount** available to RSA members on books in the ***Regions and Cities*** series, and other subject-related Taylor and Francis books and e-books including Routledge titles. To order, simply email Luke McNicholas (Luke.McNicholas@tandf.co.uk), or phone on +44 (0)20 701 77545 and declare your RSA membership. You can also visit the series page at www.routledge.com/Regions-and-Cities/book-series/RSA and use the discount code: **RSA225**

154 Climate Governance and Urban Planning
Implementing Low-Carbon Development Patterns
Deborah Heinen

For more information about this series, please visit: www.routledge.com/Regions-and-Cities/book-series/RSA

Climate Governance and Urban Planning

Implementing Low-Carbon Development Patterns

Deborah Heinen

Routledge
Taylor & Francis Group
LONDON AND NEW YORK

Designed cover image: edb3_16/Getty Images

First published 2023
by Routledge
4 Park Square, Milton Park, Abingdon, Oxon OX14 4RN

and by Routledge
605 Third Avenue, New York, NY 10158

Routledge is an imprint of the Taylor & Francis Group, an informa business

British Library Cataloguing-in-Publication Data
A catalogue record for this book is available from the British Library

Library of Congress Cataloging-in-Publication Data
Names: Heinen, Deborah, author.
Title: Climate governance and urban planning : implementing
low-carbon
development patterns / Deborah Heinen.
Description: Abingdon, Oxon ; New York, NY : Routledge, 2023. |
Series: Regions and cities | Includes bibliographical references and index.
Identifiers: LCCN 2022028266 (print) | LCCN 2022028267
(ebook) | ISBN 9781032214603 (hardback) | ISBN 9781032214627
(paperback) | ISBN 9781003268505 (ebook)
Subjects: LCSH: City planning. | Carbon dioxide mitigation—
Government policy.
Classification: LCC HT166 .H422 2023 (print) | LCC HT166
(ebook) | DDC 307.1/216—dc23/eng/20220831
LC record available at https://lccn.loc.gov/2022028266
LC ebook record available at https://lccn.loc.gov/2022028267

ISBN: 978-1-032-21460-3 (hbk)
ISBN: 978-1-032-21462-7 (pbk)
ISBN: 978-1-003-26850-5 (ebk)

DOI: 10.4324/9781003268505

Typeset in Bembo
by codeMantra

Dedicated to a Vibrant NEO

Contents

List of figures ix
List of tables xi
Author's biography xiii
Acknowledgments xv
Acronyms and abbreviations xvii

Introduction 1

1 **Promoting low-carbon development patterns** 8

2 **Facing a metropolitan governance challenge** 13

3 **Understanding rules-in-use as an implementation factor** 21
Rules-in-use as underexplored dimension of climate governance arrangements 21
The planning system rules-in-use that govern low-carbon development patterns 23

4 **Aligning plans in the Metro Vancouver region** 36
Low-carbon development patterns as a legislative priority 36
The regional growth strategy for the Metro Vancouver region 40
Transit implementation decisions: prioritizing and investing in new rapid transit 51
Local decision-making: planning for the urban centers 57

5 **Ensuring plan consistency in the Puget Sound region** 70
Encouraging low-carbon development patterns as part of growth management in Washington State 70
Regional growth strategy in the Puget Sound region 74
Transit implementation: unilateral transit decisions in a negotiated setting 89
Local decision-making: negotiating the transit alignment 94

6 Nesting plans in the Stuttgart region 105
Nested spatial planning system in Germany 106
Low-carbon development patterns – business as usual in Stuttgart under federal and state laws? 109
Spatial policies in the Stuttgart region to support low-carbon development patterns 114
Implementation of transit expansion 131
Local decision-making: increasing densities along transit corridors 137

7 Reflecting on spatial policies as rules-in-use in regional growth strategies 145

8 Integrating mechanisms support implementation 154
Types of integrating mechanisms based on empirical findings 154
The integrative nature of a Regional Growth Strategy between self-regulation and state-regulation 160
Implementing transit-connected urban centers with and without a binding Regional Growth Strategy 165
The trouble with rezoning around any rapid transit station 168

9 Implementing low-carbon development patterns 172
Findings for urban planning 173
Findings for climate governance 179
Conclusion 184

Bibliography 187
Glossary 221
Index 229

Figures

1.1	Four characteristics of low-carbon development patterns. Adopted from IPCC 2014, p. 953	9
2.1	Five dimensions of governing low-carbon development patterns	16
2.2	Levels of government involved by law in creating low-carbon development patterns	17
3.1	Illustration of assumptions about integrating mechanisms as an intermediary between the spatial vision in the RGS and the implementing entities	30
3.2	Types of policy arrangements in planning systems	32
3.3	Degrees of dependency between self-regulation and state-regulation	34
4.1	Responsibilities in land use and transportation in Metro Vancouver region	41
4.2	Regional land use designations map	46
4.3	Pictures of redevelopment near Burquitlam-Lougheed FTDA	62
4.4	Current and future transit network	63
4.5	Pictures from Surrey City Hall near Surrey Central Station	66
4.6	Pictures along the corridor for the Newton-Guildford Line	68
5.1	Responsibilities in land use and transportation in the Puget Sound region	75
5.2	Map showing regional geographies and urban centers designated by PSRC	83
5.3	Pictures of Tukwila International Boulevard Station	96
5.4	Pictures of South Center in Tukwila (designated regional growth center)	98
5.5	Pictures of neighborhoods around future transit stations in the City of Shoreline	102
6.1	Responsibilities in land use and transportation in the Stuttgart region	116
6.2	Development pattern map showing primary development corridors and community classifications for the Stuttgart region	124

6.3 Map of rapid transit in Stuttgart region showing new construction along S4 and S60 with yellow highlight 134
6.4 Pictures of redevelopment near new S-60 transit stop in Sindelfingen (Maichingen) 141
7.1 Conceptualizing spatial policies targeting various geographies 148
8.1 Types of integrating mechanisms 155
8.2 The integrative nature of a planning document based on the integrating mechanisms 161
8.3 Determining corridor alignment in metropolitan Vancouver and in the Puget Sound region 167
9.1 State agenda setting for local land use actions to foster GHG reductions 181

Tables

3.1 Analytical framework to analyze planning system along the five governance dimensions 25
7.1 Types of spatial policies to direct growth 147
7.2 Connecting spatial policies in RGS to low-carbon development patterns 149
8.1 Definition of types of integration requirements 156
8.2 Overview of integrating procedures 160

Author's biography

Deborah Heinen is a Regional Planner in the Hamburg metropolitan area (Germany). Her personal experience of having lived, studied, and worked in the USA for six years has given her unique insights into metropolitan planning in the United States. Her work experience inspired her to dive deep into the challenges of plan implementation in polycentric governance arrangements as part of her PhD work. Learning from planners in the three regions of Seattle, Vancouver, and Stuttgart about plan implementation, climate governance, and growth management has been a rewarding experience that she is excited to share in her book, *Climate Governance and Urban Planning*. Deborah received her PhD from HafenCity University Hamburg in urban and regional planning. Her expertise includes climate governance, growth management, shrinking cities, and spatial planning. When Deborah isn't working or writing about planning, she is exploring cities with her husband and two children.

Author's biography

Acknowledgments

I very much appreciate the support of Prof. Joan Fitzgerald and Kristina Abbotts and Joe Petrozzi in helping me convert my PhD thesis to this book publication.

I would like to acknowledge all the people that have supported me academically and personally while writing my PhD. I would like to offer my special thanks to Prof. Dr.-Ing. Jörg Knieling (HafenCity University) and Prof. Dr. Stefan Siedentop (ILS – Research Institute for Urban and Regional Development) for their guidance and feedback. I would also like to thank the anonymous reviewers for their thoughtful and insightful reviews of conference papers, related journal publications, and the book proposal.

My research is based in large parts on expert interviews; therefore, I would like to particularly thank all of the interviewed planners, practitioners, mayors, and professors who were so generous with their time and knowledge. The insights from the 79 qualitative interviews have helped draw clear pictures of the three planning systems. I would also like to thank my colleagues from HafenCity University for their willingness to impart their knowledge in colloquia at the institute of urban planning and regional development at HafenCity University (Hamburg, Germany). My very special thanks go to Kimberly Tatum, Alessandro Arlati, Nancy Kretschmann, Andreas Obersteg, Thomas Zimmermann, and Corinna Marquart for their continued encouragement and advice. Furthermore, I would like to express my sincere gratitude for the funding received by the German Academic Scholarship Foundation which made the research trips and participation in conferences possible.

I would also like to thank one of my best friends, Saskia Trescher, for her encouragement, ideas, and support as part of our winning team. Most importantly, I am deeply grateful for the support of my family. To my parents and grandparents: Thank you for always encouraging my curiosity. For my kids: I am very excited for you to finally see the "book" I have been talking about. But most importantly, I owe my deepest gratitude to my husband Rob for his unconditional support, constructive feedback on my writing, and his encouragement throughout this learning process.

Lastly, I am hopeful that this book helps planners and policy-makers in finding creative ways to implement low-carbon development patterns.

Acknowledgments

Acronyms and abbreviations

BC	British Columbia
CAP	Climate Action Plan
FHWA	Federal Highway Administration (United States)
FNP	Flächennutzungsplan (land use designations map)
FTDA	Frequent Transit Development Areas
GTC	Growing Transit Communities plan
GVP	Generalverkehrsplan (Statewide transportation plan)
LEP	Landesentwicklungsplan (Statewide development plan)
LRT	Light Rail Transit
MLG	Multi-level governance
MPO	Metropolitan Planning Organizations
MV	Metro Vancouver
NEPA	National Environmental Protection Act
NRC	National Research Council
NVP	Nahverkehrsplan (Countywide transportation plan)
OCP	Official Community Plan
PCG	Polycentric climate governance
PSRC	Puget Sound Regional Council
RCS	Regional Context Statement
RGS	Regional Growth Strategy
RTP	Regional Transportation Plan
RTS	Regional Transportation Strategy
SEPA	State Environmental Protection Act
SCPEA	Standard City Planning Enabling Act
SSZEA	Standard State Zoning Enabling Act
TIB	Tukwila International Boulevard
USA	United States of America
VMT	Vehicle-miles traveled
VRS	Verband Region Stuttgart

Introduction

Reducing greenhouse gas emissions in urbanized areas is one of the key challenges for planners in the 21st century. Over the past decades, planners, policy-makers, and academics have explored various approaches to reducing greenhouse gas emissions (Knieling & Leal Filho 2009; Bassett & Shandas 2010; Boswell et al. 2012). One approach includes planning for transit-connected communities in urbanized areas. Transit-connected communities are characterized by higher densities and mixed uses around rapid transit stations. By planning for transit-connected communities, planners can pave the way for residents to live a climate-friendly lifestyle. However, actually implementing transit-connected communities presents a metropolitan governance challenge since people tend to live and work in different communities. To ensure a functioning transit system, multiple levels of government responsible for land use and transit decisions must continuously cooperate and collaborate. This book unfolds this governance challenge and provides insights for practitioners and policy-makers interested in facilitating a low-carbon future.

Implementing low-carbon development patterns requires actions taken in the land use sector to spatially align with actions taken in the transportation sector. Broadly speaking, new investment in rapid transit lines (*S- und U-Bahn*) should ideally be directed to locations that are suitable for higher densities. If they are not, a rapid transit station might be underutilized (low ridership) or a densely populated area might be car reliant. In some cities, we can observe transit investments dormantly waiting for investors to build mixed-use developments while in other cities, densely populated and used areas are eagerly waiting to be connected to rapid transit. But when the objective is to reduce emissions and accumulate benefits from denser development around a transit stop, there is a heightened need for integrated decision-making between actors at multiple levels of government. To achieve emission reductions from investments in transit, it is crucial to ensure that land uses and transit investment support one another.

Rapid transit systems often connect residents living in one city to jobs and destinations in another city; all within the same urbanized area. If there is a spatial mismatch between transit investment and new development, the performance of the transit system can be jeopardized. Some metropolitan

DOI: 10.4324/9781003268505-1

regions already have phenomenal transit systems with desirable housing, recreation, jobs and good schools within a ½ mile radius of rapid transit stations. In a global market for a talented workforce, these metropolitan regions are able to attract young professionals. Other metropolitan regions lag behind as they work through the challenges of coordinating land use and transportation decision-making between multiple levels of government. Ensuring that housing, jobs, retail, and services are located in close proximity to rapid transit access is a complex governance challenge that requires coordinated efforts among multiple governmental agencies and market actors.

When I began this research journey, my initial goal was to better understand how to alleviate this type of spatial mismatch and to ensure that transit investment and land use decisions are made jointly and cooperatively. Frequently, this discussion is framed as a chicken and egg problem: what comes first – transit investment or changes to land use. From my research, I would argue that the initial step is cooperation and coordination between local governments at a regional scale which results in the ability to envision transit-oriented growth for the urbanized area. Implementing low-carbon development patterns requires the concerted effort of many actors in the urbanized area, including millions of dollars in transit investments and changes to zoning that encourage context-sensitive higher densities. While some researchers point to local zoning powers for implementation of low-carbon development patterns (Boswell et al. 2012; McCarney 2013), I found that transit systems actually serve local land uses better if there is a Regional Growth Strategy that was prepared in very close coordination with local governments at the regional level.

The term "regional level" refers to the semi-governmental layer between local governments (cities and counties) and senior-level governments (state and federal). The regional level can have a footprint ranging from 3 to more than 20 counties and can include hundreds of local governments. At the regional level, semi-governmental entities have a variety of responsibilities – some specialize in transit, others are responsible for water and sewers, while others are focused on comprehensive planning. The different responsibilities and footprint of the regional level make metropolitan governance a diverse field of study with many organizational models. The three regions presented in Chapters 4 to 6 demonstrate the wide variety of metropolitan governance of low-carbon development patterns.

To my surprise, I found that negotiations between local governments and transit providers over the location of a new rapid transit station can benefit from having a regional planning document, such as a Regional Growth Strategy (RGS), in place. An RGS can create ground rules for negotiations between a transit provider and a municipality over the alignment of a rapid transit project. In fact, having a binding RGS can strengthened the positions of the local governments to ensure that transit providers connected locally preferred sites with rapid transit, rather than picking other locations for cost reasons. However, an RGS can only have these positive impacts if supported as a planning document within the state planning enabling legislation.

I spoke to almost 80 planners in 3 metropolitan regions (all in federally organized countries) to better understand how the rules-in-use in a planning system shape the implementation of low-carbon development patterns. The rules-in-use as a factor in climate governance arrangements has not been explored thoroughly (Thiel 2017; Setzer & Nachmany 2018). This book seeks to remedy that. With its in-depth study of the rules-in-use for three planning systems, the book offers relevant policy recommendations that can propel climate actions in metropolitan regions. Its multi-level and polycentric climate governance perspective provides relevant recommendations for policy-makers and planning practitioners across all levels of government.

While reading, keep in mind that creating low-carbon development patterns and transit-connected communities is a particular spatial vision for an urbanized area that can only be achieved through a political process. Also keep in mind that there is an ongoing debate as to the extent of actual reductions in GHG emissions achievable from implementing low-carbon development patterns. Regions that have historically been characterized by low-density and car-reliant environments have estimated higher reductions than already densely populated areas. Nevertheless, by examining the integration of decision-making across multiple levels and sectors of government, this book offers insights into a "black box" of land use and transportation governance which mediates between policy goals in climate action plans (CAPs) and observable outcomes in the development patterns of urbanized areas.

This book examines actors, plans, and planning legislation in three different metropolitan areas.

The three areas I explore in the book are the metropolitan regions of Vancouver (Province of British Columbia, Canada), Stuttgart (Baden-Württemberg, Germany), and Seattle (Washington State, USA). In all three, decision-makers at multiple levels of government are generally supportive of climate actions and are involved in land use and transportation questions. The three regions are similar in population, between 2.5 and 5 million residents, with about 600,000 in the core city. Alongside these similarities are ample differences in each region's governance arrangements for implementing low-carbon development patterns.

Metropolitan areas in federally organized countries are ideal for revealing how rules-in-use at multiple levels of government interact and influence the implementation of low-carbon development patterns. Each metropolitan area presents different cultural values about power sharing across multiple levels of government. All three metropolitan areas are rooted in deep respect for local autonomy but with different notions about the role of senior-level governments, which include federal and state levels. In between the local and senior level, each metropolitan area has a regional level with a myriad of organizations that are responsible for planning and services in the urbanized areas.

The three regions vary in the role played by their respective regional planning bodies. Regional planning organizations come in all forms and shapes. They are often associations of local governments who make joint decisions through a board of directors. However, there is a wide variety in terms of representation of local governments, issues, and policy sectors covered as well as granted authority of the regional organizations. The organizations are usually hybrids that formed when the state devolved powers or local governments delegated responsibilities. I was astonished how state legal frameworks that pertain to the regional level shape the ability of regional organizations to foster low-carbon development patterns.

My analysis of the three metropolitan areas suggests that a regional planning organization can assume a vital coordination role by bringing together land use and transportation planning. This book illustrates the variety of responsibilities that go into creating low-carbon development patterns and highlights the intricacies of power struggles between levels of government over responsibilities. A central factor is, obviously, the constitutional rights of different levels of government as well as the constitutional approach to property rights. Each of these regions, all in Western federally organized countries, has high regard for local zoning powers and private property rights, yet over the years legal interpretations and cultural values have led to different ideas of what can be done at the regional level.

In fact, a challenge in writing this book has been conveying the differences in cultural understandings and rationales for planning system structures in a neutral and objective manner. I tried carefully to avoid labels and paid attention to developing a more generalized theoretical language that sees each planning system expressed through a set of variables (see Chapter 2 for comparative framework). A planning system encompasses the planning enabling legislation, the organizations involved in planning, the types of planning documents, procedures and policies that impact development patterns in a given area, and the cultural values explaining the configurations of the planning systems.

Anchored by the planning enabling legislation, regional planning organization can have very different responsibilities, prepare different types of plans, and have different "relationships" with local governments. A similarity across the three regions is that the regional planning organizations are authorized to engage in growth management and to create an RGS. Furthermore, the three regions share a spatial vision to direct new growth (jobs, housing, and retail) to transit-accessible locations (see Chapter 7). This spatial vision is underwritten by different spatial policies that actively shape the development patterns in the three regions. Spatial policies are more general than land use designations or zoning policies. Spatial policies guide local decisions on permitting new development and the location of public investments. Spatial policies evolve within the context of unique cultural and political preferences. Frequently, spatial policies are authorized within "Planning Enabling Legislation" in growth-managing states in the United States and in European Union countries that do spatial planning. Chapters 4 through 7 present multiple examples of spatial policies.

For the three regions, I found that spatial policies in the RGS were similar in the sense that they were promoting transit-connected communities in an attempt to reduce emissions from transportation (see Chapter 7 for details on types of spatial policies). Yet, I found that the spatial policies were differently legally applicable when transit providers were negotiating with municipalities over the location of new rapid transit stops. These bilateral negotiations were clearly influenced by the rules-in-use in the planning system. As I was trying to find terminology for the particular set of rules-in-use that differed between the regions, I started creating a typology of integrating mechanisms (see Chapter 8). Integrating mechanisms create interdependencies between the various decision-makers in urbanized areas and structure interactions by defining procedures for coordination. Spatial policies can have a bearing on decisions by local and transit decision-makers if they are supported by integrating mechanisms that hold implementing entities accountable to the agreed-upon spatial policies. One might think that integrating mechanisms are based on command-and-control but I learned from studying the regions that there are a wide variety of integrating mechanisms that do not simply rely on command-and-control. Chapter 8 will demonstrate the nuances in how integrating mechanisms can be applied to ensure that local interests are reflected at the regional scale.

Each of the regional chapters begins with a discussion of the relevance of low-carbon development patterns within the statewide approach to climate mitigation. I then briefly describe the planning system for each region, the responsibilities of various levels of government, and the integrating mechanisms that connect decisions across levels and sectors of government. Next, I discuss the regional and county spatial policies designed to foster low-carbon development patterns. I conclude by considering the extent to which the regional spatial policies shape transit and local decisions, paying particular attention to the redevelopment efforts around two transit stops for each region. Each regional chapter presents a systematic review of how climate policy objectives are translated into action through decisions at multiple levels of government.

The Metro Vancouver region is located in the Province of British Columbia in the Western part of Canada (Chapter 4). The provincial planning legislation (Local Government Act) is conducive to integrated decision-making between municipalities, the transit provider TransLink and the regional planning organization Metro Vancouver. The RGS serves as the primary coordinating mechanisms on broad development patterns in the region. Within the RGS fostering low-carbon development patterns is a primary objective. Several conditions foster a focus on creating low-carbon development patterns within metropolitan Vancouver. The provincial government clearly supports climate actions and incentivizes local governments to pursue changes in land use patterns as part of their climate agendas. Furthermore, the integrating mechanisms around the RGS create a framework for negotiations of local governments at the regional level. The experts I interviewed agreed that provincial legislation has created a system in which the 21 local governments can jointly influence regional development patterns within the urbanized area. Throughout the Vancouver region, one can observe new high-rise residential towers with retail on the ground floors within a ¼ mile radius of new transit stations.

The Stuttgart region is located in the state (*Bundesland*) of Baden-Württemberg in the southwest corner of Germany (Chapter 5). By federal and state laws, planning is intentionally integrated across levels and sectors of government. The RGS (*Regionalplan*) and affiliated integrating mechanisms are at the center of coordinating land use and infrastructure decisions to direct growth. State-wide and regional spatial policies direct growth to communities along priority development corridors which are serviced by transit. The planning system and spatial policies have been in place for decades and have not seen much change due to climate considerations. Throughout the region, one can observe that communities along the transit lines are growing more than other communities; however, growth is not consistently occurring adjacent to the transit stops.

The Puget Sound region derives its name from an inlet that connects the City of Seattle to the Pacific Ocean. Located in Washington State, the Puget Sound region is one of the few regions within the United States that is authorized by state legislation to engage in locally-organized and regionally-coordinated growth management. It's an example that shows that actions at the regional level can also evolve from local efforts with only rudimentary support by state legislation. Hence, the Puget Sound region represents a self-regulated approach between counties and local governments to ensure integrated decision-making on questions of land use and transportation. The RGS is established as a guiding framework for local, county, and transit decisions. The experts I interviewed did not think that the RGS played a vital role during the negotiation of the preferred alignment of the rapid transit corridor between the municipality and the transit provider. Low-carbon development patterns are a part of the regional discourse and are included, to varying degrees, in local, county, and regional agendas. Throughout the Puget Sound region, one can observe that the neighborhoods around new transit stations see mixed results – some have changes to adjacent land uses while others do not.

The climate discourse has been embroiled in a debate as to which level of government might be most suitable to take climate actions. In my research I find that besides the responsibilities at various governmental scales, the integrating mechanisms actually have a crucial role in fostering implementation. In all three locations, spatial policies in the RGS have different implications for local decisions and transit decisions, because of the different integrating mechanisms. When there is a state law that creates clear procedures to integrate decisions and resolve conflicts, then low-carbon development patterns are more likely to be invested in, authorized through zoning changes and ultimately build. Decisions over the location of new growth are always conflict-laden in urbanized areas. The Stuttgart and Vancouver chapters offer examples on how state legislation can support urbanized areas in resolving these conflicts and creating win-win-situations. While it is always tempting to talk about bottom-up or top-down, I challenge the reader to take a step back and start from the values and assumptions within each culture. While the planning systems in Vancouver and Stuttgart might appear to be bottom-up at first glance, they actually serve to empower local governments.

1 Promoting low-carbon development patterns

Creating low-carbon development patterns is one of many potential climate mitigation strategies. This chapter introduces low-carbon development patterns as a set of climate actions that is implemented within (urban) planning as a discipline. The chapter starts with a brief overview of the types and content of climate action plans (CAPs) in general, followed by a debate over recommended land use and transportation actions in CAPs. These land use and transportation climate actions are subsequently summarized as low-carbon development patterns. Low-carbon development patterns are characterized by increased densities and a diversity of uses in walkable, bikeable, and transit-accessible locations. While climate researchers have been promoting low-carbon development patterns such as transit-connected urban centers, they have long been a topic of smart growth and spatial planning advocates. Urban planners are still debating whether increased densities actually result in reduced vehicle miles traveled (and thus reduced transportation emissions). I review this discussion below and conclude that these debates underscore the need to ensure land use actions align with transit investments. Ensuring that multiple actions are integrated is a central challenge for implementing low-carbon development patterns.

CAPs are guiding strategies that recommend actions in several policy sectors to reduce carbon emissions and adapt to climate change (Boswell et al. 2012, p. 6). Governmental entities interested in climate action oftentimes have a corporate climate mitigation strategy which may include emissions reduction goals for government-owned facilities. Frequently, these government actions are expanded to a community-wide action plan in which governments leverage their regulatory and financial powers (e.g. incentive programs) to encourage emissions savings within the community (Wheeler 2008; Bassett & Shandas 2010, p. 436; Hughes 2016, p. 3). CAPs can range from very general strategy documents to very specific implementation strategies (Boswell et al. 2012). Some governments include climate actions in sustainability, green, or energy plans or integrate them directly into comprehensive land use plans (Boswell et al. 2012, pp. 9 and 195).

CAPs usually contain an emissions inventory identifying key sectors for emissions savings, emissions reduction targets, and policy recommendations

DOI: 10.4324/9781003268505-2

for various sectors (Wheeler 2008). The inventory and targets set the context for policy recommendations, which vary in details such as actors, required resources, possible regulatory changes, financial incentives and programs, evaluation indicators, and timelines (Wheeler 2008, p. 481; Bassett & Shandas 2010, p. 442; Boswell et al. 2012). The first generation of CAPs in the 1990s was technical documents prepared by consultants and/or universities for a government (Bassett & Shandas 2010). The more recent CAPs have extensive stakeholder involvement and are frequently created with the help of outside-of-government stakeholders (Boswell et al. 2012).

The recommendations in CAPs tend to focus on energy supply and efficiency, buildings, transportation, land use, and waste (Wheeler 2009; DIFU 2011; Boswell et al. 2012; Reckien et al. 2013; Nationale Klimaschutzinitiative 2015; Verbücheln & Dähner 2016). Each of these sectors has varying potential for emissions savings depending on the region. For instance, transportation emissions from single-occupancy vehicles account for between 20% and 50% of emissions in the cities of Seattle, Vancouver, and Stuttgart (Vancouver CAP 2015, pp. 9 and 21; Masterplan 100% 2017, p. 16; SEA-CAP 2018, p. 5; see also IPCC 2014, p. 950). The transportation emissions can partly be reduced through fuel efficiency and technology innovations. However, there are underpinning land development patterns that create demand for transportation (Boswell et al. 2012, p. 22). Accordingly, many CAPs contain recommendations for land use in addition to transportation.

Four characteristics of development patterns[1] are closely correlated with GHG emissions from transportation: density, mix of land uses, connectivity, and accessibility (IPCC 2014, p. 953, see Figure 1.1). The first three influence

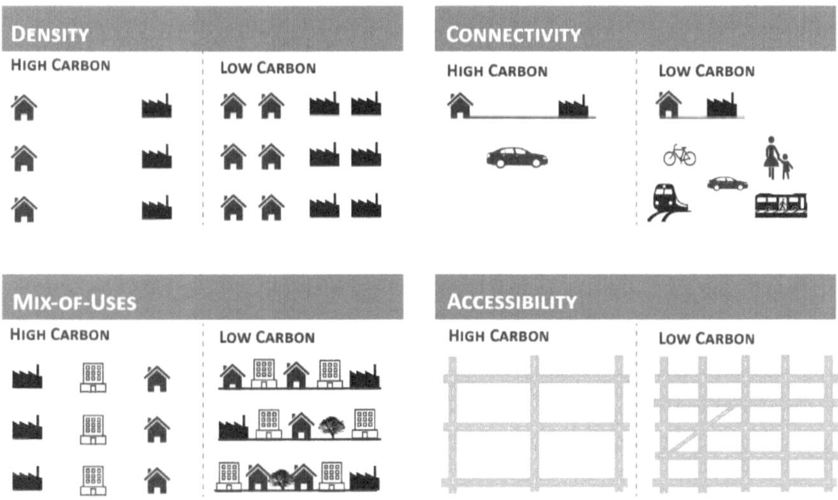

Figure 1.1 Four characteristics of low-carbon development patterns. Adopted from IPCC 2014, p. 953.

the proximity of such uses as housing, jobs, retail, and recreation. Accessibility encompasses the modal choices available to reach various destinations.

Density measures the "number of people, households or jobs per unit of land area" (Nelson 2017, p. 36). Density describes the intensity of a particular use in an area, including how many people live or work in a neighborhood. Diversity refers to the **land use mix** and job-housing balance in an area (Ewing & Cervero 2017, p. 20). It includes the mix-of-uses within an area including office, retail, and residential (single family, townhomes, apartments) as well as the use of outdoor spaces for parks, plazas, or parking. **Connectivity** (design) means the configuration of the street network, including the intersection and street density (Ewing & Cervero 2017, p. 20). The design of the street network impacts, for instance, walkability. The further apart the uses are within a region, the more relevant **accessibility** by different modes becomes. Therefore, destination accessibility refers to the accessibility of job agglomerations by car and transit within an urbanized area (Ewing & Cervero 2017, p. 20). The distance to transit measures how far away a transit stop is from a home – the nearer the stop, the more convenient the transit access (Nelson 2017, p. 36).

These four characteristics shape the individual modal choices for people living in urban areas. The individual choices of where to work, where to live, and the preferred mode of transportation are all somewhat impacted by the available infrastructure as well as housing and building stock in a region, hence by the existing development patterns. For instance, living close to work with convenient transit access might simply not be an option in a sprawling low-density region. While in higher-density mixed-use areas that connect relevant destinations by transit, residents have multiple options for how to get to and from work (car, transit, bike, scooter, walking, etc.). Therefore, from a climate perspective, desirable development patterns are characterized by pockets of higher densities with a connecting street grid and a mix of uses that are accessible by multiple modes of transportation. Throughout the book, this type of development is also referred to as low-carbon development patterns.

Low-carbon development patterns are not new to planners as these concepts have engaged researchers in smart growth, sustainability, comprehensive planning, and spatial planning in North America and Europe (Campbel 2006, p. 204; Mills 2006; Bassett & Shandas 2010, p. 441). Keywords such as smart growth, balanced growth, compact and complete communities, new urbanism, transit-oriented development are all associated with low-carbon development patterns. Besides emissions savings, compact development has other policy objectives, including reducing pedestrian and motor vehicle fatalities, increasing physical activity and reducing obesity, reducing household transportation costs, decreasing crime, and creating a sense of community (Ewing & Cervero 2017, p. 21).

Planning practitioners in metropolitan regions have been responsive to calls to include low-carbon development patterns in their efforts. In fact, some metropolitan regions have highlighted how the development patterns in their Regional Growth Strategy support a reduction in VMT and thus in emissions. This includes the metropolitan regions of Vancouver, Stuttgart, and Seattle. Within their Regional Growth Strategies, they are pursuing a spatial vision of "compact and complete communities along transit-corridors" (e.g. Surrey CAP 2013, pp. 40 and 44; SEA-CAP 2013, p. 28f; IPCC 2014, p. 959; KC-SCAP 2015, pp. 42 and 44; Vancouver CAP 2015, p. 2). This spatial vision promotes a densification and mix-of-uses at transit stop locations. While all three regions have pursued these low-carbon development patterns to achieve a variety of policy objectives, they highlight the emissions savings potential of creating compact and complete communities along transit corridors.

Since low-carbon development patterns are part of an ongoing planning debate, there are also critiques of compact and complete communities. Some in the field question the extent to which denser development actually reduces vehicle miles traveled and thus how much transportation emissions are actually lowered (Crane & Landis 2010; Bauer et al. 2013; Stevens 2017). Other factors to explain levels of fuel consumption include household size, personal wealth, price of gasoline, economic growth, and technology changes (Bauer et al. 2013, p. 2; Knaap et al. 2017, p. 34). Yet, there is a lively debate over the statistical approaches and validity of findings (Handy 2017). A common critique of studies that question the relationship of density and VMT is that they focus exclusively on density while ignoring mix-of-uses, accessibility, and connectivity (Handy 2017, p. 26).

Numerous studies have concluded that vehicle miles traveled are reduced if higher densities are complemented by a mix of uses (including retail, office, housing, open spaces) along with transit investments in the locations of higher activity (Mills 2006, p. 73; Banister & Anable 2009; Pizarro 2009; Guth et al. 2010; DIFU 2011; Boswell et al. 2012; Romero-Lankao 2012; Davoudi 2013, p. 161; IPCC 2014, p. 953; SKKK 2014). These studies underscore the importance of integrated and aligned efforts between land use and transportation decisions. Increased densities only achieve reduced emissions if complementary transit investment (access to regional job market) and a mix of uses (walkable access to retail, schools, libraries, parks, etc.) occur.

The debate on the influence of land use on transportation is ideologically charged and value-laden, with evidence supporting both viewpoints (Marzoughi & Vanderburg 2010, p. 90). As urban transportation expert Susan Handy notes, rather than more studies trying to prove or disprove the connection between development patterns and transportation, we need more in-depth case studies that point to successful compact development efforts and how they were achieved.

Achieving transit-connected communities is a metropolitan governance challenge as local, county, regional, and state actors are involved in shaping development patterns. In urbanized areas different entities are responsible for funding, planning, building, and operating transit. Additionally, land use decisions are shaped by various levels of government. While occasionally there are calls for government consolidation to reduce the complexity, the three city chapters show how well-written planning enabling legislation can foster integrated decision-making in multi-agency settings. The theoretical foundation for this discussion comes from governance researchers dealing with questions in multi-agency settings in which decisions need to be integrated towards a common goal (Wheeler 2009; Boswell et al. 2012; Brunnengräber 2013; Fröhlich & Knieling 2013; IPCC 2014; Hughes 2016, p. 8). Thus, the subsequent chapter takes on a governance perspective to examine how multiple actors can coordinate their actions to implement low-carbon development patterns.

Note

1 Development patterns are understood in the sense of general land use patterns or urban form. The IPCC (2014) report defines urban form and structure "as the patterns and spatial arrangements of land use, transportation systems, and urban design elements, including the physical urban extent, layout of streets and buildings, as well as the internal configuration of settlements (Lynch 1981; Handy 1996)" (IPCC 2014, p. 949). Development patterns refer to any uses of land within the territory of a country, including agricultural uses, transportation uses, and urban uses.

2 Facing a metropolitan governance challenge

Many people living in an urbanized area live in one city and work in another within the same metropolitan region. This chapter places low-carbon development patterns within the context of metropolitan governance and planning: Particularly in urbanized areas, administrative boundaries do not align with commuting patterns. As people live and work in different communities, one of the challenges of reducing transportation emissions is ensuring that regional transportation and local land use decisions align. This chapter examines the various government actors involved in implementing low-carbon development patterns.

An urbanized area includes several, or in some cases, hundreds of local governments that comprise one contiguous urban land cover (Mills 2007, p. 1849). This means anyone analyzing the implementation of low-carbon development patterns must include the metropolitan regional level. I use the term metropolitan region[1] in this book to mean the urbanized and adjacent rural areas governed by a unit of government responsible for coordinating between local actors (community and county) and state actors. The subsequent chapters briefly review the climate governance debate about which is the "appropriate" level of government to foster climate actions, concluding that there is a need for integrated actions across sectors and levels of government which can be facilitated by a regional planning organization.

There is conflicting evidence of the relevance of the state and local levels of government for promoting climate actions (Wheeler 2008; Dale et al. 2018; Heinen, Arlati & Knieling 2021). While some researchers promote the "cities as savior" narrative, others stress the importance of state-level actions (Van der Heijden 2019). Furthermore, research on multi-level and polycentric governance has shown the need for coordination across levels and sectors of government (Bulkeley & Betsill 2005; Brunnengräber 2013; Fröhlich & Knieling 2013; IPCC 2014; Van der Heijden 2019). Climate governance researchers globally are drawing on a wide variety of empirical evidence that are shaped by very different constitutional approaches to power sharing between different levels and sectors of government.

A common view is that since cities are responsible for the majority of emissions, they are or should be at the forefront of action on climate change

DOI: 10.4324/9781003268505-3

(Reckien et al. 2014, p. 332; Hughes 2016, p. 3; Van der Heijden 2019, p. 2). Global efforts, such as the United Nations Framework Convention on Climate Change, recognize the leadership role of local governments (Hughes 2016, p. 2). Furthermore, empirical evidence from the United States suggests that the local level is in a unique position to take action in many sectors (Wheeler 2008; Bassett & Shandas 2010; Boswell et al. 2012; Fitzgerald 2020). Authors studying Canada and Europe also echo the emphasis on local powers (Van Staden & Musco 2010, p. 5; Dale et al. 2018, p. 352).

Critics argue that the role of cities in climate action may be overemphasized in a "cities as savior" narrative that points to a few leading cities and results in overestimating the capacity or political will of most cities around the globe (Van der Heijden 2019; Fitzgerald 2020). It is misguided to apply experiments in large and highly active cities in the Global North to other cities (Van der Heijden 2018b, 2019). Actions at the local level are shaped by the regulatory and financial powers of higher levels of government (Hughes 2016, p. 13; Setzer & Nachmany 2018). In some regions, senior-level governments intentionally hinder and sabotage local abilities to pursue progressive agendas, while in other places senior-level governments actively incentivize local climate actions and create regulatory frameworks that propel local actions. But cities cannot do it alone – they need the support of higher levels of government to implement low-carbon development patterns (van Staden & Musco 2010; Hughes 2016; Setzer & Nachmany 2018; Fitzgerald 2020).

Senior-level governments typically take one of these five approaches: (1) senior levels are completely uninvolved in climate actions, (2) senior levels pursue climate actions within areas of their direct realm of influence (corporate climate actions), (3) senior levels leverage their regulatory and financial powers to engage lower levels of government in climate actions, (4) senior levels revise the power structures centralizing or devolving authority to local levels (rescaling), or (5) senior levels are opposed to climate actions and intentionally limit local actions. The empirically observable differences lead to a myriad of conclusions on the relevance of senior-level actions.

Rather than identifying the "correct" scale of climate action, we need a more nuanced analytical framework for cross-country comparative research on climate governance that is rooted in understanding of the historical, political, and economic contexts of each country (Heinen et al. 2021).

Any climate action faces the initial challenge of ensuring that climate concerns are implemented in other policy sectors (Boswell et al. 2012, p. 183; Fröhlich & Knieling 2013, p. 17). For low-carbon development patterns this involves the land use and transportation governance sectors. As discussed in Chapter 1, if not all components of transit-connected centers are implemented, there may be adverse effects such as traffic congestion (if transit investment is lacking behind land-use changes) or low-transit ridership (if land use changes lack behind transit investments). Thus, there is a heightened need for integrated decision-making by multiple actors at various levels and in various sectors of government within metropolitan regions. The case studies will provide detailed accounts on how many actors are actually involved in implementation.

This section takes a step back from the particularities in various countries to reflect theoretically on how empirically observable climate governance arrangements might diverge. Employing a multi-level and polycentric governance perspective allows us to understand the implementation of low-carbon development patterns from a theoretical viewpoint and is able to identify systematic differences across empirically observable climate governance arrangements. Polycentric and multi-level governance perspectives oscillate along five dimensions within which empirically observable governance arrangements can diverge (Heinen et al. 2021):

A A particular **issue** (interdependent policy problem/collective action problem) that needs resolving.
B **Decision-makers** and their statutory responsibilities that contribute to solving a particular issue.
C The decision-making centers may be formally independent or formally interdependent in their decision-making. Decision-making centers may choose to interrelate decisions in a self-regulated effort (**degree of dependencies** in decision-making).
D The decision-makers may **interact** in a variety of different ways including competition, conflict, conflict resolution, and cooperation (type of interaction).
E The **rules-in-use** shape the other four governance dimensions (issue, the statutory responsibilities, the degree of dependency, and the types of interactions). The rules-in-use include legislative rules, self-regulation, and cultural rules.

At the foundation of the analysis of any governance arrangement is the definition of the interdependent policy problem that needs resolving (Dimension A). Creating low-carbon development patterns is one such interdependent policy problem which involves integrated transportation and land use decision-making. Peters and Hoornbeek (2007) highlight how difficult it is to resolve interdependent policy problems because of, for instance, competition among various agencies for limited resources, selection of the lowest common denominator solution (joint-decision trap), and disagreements over framing of the problem (p. 98f.). In fact, a primary challenge is ensuring that all relevant decision-making centers pursue a common goal. Within this context, spatial policies can serve as common goals if supported by multiple actors that are part of the governance arrangement.

Employing a multi-level and polycentric governance perspective allows me to analyze a multitude of governmental actors that are or may be involved at various levels of government in implementing low-carbon development patterns (Dimension B). Mayntz (2008) describes this as the constitutionally preserved power structures within a political system (p. 48). Rather

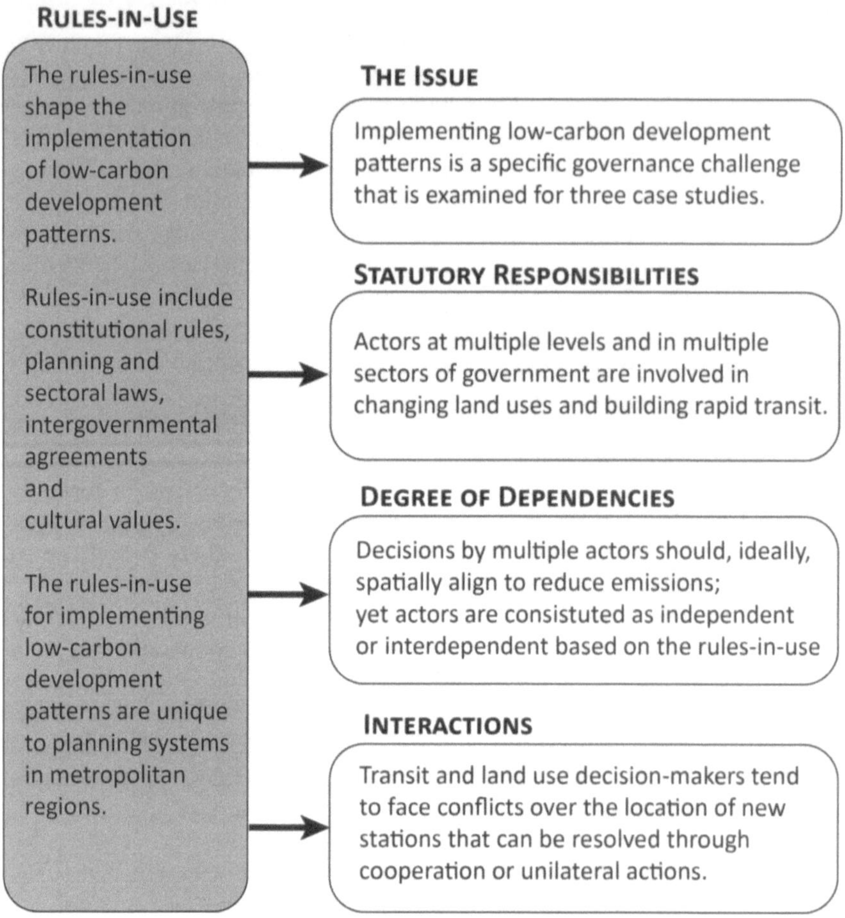

Figure 2.1 Five dimensions of governing low-carbon development patterns.

than asking what level of government should implement climate action, Dimension B calls attention to the statutory responsibilities distributed across levels of government in different countries.

As responsibilities are distributed differently, so are power relationships. Dimension C draws attention to the degree of dependencies in decision-making. Decision-makers may be independent or interdependent in their decisions based on the rules-in-use. Some governance researchers are interested in studying decision-making centers that have independent and autonomous actors, while others focus on decision-makers that are interdependent by law. The region chapters will demonstrate how state laws can create interdependencies among decision-makers through integrating mechanisms.

Generally speaking, decision-makers can interact (Dimension D) in many different ways to govern an issue. They may cooperate to manage interdependencies but frequently they compete, face conflicts, resolve conflicts and/or enter into contracts (Ostrom 2010a; Cole 2015; Carlisle & Gruby 2017; Dorsch & Flachsland 2017; Marquardt 2017; Thiel 2017; Jordan et al. 2018a, b). The rules-in-use can have a profound impact on interactions. For instance, collaboration may occur because actors are required by law to coordinate on a particular issue. However, decision-makers may also voluntarily choose to coordinate in order to reach a collective goal. A legislator might anticipate conflicts across levels of government and create legislation for resolving such conflicts.

Regarding Dimension E, the rules-in-use are fundamental to shaping the other four dimensions. The rules-in-use address who the decision-makers are, how interdependent their decisions are, and how they interact. These rules-in-use can be a set of senior-level government laws, but they can also be part of a self-regulated effort by the actors. Furthermore, rules-in-use may include cultural values that shape the dimensions of governance arrangements. The particular rules-in-use relevant for implementing low-carbon development patterns will be discussed in Chapter 3. The analytical framework presented in Figure 2.1 is intended to help understand the conditions of governance arrangement of low-carbon development patterns.

Identifying the relevant actors in any region requires a clear understanding of the statutory responsibilities involved in creating low-carbon development patterns. Figure 2.2 shows the particular decisions in land use and transportation governance needed to implement low-carbon development patterns. Depending on a country's planning system, various governmental entities may be responsible for these decisions. The governmental entities responsible for zoning must be involved in connecting urban centers with transit. Furthermore, the governmental entity responsible for funding

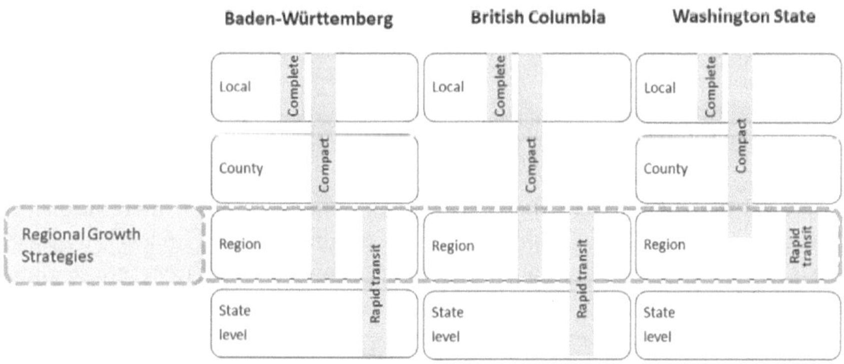

Figure 2.2 Levels of government involved by law in creating low-carbon development patterns.

Source: Own illustration.

transit needs to authorize investment into transit projects that connect locations of higher job and population densities. The region chapters will show that the metropolitan level can play a central role in ensuring that zoning decisions align with transit investments within a growth management context. Subsequently, each decision area will be described in more detail.

Building new rapid transit involves decisions at multiple levels of government, including to secure funding, prioritize corridors and engineer the specifics: Someone needs to provide the funding for new rapid transit, someone else needs to prioritize a specific corridor to receive the investment (e.g. do we connect to the north of the core city or to the south), someone else needs to decide on the specific route (including the location of stations – meaning the particular land parcels touched and covered by the route). Technology also plays a role but I do not explore it further as each of the metropolitan regions has light rail or rapid transit corridors. Additionally, the land use decisions need to align.

To ensure that transit stops are served by higher densities and mix of uses, several levels of government might play a role: Someone needs to permit higher density and allow a greater mix of uses around a transit station. The level of government that makes these types of land use decisions can set the parameters for, among other things, lot size, floor area ratios, building height, permitted density, permitted uses, and permitted housing types (duplex, triplex, cottages, apartment buildings). Through rezoning, a government sends a clear signal to the market (real estate developers) that an area can be redeveloped at higher intensity and mix of uses. One consultant in the Seattle region indicated that developers prefer when the municipality proactively rezones land because it saves time and costs spent applying for zoning amendments which often face neighborhood opposition.

While zoning is one aspect of land use decisions, there is another type of land use decision that does not get as much attention: namely, regional growth management which involves to direct new housing and job growth to specific locations within an urbanized area. Intentionally directing growth within metropolitan areas is a value-laden and highly polarized topic in North America. Traditionally, many metropolitan areas across the United States have preferred market-led development. In market-led dispersal, real estate developers determine the location of new growth based on business cases. Frequently, the result of **market-led expansion** is sprawl since greenfield development tends to be cheaper (cheap land, no demolition or cleanup needed) than redevelopment within the urbanized area (Echenique et al. 2012). Market-led dispersal proposes minimal regulatory constraints on available land within an urbanized area in order to ensure competitively priced land (see e.g. Echenique et al. 2012, p. 125).

In contrast, **growth management** is about governmental entities deliberately intervening in land markets by directing growth to prioritized locations of various sizes. In some regions, local governments jointly prepare a Regional Growth Strategy to discuss suitable locations for employment and population growths. Negotiating win-win situations between the many local interests is a core expertise of regional planning organizations. Content in Regional Growth Strategies includes policies about economic development, housing development, natural areas and parks, and infrastructure investments. Usually contentious issues such as projections of future population growth for communities or priority locations for regional-scale economic development are discussed and negotiated. Some Regional Growth Strategies might also include policies and questions pertaining to growth boundaries (see Chapter 7). Particularly growth boundaries represent a contentious issue within the United States but frequently any type of intervention is frowned upon in market-led planning systems.

Proponents of market-led development have frequently critiqued compact development for potential increases in property prices, reduced dwelling space per person, insufficient affordable housing, and exacerbated congestion within cities (Echenique et al. 2012, p. 122; for a discussion, see Nelson et al. 2004). Practitioners have contested these concerns by arguing that affordability is more a challenge of permitting enough density within the urbanized area rather than an issue of limiting land supply in a region. Furthermore, the increased congestion may point to the lack of transit investment to support the density increases. The critique of growth managements seems to also point to the challenge of getting all decision-making centers to move in the same direction. If a senior-level government limits land supply without engaging the local level in rezoning for higher densities in locally-preferred locations, there will be affordability problems. If a transit provider does not connect the places of higher densities, there will be congestion. This demonstrates the heightened need for integrated decision-making when pursuing low-carbon development patterns.

Ultimately, deciding on low-carbon development patterns and the extent of governmental intervention in land markets to achieve these patterns is a value-driven political decision. The book does not further address the dynamics in market-led systems but rather studies the mechanisms in growth managing planning systems in more detail. Having personally worked as a planner in a market-led planning system, it was mostly curiosity that drove me to better understand how a regional level can help coordinate development patterns among local governments. Commuters usually cross municipalities on a daily basis, yet planning is hyper localized in market-led planning systems. In growth managing planning systems, governmental entities deliberately encourage coordination at the county or regional level to achieve compact development patterns. This means that the findings may only be applicable in places where the government is comfortable to take a proactive role in land development to achieve other social goods such as the protection of agricultural land and environmentally sensitive areas, as well as a reduction in vehicle miles traveled. The regional chapters actually show that local government can be highly valued if growth management legislation is drafted carefully. The regional chapters will demonstrate very different approaches to growth management at the regional level, some of them even empowering the local level in negotiations with the transit provider.

As discussed above, a practical challenge is to ensure integrated decision-making on transit investments and land use changes. This book focuses on cities that provide opportunities for regional coordination on development patterns that facilitate integrated decision-making. The regional chapters will show that the rules-in-use for integrated decision-making in the planning system are a relevant factor in implementing low-carbon development patterns. By focusing on planning systems that direct growth, this book adds to the discourse on how the regional level can be established through state legislation as a collaborative entity that can support the implementation of low-carbon development patterns.

Note

1 In the United States, metropolitan regions often align with Metropolitan Statistical Areas as defined by the US Census: "The general concept of a metropolitan area (MA) is that of a core area containing a large population nucleus, together with adjacent communities that have a high degree of economic and social integration with that core" (US Census 2013).

3 Understanding rules-in-use as an implementation factor

When implementing low-carbon development patterns, a key question is: How do we align the decisions of multiple actors? Structuring the planning process around a Regional Growth Strategy (RGS) is one answer. Planning enabling legislation shapes the planning process with rules-in use. This chapter introduces rules-in-use as a crucial factor for implementing low-carbon development patterns and provides a theoretical framework for my comparative analysis of the rules-in-use in three metropolitan regions. All three regions have committed to low-carbon development patterns in their RGS; however, the RGS in each region has a different significance and role based on the respective planning enabling legislation. The three regions' approaches range from self-regulation (Puget Sound region) to state-regulation (Stuttgart and Vancouver regions).

Rules-in-use as underexplored dimension of climate governance arrangements

The rules-in-use have not been thoroughly explored in the climate governance discourse (Thiel 2017; Setzer & Nachmany 2018; Van der Heijden 2019). The rules-in-use are particularly interesting because they influence who the decision-makers are, how interdependent they are, and how they interact. Thus, rules-in-use may fundamentally shape the ability to implement low-carbon development patterns in specific governance arrangements. However, most researchers of governance arrangements treat the rules-in-use as given conditions of a particular arrangement and then study, for instance, the interactions among decision-making centers. Rarely do they focus on the rules-in-use to understand how they shape integrated decision-making in governance arrangements. Understanding the impact of the rules-in-use may help inform the discussion on the role of various levels of government in implementing low-carbon development patterns in metropolitan regions.

I use the term rules-in-use in this book in the sense of Elinor Ostrom's (1990) definition of "working rules," a characteristic of which is that they are "actually used, monitored, and enforced when individuals make choices about the action they will take" (loc 1282). The rules-in-use are therefore

DOI: 10.4324/9781003268505-4

known to all the actors in a particular governance arrangement and there is a mechanism to monitor behavior and there is recourse for non-compliance. Rules-in-use are often said to establish the following features of governance arrangements: clarity of purpose, clear roles and responsibilities, alignment of goals among decision-makers, and acceptable and unacceptable actions, procedures, and information flows (Ostrom 1990, loc. 1279f; Amundsen et al. 2010, p. 278; Sovacool & Van de Graaf 2018, p. 318).

The rules-in-use can partly be self-regulated among decision-makers or "given" as rule of law (Ostrom 1990, loc 1293; Mayntz & Scharpf 1995, p. 20; Mayntz & Schneider 1995, p. 92). Ostrom (1990) calls the approach relying on the rule of law "externally organized collective action" and the other relying on self-regulation "self-organized collective action" (loc 1293 and 1346). Ostrom (1990) is particularly interested in "self-organized collective action" (loc 1346) which has influenced both the polycentric governance and climate governance research agendas. In self-organized settings, multiple decision-making centers may agree on a set of rules for their dependencies and interactions beforehand. The rules-in-use are essentially self-imposed by the actors (Peters & Pierre 2016, p. 124). For instance, several cities in a region may decide to collectively purchase renewable energy from a wind farm. The cities self-organize as a group and enter into contracts with a third party provider.

Although the discussion on legal rules often equates them to command-and-control type systems, many multi-level governance researchers take care to differentiate the rules-in-use in multi-level governance from command-and-control systems (Hooghe & Marks 2003, p. 233; Betsill & Bulkeley 2006; Newig & Fritsch 2009, p. 199; Cole 2015, p. 114; Homsy & Warner 2015, p. 53). In contrast to a command-and-control-system, legal rules in multi-level governance do not create one all-powerful actor that can override other decisions (Jordan et al. 2018b, p. 363). Rather, federal and state levels create "rules of the game" and set a framework that other actors follow (Homsy & Warner 2015, p. 53). They may be a mix of various policy instruments, including several substantive and procedural instruments to achieve a certain objective (Howlett 2007, p. 49).

Legal rules relate to the regulatory power of the state. The regulatory power is one of four governing resources (instruments) that governments can employ to achieve desirable outcomes (Eliadis et al. 2007). The four governing resources are: information, regulation, treasure, and organization (Howlett 2009, 2007 – builds Hood (1986)). Certainly, active national and state governments have employed a mix of these governing resources to foster climate actions and to structure land use and transportation governance arrangements. To implement low-carbon development patterns, a senior-level government may decide to leverage its financial powers and authorize additional funding for transit projects (see Vancouver and Stuttgart chapters). Conversely, a senior-level government could authorize a lower-level government to implement a regional or local tax to fund a transit system. In that case, the senior-level government leverages its regulatory powers and delegates treasure powers to a lower level (see Seattle chapter).

The instrument choice researcher Howlett (2007, 2009) highlights the fact that governments may choose various combinations of instruments and may, in fact, have a preferred instrument. Various policy objectives might be achieved using differing instruments – for instance, national and state governments may employ regulation, information, organization, or funding to reduce GHG emissions. Governments may choose any of these instruments to implement policies. Peters writes:

> Understanding the independent influence of instrument choice is important because policies that appear to be failures because they have chosen goals that are not achievable through collective action may, in fact, be quiet feasible and even popular if they were attempted utilizing different instruments.
>
> (Peters 2007, p. 353)

Therefore, in a global context, where reducing GHG emissions is a shared policy objective among many actors, understanding how the rules-in-use shape implementation in different metropolitan regions may provide valuable insights into a senior-level government's instrument choice. The subsequent section will discuss the planning system as a source for the rules-in-use that govern the implementation of low-carbon development patterns.

The planning system rules-in-use that govern low-carbon development patterns

A planning system contains rules-in-use for the governance of territorial development in a country. Planning systems are governance arrangements concerned with the use of land in a wider sense – meaning the activities and uses in a territory. These uses can encompass agricultural uses, ecosystem services, recreational purposes, resource extraction, urban uses, and transportation infrastructure. In fact, planning systems diverge in what uses they consider part of the "formalized" planning system. Furthermore, planning systems across the globe differ in the extent to which these uses are regulated by various levels of government. This leads to narrower or wider interpretations of planning systems (CEC 1997; Alterman 2001). A narrower understanding of a planning system may only focus on local land use planning and zoning which primarily handles urban uses. A wider understanding may encompass sectoral planning efforts (agriculture, transportation, mining, energy facilities) and activities at multiple levels of government. These differences are manifested in the legislation governing planning.

In most countries there is a legal basis for planning which may include planning enabling legislation, sectoral laws, and constitutional rights of property owners and levels of government (CEC 1997, p. 34; Stead & Nadin 2009, pp. 287 and 290). Planning enabling legislation frequently delegates planning and zoning powers to local levels of government. The legislation

> permits the local government to do something, but in a certain way and through certain mechanisms. [...] Such legislation will include definitions, a grant of authority, an organizational framework, a set of procedures, and, often, a set of duties that accompanies the delegation.
>
> (Meck 2006, p. 589)

These laws regulate aspects along the five governance dimensions to varying degrees.

While governance researchers primarily examine legal rules and self-regulation, planning researchers call attention to a **third source of rules: cultural values** (Knieling & Othengrafen 2009). The particularities of a planning system are shaped by the values and attitudes within the larger society on topics such as property rights, government involvement in markets, and senior-level government involvement in local matters. Cultural and societal values in planning may include attitudes towards acceptable government intervention in land markets, appropriate senior-level involvement in local decisions, extent of administrative discretion, and acceptability of a "common good" (Hardinghaus 2004; Booth 2005, p. 260ff; Heinen 2020).

The cultural preferences of different countries do, in fact, shape the legislative rules. A market-led system, as described in Chapter 1, is likely supported by a cultural preference for private actors rather than governmental actors to determine locations of new growth. Similarly, the relationship between local and senior levels is shaped by cultural expectations of the "appropriate" amount of senior-level government involvement. Therefore I include the cultural rules as an explanatory factor in the analytical framework, as they are crucial to understanding the differences in the observable features (e.g. legislation). One could easily argue that the decision-making centers involved and their influence on planning are a direct expression of cultural preference on the roles of the private sector and various levels of government.

Shaped by cultural preferences, planning systems are unique to specific geopolitical territories with distinct legal foundations and distinct vocabularies to speak about planning (CEC 1997, p. 34; Boswell et al. 2012, p. 195). Studying the rules-in-use within each planning system through a comparative framework may shed light on legislative tools that state governments can utilize to integrate decisions in land use and transportation planning to achieve low-carbon development patterns. All three types of rules-in-use (cultural values, state-regulation, self-regulation) speak to the five governance dimensions of planning systems. All five dimensions shape the

Table 3.1 Analytical framework to analyze planning system along the five governance dimensions

Dimensions of governance arrangements	*Governance variables*	*Rules-in-use in the planning system*	*Description*
Sources of rules-in-use	Legal frameworks (state-regulated)	Legal tradition (case law vs common law) Constitution Planning enabling legislation Sectoral planning laws	Legislation may set rules for statutory responsibilities of decision-makers, degrees of interdependencies and interactions among decision-makers across levels and sectors of government. The sectoral focus here will be on land use and transportation.
	Self-regulated	Intergovernmental agreements and contracts	Self-regulated agreements may fill in aspects of governance arrangements not regulated by law.
	Cultural values	Planning culture	Extent of legal framework is shaped by cultural values on government intervention in land markets, senior-level involvement in local decisions, and protecting a "common good" or individual property rights.
Common goal	Common goal or no common goal	Spatial policies	Spatial policies describing desirable development patterns are frequently contained in a planning document.
Multiple decision-making centers and their realm of influence	Vertical governance	Scale of planning	Statutory responsibilities of levels of government
	Horizontal governance	Scope of planning	Statutory responsibilities of sectoral agencies (e.g. transit providers)
	Private actors	Private vs public actors	Extent of public responsibilities for new development in contrast to private market

(*Continued*)

Dimensions of governance arrangements	*Governance variables*	*Rules-in-use in the planning system*	*Description*
Degree of dependencies	Interdependent by law	Legislatively-defined integrating requirements	Extent by which decision-making centers are formally independent or interdependent. This is expressed through the locus of power residing with one particular actor, or in contrast being shared or dispersed among multiple actors. Decision-making that is dispersed across multiple actors can be tied together through integrating requirements.
	Independent by law	No mechanisms	
	Interrelated by self-regulation	Self-regulated integrating requirements	
Interactions	Coordination	Mechanisms to coordinate decision-making	Rules-in-use (self- or state-regulated) to foster coordinated actions among decision-making centers.
	Conflicts and conflict resolution	Mechanisms to resolve disagreements	Rules-in-use (self- or state-regulated) to ensure conflict resolution.
	Competition	No mechanisms	Decision-makers may take unilateral actions without coordination or conflict resolution mechanisms.

implementation of low-carbon development patterns. Table 3.1 provides an overview of the rules-in-use I examined for my analysis of how existing planning systems integrate decisions to implement low-carbon development patterns. Each dimension is explained in more detail below.

Defining spatial policies as common goals for territorial development

Spatial policies (*raumstrukturelle Festlegungen*) are the rules-in-use applied when actors make decisions about infrastructure investments and areas for new residential, commercial, and industrial development. Spatial policies can be included in planning enabling legislation and regional growth strategies or in local comprehensive plans, but may also simply be scoring criteria for prioritizing infrastructure projects. Spatial policies actively shape the development patterns in metropolitan regions by guiding the location of public investments and new development. Spatial policies are shaped by unique cultural and political preferences. Frequently, spatial policies are authorized within "Planning Enabling Legislation" in growth managing states.

Low-carbon development patterns can be operationalized through a variety of spatial policies, including the designation of urban centers along transit corridors, the designation of an urban growth area, and/or growth projections and density requirements for certain areas. All of these are policy statements that could be contained in an RGS and/or in local comprehensive plans. Spatial policies have implications for other governmental actors that decide about zoning and land use designations. The different types of spatial policies observed in the metropolitan regions are presented in Chapters 4 through 6 and compared in Chapter 7.

Decision-making centers

Planning systems are characterized by the decision-making centers involved. Three types of decision-making centers shape development patterns. These are the levels of government involved in planning **(scale of planning)**, the sectors of government **(scope of planning)**, and developers, property owners and the land markets (the role of the private sector). (1) The scale of planning is defined as the levels of government involved in planning, (2) the scope of planning (*Fachplanungen*) describes the "range of policy topics over which the planning system has some competence," and (3) the **role of the private sector** examines to what extent implementation relies on private or public resources (CEC 1997, p. 34; Birch 2005; Stead & Nadin 2009, pp. 287 and 290). The involvement of these three types of decision-making centers in questions that cover implementing low-carbon development patterns is shaped by the rules-in-use in a planning system.

A level of government's ability to influence development patterns is shaped by the authority granted to it in the planning enabling legislation. As discussed in Chapter 1, market-led systems usually have fewer government restrictions on land markets. Therefore in market-led systems, it is likely harder to achieve low-carbon development patterns. In growth management systems, planning enabling legislation authorizes a level of government above the local level to coordinate the locations of new growth in metropolitan areas. This can be done through a variety of spatial policies that incentivize and guide developers' choices to certain locations more suitable for new development from a public infrastructure perspective. In the second instance, developers still play an important role in investing but are less important in steering the spatial development patterns of a metropolitan area. Planning systems with more government involvement are occasionally considered "top-down." The regional chapters will show that there is much nuance in structuring government involvement in development patterns. These nuances derive from the way interdependencies are structured.

Interdependencies: power sharing through integrating mechanisms

Planning systems differ based on the "locus of power" and interdependencies in decision-making among actors (CEC 1997; Alterman 2001). Frequently, the distribution of powers among decision-making centers is framed in a simple dichotomy of centralized and decentralized authority. Using binary labels such as "centralized" and "decentralized" does not fully capture the diversity and nuances in empirically observable planning systems. All three regions present a variety of examples on how to share powers across levels and sectors of government. At the center of this power sharing are integrating mechanisms that connect decisions by one entity to decisions of another entity. The integrating mechanisms also clearly protect and preserve the rights of each level of government.

Integrating mechanisms have practical implications for the implementation of low-carbon development patterns. Such mechanisms can be organized around planning documents. Planning documents usually include spatial policies or identify actions that ought to be implemented. For instance, a Regional Growth Strategy is a planning document which might encourage low-carbon development patterns. The spatial policies set out in a Regional Growth Strategy are frequently implemented by other actors (implementing entities). Some planning systems have intentionally created integrating mechanisms around a Regional Growth Strategy to ensure that implementing entities are accountable to the spatial policies therein. Integrating mechanisms can ensure accountability during implementation decisions.

Some planning systems legislatively define integrating mechanisms to ensure integrated decision-making and power sharing across levels and sectors of government. Integrating mechanisms are the medium by which a policy objective is translated into actions (Diller 2018, p. 1024). Integrating mechanisms are understood as "generalized interdependencies [...] of interactions" (Heinelt & Lamping 2015b, p. 286f.). As generalized interdependencies, integrating mechanisms stand in contrast to specific observable interactions (Heinelt & Lamping 2015b, p. 286f.). For instance, planning enabling legislation may require coordination or require plan consistency across levels and sectors of government (Heinen 2020). In the United States, plan consistency requirements in growth managing states mandate consistency among state, regional, and/or local plans (Ben-Zadok 2005, p. 2167). These consistency requirements can vary; some states may only require county-local plan consistency while others may include the regional level (Gale 1992, p. 429).

While growth management researchers in the United States discuss consistency requirements as integrating mechanisms, German spatial planning researchers study the legal status of planning documents (*Rechtswirksamkeit*). The German debate distinguishes between plans that are legislatively-binding (*Formelle Pläne mit rechtlicher Bindungswirkung*) and plans that have a guiding character (*Informelle Pläne*). The spatial policies in a legislatively-binding plan in Germany are applied to subsequent decisions like a law would be. This distinction between guiding plans and legislatively-binding plans fits neatly into the monochromatic perspective of "centralized" and "decentralized" power structures. However, this perspective fails to accommodate plan consistency requirements as they do not establish a hierarchical structure of plans (legislatively-binding) and are not guiding. Accordingly, there is a need in comparative planning research to develop theoretical frameworks to examine the nuances in how implementing entities are held accountable to spatial policies in planning documents.

As Elinor Ostrom points out, there are multiple layers of rules-in-use structuring governance arrangements. Integrating mechanisms are a layer above spatial policies. While spatial policies define the desirable development patterns in an area, integrating mechanisms contain details on how implementing entities will be held accountable to these spatial policies. Whether there are such requirements in the planning legislation depends on how narrowly or broadly state legislators have drafted the planning legislation. In a planning system designed to be comprehensive and integrated, integrating mechanisms tend to create interdependencies to foster integrated decision-making across levels and sectors of government. In instances with such mechanisms, decision-makers are formally interdependent. In absence of such integration requirements, decision-makers are formally independent. Nevertheless, decision-makers at the local or regional level may choose to voluntarily interrelate decisions in a self-regulated effort. Actors may then create integrating mechanisms by themselves rather than through legislation. This means that integrating mechanisms can be created either by legislation or from a self-regulated effort. The regional chapters will present several integrating mechanisms that I examine as part of a typology in Chapter 8.

To summarize, integrating mechanisms are defined as rules-in-use in a governance arrangement that connect decisions by one set of decision-makers to those of another set of decision-makers. Integrating mechanisms can establish interdependencies among decision-making centers and can structure interactions. For this book, I examined in detail the integrating mechanisms that evolve around RGS (Figure 3.1).

Interactions among decision-makers and integrating procedures

The rules-in-use described above likely shape the interactions among decision-making centers working on implementing low-carbon development patterns. This section briefly explores concepts from actor-centered institutionalism to demonstrate how rules-in-use may shape interactions among local governments and transit providers in determining the locations of transit-accessible higher-density and mixed uses. Interactions among decision-makers are a central dimension of governance arrangements. Interactions in this context do not refer to the daily interactions and relationships of, for instance, staffers or politicians. Interactions in this context refer to situations in which decision-makers (organizations) have to formally interact to solve

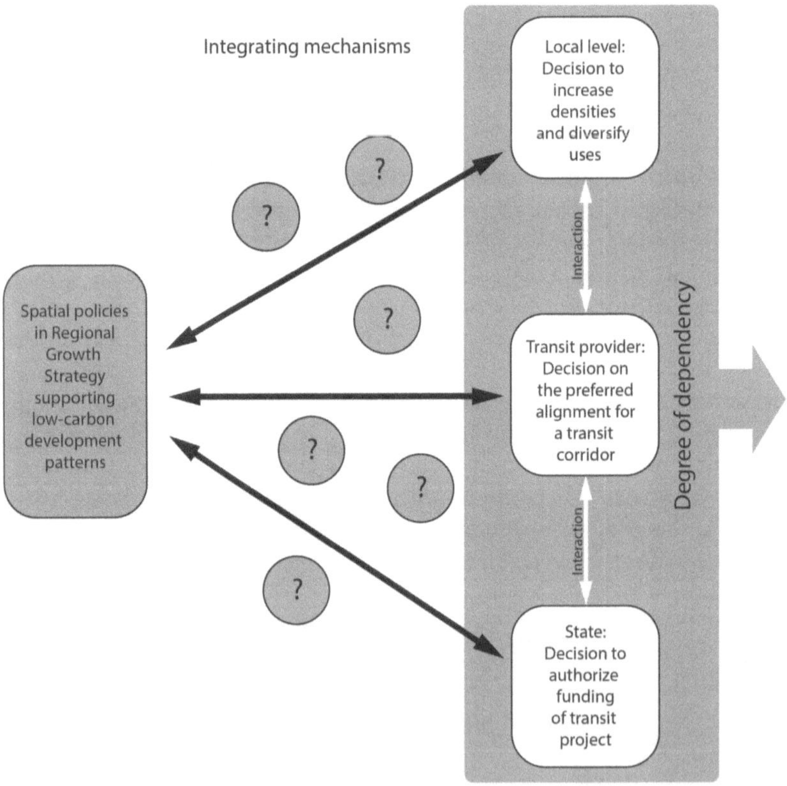

Figure 3.1 Illustration of assumptions about integrating mechanisms as an intermediary between the spatial vision in an RGS and the implementing entities.

Source: Own illustration.

an issue. These interactions may be embedded in specific rules-in-use, setting a framework for actions that are possible (Scharpf 2000).

For instance, a local government may interact with a transit provider in negotiations to determine the location of a new transit stop. In this interaction, the transit provider has an interest in his investment being maximized by ensuring appropriate ridership levels which are impacted by current and future densities and uses around the station. At the same time, the community has an interest in a transit stop supporting its preferred location for businesses and density-supporting transit. The local government and the transit provider may then negotiate the location of the transit stop. The actual interactions may be plagued by disagreement and conflict among the decision-makers; however, the resolution of these disagreements depends on the rules-in-use. The conflict resolution itself may depend on whether the legislative framework establishes procedures for conflict resolution or grants one decision-maker certain rights (Scharpf 2000).

According to game theory, in a setting with no binding agreements or shared decisions, individual actors are able to take unilateral actions in situations where they can increase their own benefits (Scharpf 2000, p. 187f.). The prisoner's dilemma is one example of the problems decision-makers face in unilateral action situations when there are no binding agreements or opportunities to communicate (Scharpf 2000). Unilateral actions typically occur in competitive arrangements where actors focus on increasing their own benefit rather than achieving a common goal. A unilateral action impacting low-carbon development patterns would be if the transit provider does not invest at the location preferred by the community or if the community decides to not focus redevelopment efforts around the newly built transit station. The extent to which unilateral actions are actually possible is intimately related to the rules-in-use within the planning system.

In comparative research, Looking at conflicts and their resolution provides insights into the functioning of legislatively created mechanisms. For instance, when it comes to creating low-carbon development patterns, a city and a transit provider may disagree on the location of a transit stop. If unilateral action is allowed, the transit provider can go ahead with its preferred choice. In contrast, if coordination is mandatory or if clear review and enforcement procedures are established, a mutually agreeable solution must be developed. However, there needs to be more research on how planning legislation can foster mutually agreeable solutions. Chapters 4–6 will focus on the unique approaches in each metropolitan region and the implications for implementing low-carbon development patterns. A particular focus will be on the spatial policies and integrating mechanisms enabled under state planning laws or by self-regulation in each metropolitan region.

Rules-in-use in three metropolitan regions

Analyzing the planning law for spatial policies and integrating mechanisms can provide insights into the fundamental differences between planning systems along the five governance dimensions discussed above. Hypothetically,

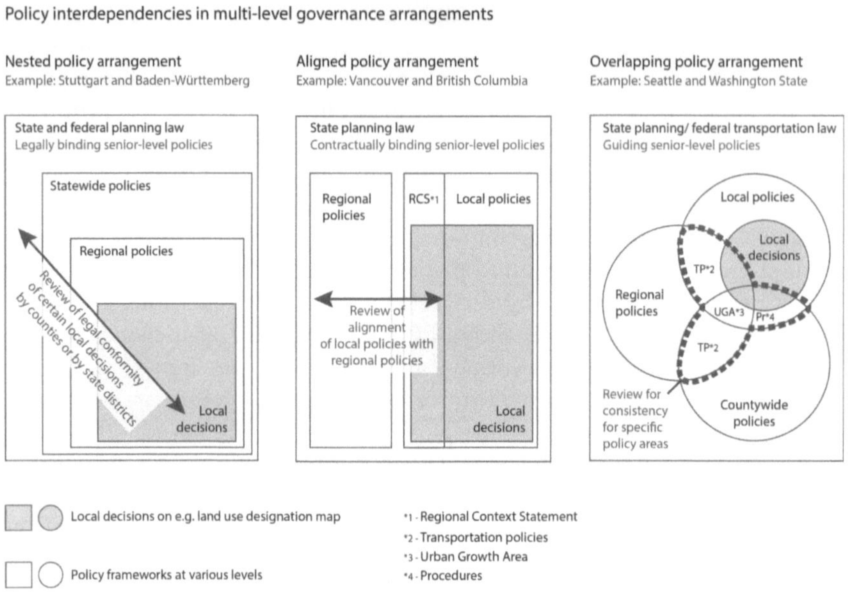

Figure 3.2 Types of policy arrangements in planning systems.
Source: Own illustration modified from published illustration in Heinen (2020).

the extent of legislative provisions regarding planning is inversely related to the extent of self-regulation required to achieve similar outcomes. If there are few substantive and procedural laws, decision-makers at the local, county, and regional levels may jointly collaborate to develop such rules for the territorial development of the region.

The extent to which spatial policies are binding on other actors greatly depends on the rules-in-use in the planning system. The regional chapters show three different examples of how the spatial policies in the RGS in each region have implications for local and transit decision-making. Figure 3.2 provides an overview on the different approaches in each region based on the planning laws. Washington State legislation enables counties to work together with communities in order to direct growth into the urbanized area. While Washington State law encourages coordination and consistency both levels (cities and counties) stand as equals next to one another, creating an overlapping policy arrangement. A different approach is taken by British Columbia where the Local Government Act creates an aligned policy arrangement. British Columbia grants Metro Vancouver the authority to direct growth into the urbanized area and to coordinate with communities on locations of urban centers. Yet another approach is taken by Baden-Württemberg. Under federal law, responsibilities are functionally separated by levels of government creating a nested policy arrangement. Within this context, Baden-Württemberg permits the regional planning organization

(VRS) to allocate expected new growth to specific community types and to set policies such as density requirements for the entire region.

The varying extent of senior-level government involvement in local decisions can be explained by looking at each of the respective senior-level constitutions. The constitution is one source of rules-in-use that shape the rights of each level of government, including the rights of cities. The constitutional rights of cities influence the extent of their regulatory and financial independence (Figure 3.2). The right to self-administration in Germany grants cities implementing powers, whereas senior levels retain regulating powers. This is reflected in the **nested planning systems**: cities make zoning decisions by applying laws and policies created by senior levels to specific parcels. In Washington State, home-rule is also reflected by the regulatory powers granted to the local level. Cities do not just implement, but they also regulate their own zoning decisions. Planning policies are not just drafted by senior levels of government like in Germany, but they are also drafted by the local level. Nevertheless, Within the United States, Washington State has chosen a rare path as the state government grants counties, as well as regions, planning policy powers which creates an **overlapping planning systems**. Lastly, in British Columbia, cities have no constitutionally protected rights. Accordingly, the province delegates some powers to the cities (zoning), while maintaining other powers at the regional level. The regional level is explicitly authorized to plan for matters of regional significance. Furthermore, the province also regulates many procedural aspects, which in Washington State are self-regulated by the county and region.

By focusing on rules-in-use, this book untangles an overlooked dimension in implementing climate actions. While the climate discourse at times promotes self-regulation at the local level, my research finds that state-regulation can significantly shape how multiple decision-making centers integrate their decisions – particularly for an issue with a heightened need for integrated decision-making such as implementing transit-connected communities to achieve emission reductions. A primary difference across the three regions is the extent to which senior-level governments create rules-in-use along the five governance dimensions. The regional chapters will show that each governance arrangement is characterized by a mix of both self-regulated and state-regulated rules-in-use, with some instances where self-regulation is required by state-regulation. The rules-in-use were long assumed to be either self-regulated or state-regulated. However, the three regions demonstrate that actual empirically observable examples are more nuanced in the extent to which state-regulation structures self-regulation at lower levels. Rather than decision-making centers that are either formally independent or formally interdependent, metropolitan regions demonstrate varying degrees of interdependencies and power sharing based on the level of detail in state legislation.

When we compare the regions, the Baden-Württemberg[1] legislation specifies the most details in state law, while Washington State law is the least specific. Baden-Württemberg and British Columbia actually create integrating procedures while Washington State encourages self-regulation of integrating procedures.

Figure 3.3 shows the hypothetically possible combinations of state-regulation and self-regulation for the rules-in-use in a planning system. The metropolitan regions are displayed in blue on the chart. The y-axis contains the rules-in-use along the governance dimensions. The x-axis describes the degree of dependency among decision-making centers. The graph delineates instances of state-regulation from instances of self-regulation, including the in-between case of state-mandated self-regulation. The graph shows that any of these rules-in-use may be state-regulated, self-regulated, or required to be self-regulated. The chart shows that the three regions only represent a fraction of possible combinations of self-regulation and state-regulation in a planning system. This means that there is likely a wide variety of empirically observable degrees of dependencies among decision-making centers.

Overall, the extent of self-regulation and state-regulation is likely based on cultural preferences. Culturally, Germans prefer state-regulated integrating mechanisms for their capacity to reduce power struggles and to create clear expectations for all actors. In Washington State, state-level action is generally viewed with more suspicion because local regulatory autonomy is highly valued. Therefore, there is likely a cultural preference in Washington State for self-regulated integrating mechanisms and spatial policies. Nevertheless, in contrast to other states in United States, Washington State opted to pre-structure spatial policies through content categories and to require

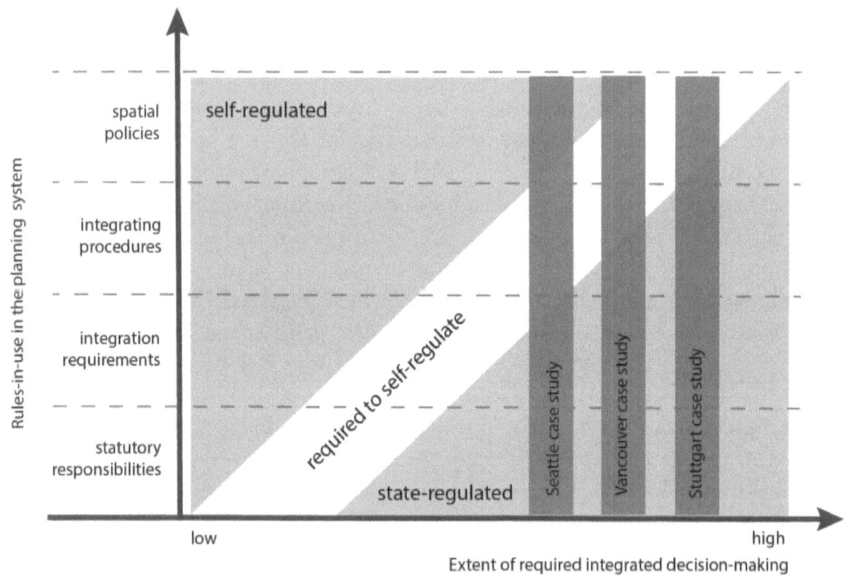

Figure 3.3 Degrees of dependency between self-regulation and state-regulation.
Source: Own illustration.

integrated decision-making. Vancouver operates in between both of those cultural preferences. The senior-level government establishes clear integrating procedures around the RGS, but with substantially lower involvement in creating the actual spatial policies.

To summarize, Washington State delegates parts of its regulatory responsibilities to the county and regional levels to create integrating mechanisms and spatial policies. Therefore, integrating mechanisms and spatial policies are de facto self-regulated by state-mandate in Washington State. In contrast, in Baden-Württemberg, state-regulation creates the integrating mechanisms and enables specific spatial policies. Lastly, British Columbia defines the integrating mechanisms but not the spatial policies. These different approaches by state legislators explain the different degree to which spatial policies in an RGS can have a bearing on decisions by local and transit decision-makers. The subsequent chapters discuss each region in detail, examining how low-carbon development patterns are implemented within multi-level growth managing planning systems.

Note

1 For ease of reading, when referring to Baden-Württemberg legislation, the German federal legislation is implied as the state law refers to the federal law.

4 Aligning plans in the Metro Vancouver region

The Metro Vancouver region is an example of a metropolitan area pursuing a clear land use agenda to foster a low-carbon future. Governmental entities at all levels (local, regional, provincial) are committed to low-carbon development patterns. The provincial government takes several approaches to engage communities in climate action, including mandatory requirements and voluntary commitments. Updates to the provincial planning law ensure that climate actions are included in plans at subsequent levels of government.

This chapter provides a deep dive into the rules-in-use empowering local governments to jointly implement low-carbon development patterns in the Metro Vancouver region. The provincial planning legislation provides a unique framework that enables the creation of a Regional Growth Strategy (RGS) as a contract among local governments which has implications for the regional transit provider's investment decisions. Within this context, the regional level in the Metro Vancouver region finds itself in an interesting position to promote low-carbon development patterns across the region based on provincial laws. Understanding the rules-in-use in the Metro Vancouver region gives a fresh perspective on how to empower local land use interests within a regional framework.

Subsequently, I will introduce the interactive planning system under the provincial Local Government Act (LGA) and discuss how the Province leveraged the interactive planning system to foster climate actions. I then present the specific spatial policies within the RGS that foster low-carbon development patterns and end with the local governments and the transportation provider (TransLink) implementing that regional vision. The Metro Vancouver region is an interesting example of provincially empowered local collaboration and coordination at the regional level. Under provincial law, the RGS serves as a contract that holds the implementing entities accountable to its policies through the integrating mechanisms.

Low-carbon development patterns as a legislative priority

Leveraging the Local Government Act

British Columbia intentionally leveraged the planning enabling legislation to promote climate mitigation actions across the Province. In the early 2000s,

DOI: 10.4324/9781003268505-5

the Province set an agenda around fostering the creation of low-carbon development patterns in order to reduce GHG emissions. One provincial employee recalled that in the early 2000s, each provincial ministry was developing ideas on how climate actions could be pursued within their sector. The Ministry of Municipal Affairs and Housing developed an enabling framework that would give clear direction to local governments without imposing. They combined legal requirements with incentivized voluntary commitments. The employee said, "It was part of a bigger philosophy that we all have to pitch in to solve climate change" (VAN-S-LU expert).

In an effort to achieve GHG emissions reductions, the provincial legislature included climate considerations in the planning system. More specifically, in 2007, the British Columbia legislature passed the "Greenhouse Gas Reduction Targets Act" (Bill 44). The law sets emissions reduction targets for public sector organizations (BC Bill 44 (2) (1) (a) and (b)). A year later, the Local Government (Green Communities) Statutes Amendment Act was passed (BC-Bill 27–2008). That Act requires communities and regional districts to include their own GHG targets, policies and actions to reduce emissions in their Official Development Plan (OCP) and in the RGS – two cornerstones of the interactive planning system (see BC Vancouver Charter 1953-Section 652.01; BC-Bill 27–2008, parts 14, 20, and 38; BC-LGA 2018-Sections 473 and 429). By adopting this requirement, the legislature included climate considerations "by default" into the formal planning system at the local and regional levels.

A provincial employee said that "the GHG targets requirement for OCPs created green light for administrators in municipalities to work on that" (VAN-S-LU expert). In fact, several local planners indicated that having the provincial mandate allowed them to start a conversation with city council officials about climate issues. The Province does not verify if communities actually include climate actions in their local plans, but the interactive planning system subjects them to several procedures that provide checking points.

Additionally, the Province of British Columbia engages its local government to commit to climate mitigation and adaptation in general and low-carbon development patterns in particular through a voluntary agreement – the "British Columbia Climate Action Charter" (BCCAC). So far, 187 of the 190 communities in British Columbia have signed the BCCAC (BC-CSCD 2018a), which was developed in cooperation with the Union of British Columbia Municipalities (UBCM). Signing the agreement is incentivized through the Climate Action Revenue Incentive Program (CARIP). Actions in the charter include the reduction of community-wide emissions as well as a reduction in emissions from local government operations (BC-CAC 2011, p. 2; BC-CSCD 2018a). Most importantly, the BCCAC sets a clear land use agenda for communities. By signing the BCCAC, communities commit to

> creating complete, compact, more energy efficient rural and urban communities [...] that support a reduction in car dependency, [...and], that encourage development patterns that increase density and reduce sprawl.
> (BC-CAC 2011, Section 5(a)(iii))

A toolkit advises communities to leverage the RGS and planning process:

> An effective RGS guides growth in a way that minimizes emissions through efficient use of land and water resources, infrastructure and transportation systems. [...] An RGS can guide land use across a region to [...] set a direction for 'complete community development patterns' that create the highest density and diversity of land uses possible in each community.
>
> (BC-Toolkit 2018b)

The combination of legislative requirements and incentivized voluntary commitment creates a framework for the local level to focus on changing development patterns. Supporting changes in development patterns that result in compact and complete communities along transit corridors is a central component of British Columbia's climate action strategy. Mandating the inclusion of GHG targets, actions, and policies in RGS and Official Community Plans legally enshrines climate mitigation in the planning system at the regional and local levels. Furthermore, by signing the BCCAC, communities commit to low-carbon development patterns to reduce emissions. The subsequent sections review how this provincial guidance materializes and is implemented in the planning process.

Tapping the interactive planning system

In Canada, regulating municipalities and regional governance is a provincial task, meaning that the federal government has no influence over urban affairs (Canadian Constitution of 1982, Article 92, clause 8; Quesnel 2000, p. 124; Wichern 2004, p. 50; Hamel 2017, p. 182; Miller 2017, p. 217). Metropolitan and local areas are governed by provincial legislative frameworks with the extent of control at the local and metropolitan levels constantly in flux (Wichern 2004, p. 51f; Hodge, Hall & Robinson 2017, p. 265). Over time, Provinces have tried different approaches to metropolitan governance. While some Provinces have chosen to create larger all-purpose jurisdictions such as new counties, others have chosen to create special districts to foster regional coordination on issues such as waste, water, and transportation (Quesnel 2000, p. 136; Sancton 2009, p. 5). Creating larger footprints of local governments through annexations is especially common in the Provinces of Ontario and Quebec (Krawchenko 2012, p. 111f.). In contrast, the Province of British Columbia has established a framework for regional coordination among local governments (Smith & Oberlander 1998, p. 372).

Canadian cities are considered creatures of the provinces which exert legislative control (interview Canadian Practitioners, Deangelo & Harvey

1998, p. 121; Quesnel 2000, p. 126). Canadian Provinces may choose to maintain their authority or delegate it to local governments (Quesnel 2000, p. 128). For instance, cities in British Columbia establish their own zoning bylaws, but local zoning is part of an interactive planning system with regional policies that provide contractually-binding guidance on matters of regional significance. The concept of "regional significance" is a central justification for the involvement of the regional level (Metro Vancouver) in land use decision-making.

Overall, regional planning in the Metro Vancouver region operates under a strong legal framework for collaborative land use planning between Metro Vancouver and its member municipalities. It is a system designed to balance local and regional interest. In British Columbia, under the current LGA, regional planning is seen as "interactive planning–a system that relies on a cooperative process, rather than hierarchy, to ensure that plans [at multiple levels of government] fit together" (BC RGS Guide 2005, pp. 2 and 18). Therefore, the British Columbia Local Government Act covers more procedural issues for guiding regional development (BC-LGA 2018–Part 13). The LGA details clear rules and procedures on how locals are to coordinate and resolve conflicts on matters of regional significance within the regional districts (BC-LGA-Parts 13, Division 3, Sections 432–444). Therefore, the planning approach in BC has been called "one of 'gentle imposition' by the province" (Artibise et al. 2004, 199). Planning at the regional level is limited to regional matters by provincial law (BC-RGS Guide 2005, 34 referencing 429(2) (c) Local Government Act). Regional matters are defined by the federation. If a matter is found in the RGS, it is a regional matter. Zoning and development permits remain primarily a local responsibility in the Metro Vancouver region; however, local OCP activities are embedded in a robust regional planning framework. The region has no involvement with zoning – only alignment between the OCP and RGS are important. Two procedures in particular hold local decision-makers accountable to regionally agreed upon policies. The two procedures are the adoption of the RGS and the review process around the Regional Context Statement (RCS). Both procedures create interdependencies in decision-making and are therefore integrating mechanisms.

While there is no constitutional protection of local rights, a provincial employee in BC highlighted that "there is a real respect for local autonomy" (VAN-S-LU expert). At the same time, a higher value is placed on collective and government actions (Krawchenko 2012) which justifies the senior-level government's involvement in land-use issues such as the protection of natural resources. Both the need for local autonomy and the need to coordinate on regionally significant issues are addressed within the interactive planning system as the integrating mechanisms are intended to balance local and regional interests. Rather than prioritizing one over the other, the interactive planning system creates clear rules for negotiations among the levels. My subsequent analysis will provide more details on the integrating mechanisms that create the framework for integrated decision-making.

The regional growth strategy for the Metro Vancouver region

Regional planning and integrating mechanisms

The provincial guidance on climate actions is implemented through the interactive planning process. Implementation evolves around the planning procedures that use the Regional Growth Strategy (RGS), Regional Context Statements (RCSs), and Official Community Plans (OCPs). The subsequent sections examine the details for the Metro Vancouver region to understand how implementation of low-carbon development patterns takes shape under the British Columbia Local Government Act.

In British Columbia, RGS are considered a crucial tool to implement climate action (BC-Toolkit 2018b). As discussed above, the Province legislatively mandates the inclusion of GHG emissions reduction targets and climate actions into RGSs and OCPs across the Province. Within an RGS, municipalities in a region agree on issues concerning land use, housing, transportation, water, sewer, parks and natural areas, and economic development (BC-RGS Guide 2005, p. 7; BC-LGA 2018, Section 429). In the Metro Vancouver region, the organization Metro Vancouver is responsible for preparing and administering the RGS.

Metro Vancouver is a regional federation of local governments responsible for sewer, water, housing, and most importantly broad planning which involves preparing the RGS (BC-LGA 2018, Section 430; MV-Board Strategy 2015–2018). Metro Vancouver is a federation of 21 municipalities, one Treaty First Nation, and one Electoral Area. Within Metro Vancouver, each entity (sewer, water, housing, and regional planning) has its own governing boards composed of elected representatives from municipalities participating in the service. For regional planning, all local governments are represented on the board preparing the RGS. The first regional plan was prepared in 1966. Over the decades, the planning enabling legislation changed multiple times. The current approach of the interactive planning system evolved in the 1990s (Wichern 2004, p. 48f.).

Besides Metro Vancouver, another regional organization is crucial for the implementation of low-carbon development patterns: TransLink. TransLink is responsible for transportation planning and operation in the region, including investments in new rapid transit services. TransLink was established in 1999 as a regional transportation authority responsible for providing an integrated multi-modal regional transportation system (TL-RTS 2013, p. 2). Accordingly, TransLink manages all public transit and construction on major roads (TL 2018). Investments by TransLink are funded by property taxes, fuel tax, charges and fees, and a tax on parking rights (BC-SCBCTAA 1998-Part 3).

For a brief period in the early 2000s, TransLink was closely connected to Metro Vancouver.[1] This connection came undone due to a conflict over transit funding between the Ministry of Transportation and the mayors represented at Metro Vancouver (Krawchenko 2012). Nowadays, Metro Vancouver is in the land use governance arena and TransLink is in the transportation governance space (Figure 4.1). Figure 4.1 shows the responsibilities in land use and transportation and the organizations involved. Figure 4.1 also shows the planning documents and integrating mechanisms linking plans across levels and sectors of government.

As the regional transportation authority, one of TransLink's responsibilities is to prepare a regional transportation strategy (RTS) and more specific plans for particular transit corridors (MV-RGS 2011, p. 51). The RTS sets out a 30-year vision for the regional transportation system (Surrey RTAA 2013, p. 4). Within its RTS, TransLink vows to "align transportation infrastructure and services more closely with land use decisions that are the responsibility of Metro Vancouver, member municipalities, treaty first nations, electoral areas, and the Port and Airport authorities." (TL-RTS 2013, p. 2). While TransLink is a separate entity from Metro

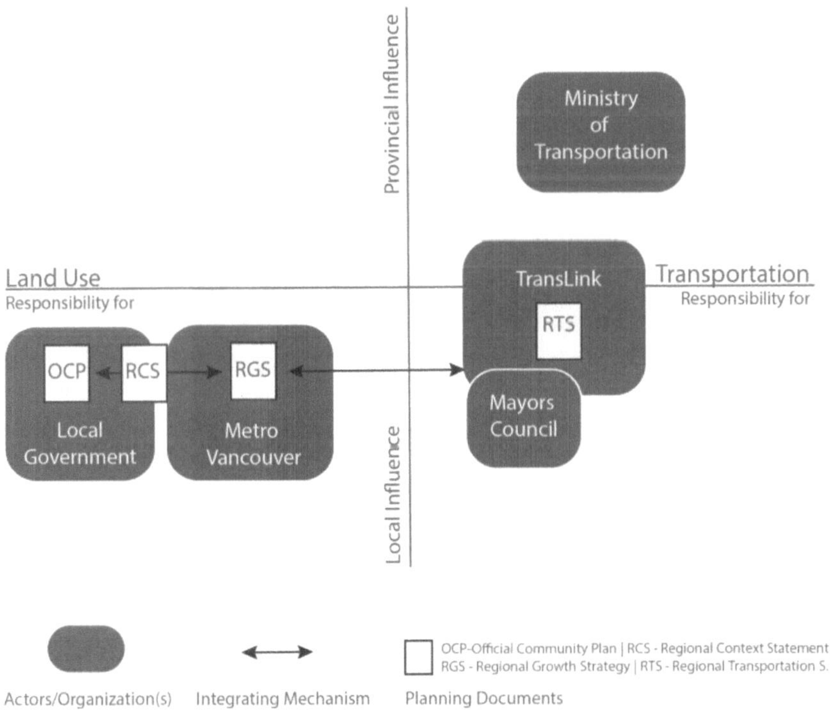

Figure 4.1 Responsibilities in land use and transportation in the Metro Vancouver region.

Source: Own illustration.

Vancouver, provincial law commits TransLink to implementing the RGS and ensures that the RTS aligns with the RGS (BC-SCBCTAA 1998-Part 1-Division 1-Section 3). This makes the RGS a central tool for fostering low-carbon development patterns - local governments and the transit provider are accountable to the RGS. The subsequent section dives into the technical details on how the legislative requirements engage all levels around specific planning documents.

The RGS is prepared by the Regional District (Metro Vancouver) with deep engagement of all member jurisdictions (staff and council), TransLink, adjacent regional districts, local First Nations, other regional agencies (e.g. the Province, health authorities, the Port, the Airport, Boards of Trade), and the general public (e.g. residents, non-profits, and advocacy groups). The latest update (Metro 2050) took three years because of the deep engagement seeking consensus across the federation. Many ideas were tested, and significant feedback was received. The RGS gains its authority by being adopted by each local government – that means that by provincial law the RGS is established as a contract among the member municipalities of Metro Vancouver (BC-RGS Guide 2005; BC-LGA 2018, Section 436(4)). This procedure is practical because it only involves 21 local governments, one Treaty First Nation and one Electoral Area. Prior to an RGS taking effect, each community has to accept the RGS and potential disputes have to be resolved through a set of provincially defined procedures (BC-RGS Guide 2005, pp. 2 and 17–20). British Columbia legislatively defines an extensive arbitration process if local governments and regional districts disagree on issues (BC-RGS Guide 2005, 18–20). This process has rarely been used because agreements tend to be reached prior to undergoing arbitration. By having each local government adopt the RGS, the document gains a contractual status. One mayor said, "If we didn't pursue policies in the RGS locally, we would be breaching a contract."

Communities demonstrate that they are aligning with the RGS through a provincially defined mechanism called a "Regional Context Statement." By provincial law, municipalities have to prepare an RCS as an appendix to their OCP (MV-RGS 2011, p. 14; BC-LGA 2018, Section 446–449). Within the RCS, communities interpret the policies and maps in the RGS for the local context. If the local government identifies any inconsistencies between the OCP and the RGS, it must specify in the RCS how they will be made consistent (BC-LGA 2018, Section 447(1)). This fosters local autonomy and achieves agreement between communities on matters of regional significance.

The procedures around the RCSs advance the local sense of responsibility pertaining to the RGS. The Province established an alignment mechanism for the regional district to verify if the local Official Community Plan (OCP) aligns with the RGS (BC-LGA 2018–Sections 446 and 449). The relevant section reads as following:

> (1) A regional context statement must specifically identify (a) the relationship between the official community plan and the matters referred to in

> section 429(2) [required content for RGS] and any other regional matters included under section 429(3), and (b) if applicable, how the official community plan is to be made consistent with the RGS over time.
>
> (BC-LGA 2018, Section 447)

By requiring the local-level government to prepare an RCS as part of the OCP, the provincial-level government essentially asks the local level for a self-review of its policies and how they relate to the RGS. Inconsistency between the RGS and OCP can be addressed within the RCS. This was an important component for local planners – in instances of inconsistencies, the RCS can detail how the inconsistencies will be addressed over time.

Ultimately, however, this is accompanied by another requirement that the RCS needs to be consistent with the OCP (Division 5–447(2)). Thus, there is an expectation that the OCP will be adjusted at some point in the future. Through the alignment mechanisms of the RCS, the local level is in a position to demonstrate how its locally developed OCP aligns with the RGS. Inconsistencies can then be addressed after the RCS is approved by Metro Vancouver. Thus, the RGS is "enforced" not through oversight by the province, but through a contractual obligation verified by Metro Vancouver through alignment mechanisms. In case of inconsistencies, the RCS sets out specific steps on how an OCP will be edited to conform to the RGS. The legal requirements around the RCS essentially create formal interdependencies between the local level and Metro Vancouver by engaging them in a conversation around local and regional policies.

Furthermore, the Province legislatively ensured that if conflicts in the preparation of the RGS and RCS arise, there is clear guidance on how to resolve them (BC-RGS Guide 2005, pp. 20–27; BC-LGA 2018, Sections 438–442). Smith and Oberlander (1998) write that the legislation "required municipalities to plan regionally and allowed the province to establish mediative forms when local-regional agreement was not forthcoming" (p. 372). As a result of the provincial mandate, most communities proactively engage with the regional district to prepare their RCSs. This allows regional and local planners to discuss growth projections for a community prior to specific development considerations. One aspect of the planning system in British Columbia is that the local level creates its own policies which are more specific than regional policies. However, for matters of regional significance, the procedures around the RGS and RCS ensure that local policies comply with the intent of regional policies. The provincial legislation provides a process around the RCS to check the alignment of policies between the local and regional levels. Through the RCS, local governments then demonstrate how their policies align with regional policies. The local policies then guide local decisions on zoning. To some extent, the interactive planning process in the Metro Vancouver region is designed to facilitate negotiation between communities on land use and other regional issues at the regional level. Therefore the RGS provides a framework for negotiations among locals on regional matters such as development patterns.

Spatial policies supporting low-carbon development patterns

Metro Vancouver develops the content of the RGS through an engagement process of the board members and the public. The spatial policies in the RGS are framed by provincial law that describes the purpose of the RGS as working towards "settlement patterns that minimize the use of automobiles and encourage walking, bicycling and the efficient use of public transit" (BC-LGA 2018, Section 428 (2)). While the provincial law provides a broad direction for the spatial policies, the specific policies are self-regulated by Metro Vancouver. This next section examines the spatial policies for the creation of desirable development patterns in Metro Vancouver's RGS and discusses how the spatial policies are connected with the integrating mechanisms.

The RGS (2011) envisions a region of compact and complete communities along transit corridors. Within the RGS, Metro Vancouver stresses that fostering compact and complete communities along transit corridors is a vital component of achieving GHG emissions reductions. Metro Vancouver included the following language in the RGS:

> The most significant contributions of the RGS to climate change mitigation will be made through a continued focus on urban containment and development patterns that support sustainable transportation and reduce energy use.
>
> (MV-RGS 2011, p. 33)

The desired development patterns can be characterized as compact urban areas with multiple urban centers connected by transit (MV-RGS 2011; MV-Climate 2050-DP 2018, p. 45). There was a shared understanding among the interviewed planners in the region that planning for transit-connected urban centers achieves multiple policy goals such as protecting important lands (agricultural, ecologically important, and industrial), enabling a network of healthy, walkable, and affordable communities and supporting efficient use of urban infrastructure (transit and utilities). Hence, the vision of transit-connected urban centers was not specifically developed in response to climate concerns. Yet, there are clear climate benefits of this type of low-carbon development patterns.

The notion of transit-connected centers has been a vision in the region since at least the 1975 Livable Region Plan (TL-RTS 2013, p. 1). I interviewed an expert involved in creating the RGS (2011), who indicated that climate considerations were not front and center for the development patterns envisioned in the RGS. The expert said: "In regional planning we had done very little work around climate explicitly at that time and so we simply adopted the same provincial targets in the plan" (VAN-R-LU expert). More recently,

Metro Vancouver has been developing a more specific climate action strategy which reaffirms the commitment to transit-connected urban centers as a spatial vision. In a Draft Climate Action Plan for public consultation in 2018, Metro Vancouver renewed the emphasis on development patterns to reduce GHG emissions.

Considering that creating a network of transit-connected urban centers has been an objective for 40 years, Metro Vancouver's capacities to be involved in directing growth into transit-connected urban centers has evolved with changes to the provincial legislation supporting regional planning. In the 1980s, regional planning was completely voluntary, which actually resulted in the building of support for the current day configuration (VAN-R-LU expert). Today's legislation evolved in the 1990s. The province intentionally focused on creating procedures that enable regional coordination among locals (VAN-S-LU expert). While the integrating mechanisms at Metro Vancouver are provincially regulated, the spatial policies are self-regulated as part of the RGS.

Regional land use designations map

Four strategies in the RGS support this vision of transit-connected urban centers: (1) limiting outward sprawl through an urban containment boundary, (2) focusing new growth in urban centers and along transit corridors, (3) protecting rural areas from urban development, and (4) not allowing extension of sewers to areas outside the urban containment boundary (MV-RGS 2011, pp. 13, 45). Limiting outward sprawl ensures that it's attractive for developers to develop at higher densities within the urbanized areas. As land prices increase, developments need to have higher densities to make financial sense. For housing prices to not escalate in a region, it is therefore crucial for communities to permit higher densities in selected locations such as urban centers. While urban containment is certainly controversial, Metro Vancouver was able to build the political support in the region. The subsequent discussion gets into the technical planning details on setting the urban containment boundary, designating urban centers, and allocating population forecasts.

The four strategies are mapped on a regional land use designations map which clearly delineates urban from non-urban land through an urban containment boundary.[2] Furthermore, within the urban area, the map displays urban centers and Frequent Transit Development Areas (FTDAs) (MV-RGS 2011, p. 9ff.). These centers and FTDAs are (to be) connected by transit infrastructure (MV-RGS 2011, p. 10). The subsequent section first introduces the regional land use designations map as a mechanism not commonly used in North America at the regional level. Afterwards, I discuss the particular spatial policies that are on the map (Figure 4.2).

The regional land use designations map provides a broad framework for the more detailed local land use designations maps that communities include in their OCP. As shown in Figure 4.2, the regional land use designation map contains three urban designations (General Urban, Industrial, Mixed

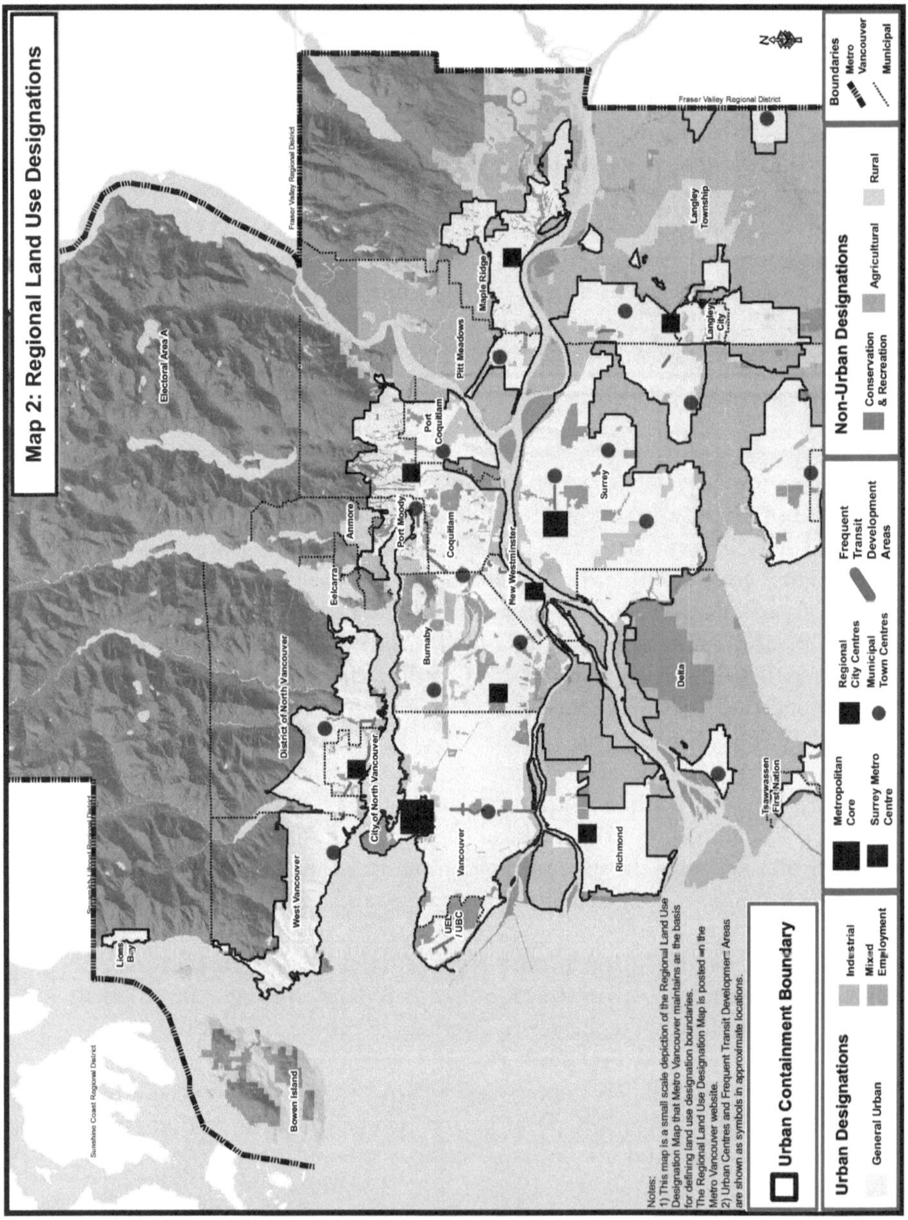

Figure 4.2 Regional land use designations map.
Source: Metro Vancouver - MV-RLUD 2020.

Employment) and three non-urban designations (Conversation & Recreation, Agricultural, Rural). When communities submit their RCS, they have to demonstrate that the local land use designations are consistent with the regional designations (MV-RGS 2011, several policies). For instance, within the RGS, Metro Vancouver is requesting municipalities to "identify the Rural areas and their boundaries on a map generally consistent with the Regional Land Use Designations map" in their RCS (MV-RGS 2011, p. 21, policy 1.3.3.a). So, local land use designations maps show rural areas in the same locations as the regional land use designations maps, however, the local maps have several sub-categories for rural lands. The local land use designations then inform local zoning decisions. Therefore, the regional land use designations map has implications for local zoning decisions.

Through the process around the RCS, municipalities are limited to the extent that they can re-designate land from one regional land use to another (MV-RGS 2011, p. 59). For instance, if a community wanted to permit an urban use on non-urban land, they would need approval by 2/3 of the regional board (MV-RGS 2011, p. 60; Type 2 amendment). Nevertheless, within the designated General Urban Area, municipalities make all decisions on zoning and land uses. One of the experts at Metro Vancouver said:

> It's really about containment. We have much less involvement within the urban containment boundary. In fact, within the general urban designation we have no involvement at all. It's local planning at its heart. So our involvement is really about limiting the conversion of industrial and agricultural land to urban uses.
>
> (VAN-R-LU expert)

It needs to be highlighted at this point that it is not just the mayors represented at Metro Vancouver's board that decided to self-impose a parcel-based urban containment boundary.[3] In fact, through the provincially-defined RGS adoption process, every jurisdictions' Council, TransLink, adjacent regional district Board, and Metro Vancouver signed on to the RGS, including the urban containment boundary and parcel-based regional land use designations. By signing on, everyone essentially agreed that if they contemplated significant land use change at the local level, they first have to come to their peers at the Metro Vancouver Board to discuss the regional implications of that local land use change (e.g. conversion of agricultural land or extension of the urban containment boundary).

To some extent, Metro Vancouver is able to create the self-regulated process around amending the land use designations because the provincial legislation mandates very clear integrating mechanisms in which both local and regional interests are protected. Having clear provincial guidelines on how conflicts are to be resolved helps to create a level of trust between local decision-makers at the regional level. By creating clear integrating mechanisms, the Province protects the interests of the local and regional levels and provides recourse to resolve disagreements.

Urban containment boundary

The urban containment boundary is supported by two other mechanisms. Metro Vancouver is responsible for water and sewers in the region. However, Metro Vancouver does "not allow connections to regional sewerage services to lands with a Rural, Agricultural or Conservation and Recreation regional land use designation [except for a few exceptions]" (MV-RGS 2011, p. 14, policy 1.1.1). One expert indicated that the limitation on the sewer extension is a strong implementation mechanism for urban containment in the region (VAN-R-LU expert).

The second mechanism was created in 1973 by the provincial government: British Columbia set up the Agricultural Land Reserve (BC-ALCA 2002) which provides an additional layer of protection for agricultural land. Therefore, in the Metro Vancouver region, the urban containment boundary is partly predetermined by the extent of the Agricultural Land Reserve (under provincial law, see BC-ALCA 2002). The Metro Vancouver expert said: "Well, the agricultural land use designation we inherit. [...] So our strategy can't take fabulous kudos for protecting agricultural land. It's there because of a provincial legislative value." Land in the Agricultural Land Reserve is protected through decisions by a separate provincial entity called the Agricultural Land Commission. Prior to Metro Vancouver permitting a re-designation of agricultural land, the provincial entity would have to agree to take land out of the Agricultural Land Reserve. If the provincial entity approved the change, then Metro Vancouver would consider a change of the land use designations map.

Overall, this use of a map to formally designate land uses at the regional level is quite unique in North America. One of the experts at Metro Vancouver remarked on the advantages and disadvantages of having a regional land use designations map:

> So I think that the land use designations map is a much stronger tool than just policy. [...] It's a lot more effective to [steer development] through the map than it is through policy. The disadvantage is that you don't want to have so many designations that you're replicating local plans. And so we have these very coarse tools [...where rural land can be underserviced mountainous area or open space agricultural land]. However, I don't think there's any appetite to have more regional land use designations.
>
> (VAN-R-LU expert)

While the six land classifications and the urban containment boundary are defined by Metro Vancouver and its members during the RGS development process, the FTDAs and Urban Centers are included in the RGS at the request of municipalities when they submit their RCS (MV-RGS 2011, p. 10).

Urban centers and frequent transit development areas

The Urban Centers and FTDA overlays (designations) complement the idea of protecting natural resources and agricultural land. As new urban development is not permitted on the fringes of the Metro Vancouver region, the Urban Centers and FTDAs are considered primary locations for redevelopment at higher densities around transit stops. Many of the 21 communities in the Metro Vancouver region has at least one urban center that is (or will be) connected with transit infrastructure to downtown Vancouver (MV-RGS 2011, p. 9). For each type of urban centers and FTDAs (e.g. Regional City Centre, Municipal Town Centre), the RGS defines growth targets for employment and housing (MV-RGS 2011, pp. 16 and 18). Communities designate the location of urban centers during their OCP development process and report them to Metro Vancouver in the RCS (MV-RGS 2011, p. 16). Within this context, communities have to show how they are contributing to the region wide target and have to adopt policies in their OCP that apply to the Urban Centers (MV-RGS 2011, pp. 16 and 19). The RGS defines the Urban Centers as follows:

> Urban Centres are intended to be the region's primary focal points for concentrated growth and transit service. They are intended as priority locations for employment and services, higher density housing, commercial, cultural, entertainment, institutional and mixed uses. Urban Centres are intended to emphasize place-making, an enriched public realm, and promote transit-oriented communities, where transit, cycling and walking are the preferred modes of transportation.
>
> (MV-RGS 2011, p. 10)

The Urban Centers are a good example of how communities further specify policies in the RGS: for instance, Strategy 1.2 in the RGS is to "Focus growth in Urban Centres and Frequent Transit Development Areas" (MV-RGS 2011, p. 16). The strategy is then supported by several action items that detail the role of Metro Vancouver and the municipalities. For instance, Metro Vancouver's role is to "Work with municipalities, TransLink, other governments and agencies to support the development and delivery of effective regional transportation networks and services that support the growth and development of Urban Centres and Frequent Transit Development Areas." (MV-RGS 2011, p. 16). The role of the communities is to

> adopt Regional Context Statements which [...] (b) include policies for Urban Centres which: i) identify the general location, boundaries and types of Urban Centres on a map [...], ii) focus growth and development in Urban Centres [...]; iii) encourage office development through policies and/or other financial incentives, such as zoning that reserves capacity for office uses and density bonus provisions.
>
> (MV-RGS 2011, p. 16)

Throughout the region there are urban centers of differing size, some serving the municipality, a sub-region or are serving as regional hubs. The regional hubs are identified as primary locations for regional-scale employment and commercial activities, for major institutional uses and for high and medium density housing (MV-RGS 2011, p. 19). In comparison, the municipal centers primarily serve the local area as focal points for employment and denser housing (MV-RGS 2011, p. 19). Lastly, in responding to development along rapid transit stops, Metro Vancouver has more recently introduced the FTDA designation. FTDAs are intended as locations for medium density housing and mixed uses along the Frequent Transit Network (MV-RGS 2011, p. 19).

Growth projections for employment and housing

For the urban centers and FTDAs, Metro Vancouver includes employment and housing growth targets in the RGS (MV-RGS 2011, p. 18). The projections are supposed to guide local decisions on infrastructure investments and rezoning that will be needed to increase capacity. Provincial law requires growth projections be included in the RGS and OCP (BC-LGA 2018, Section 429(2)); however, the projections are not targets and there is no recourse if communities do not achieve the targets. The Metro Vancouver expert explained:

> Communities have to tell us in their RCS how they're working towards the targets, towards directing growth towards centers and FTDAs and tell us what percentage of their population growth is planned in the centers and FTDAs. But we recognize that our collaborative relationship extends to those targets. And so our data team regularly goes out to members and says, here's what our model says. What do you think?
>
> (VAN-R-LU expert)

Through this collaborative process, communities recognize the need to increase the zoned density within their urban centers. As the region is planning to absorb a projected increase of 1 million residents by 2040 within the urban area (not on rural land) (MV-Climate 2050-DP 2018, p. 45), the urban centers play a crucial role in absorbing the projected growth. Focusing new growth in the designated urban centers also preserves existing single family neighborhoods, as one local planner pointed out.

Metro Vancouver does not actually provide much more detail on the urban centers other than setting a vision (transit accessible, focus of growth, with office development), identifying growth projections and requiring planning around the urban centers. Effectively, the policies in the RGS become directions for implementing the RGS. While the RGS sets the framework for planning urban centers and FTDAs in each community, the communities themselves decide specifics as long as they accommodate the projected growth. By directing communities to have a designated urban center to focus growth, Metro Vancouver guides the implementing entity (local level) towards a regionally desirable development pattern. By provincial law, the RCS process can be applied as a permitting process; however, the interviews made apparent that Metro Vancouver strives to apply the RCS process as a collaborative effort. During the development of an RCS and OCP, Metro Vancouver actively communicates with municipalities on the implications of the policies in the RGS for local planning. The emphasis led to communities on the very fringes of the metropolitan region to design new neighborhoods with five story buildings in a new urbanist style. While there is still Greenfield development, it occurs at much higher densities.

Interestingly, most cities chose to align the urban centers with existing retail locations, initially auto-oriented indoor malls or strip malls with an excess of surface parking. Currently, these locations are rapidly transforming to high-rise residential and office development. Overall in the Metro Vancouver region area, 75–80% of growth occurs through redevelopment and intensification. About 20% is on greenfields inside the urban containment boundary. (VAN-R-LU expert). One local expert said:

> The idea of centers that would eventually be linked by rapid transit was the basis – *now 40 years later we see the results. That's the type of thing that takes decades to change. The kind of vision of a Copenhagen finger plan holds for a long time.*
>
> (expert interview)

To summarize, to implement the regional vision of transit-connected centers, Metro Vancouver can work with municipalities through the RCS procedures which include the regional land use designations map as well as the urban centers designation (MV-RGS 2011, p. 46). The local policies and maps are linked to the regional policies and maps by provincial law through the process around the RCS. In a self-regulated effort, Metro Vancouver leverages this process by including the regional land use designations map and by providing specific directions on content for the Urban Centers and FTDAs. All communities have signed on to these self-regulated efforts by adopting the RGS, which is also a provincially mandated procedure. Prior to reviewing the specific local circumstances, the subsequent chapter explores the transit side of the story, including the alignment and investment decisions at TransLink.

Transit implementation decisions: prioritizing and investing in new rapid transit

TransLinks responsibility to implement the RGS

A substantial part of successfully implementing low-carbon development patterns in an urban area is the investment and successful implementation of a regional transit system that connects spots of higher density and diversified uses. As indicated above, the RGS in the Metro Vancouver region had been advocating for this type of development pattern for decades, however, when it comes to planning, building, and operating the rapid transit network, another regional player is key: TransLink. As the regional transit provider, TransLink prepares planning studies for new transit lines, prioritizes and advances new transit projects. For implementing transit-connected communities, TransLink is a crucial partner within the regional governance network.

Transportation planning at TransLink is guided by the RTS. Within the RTS, TransLink clearly commits to prioritizing transit and alternative forms of transportation over car-based transportation. One of TransLink's primary objectives is to make "it possible to make half of all trips by walking, cycling and transit; and [...] to reduce the distances people drive by one-third" (TL-RTS 2013, p. 14). While TransLink does not have GHG targets, the experts at TransLink argued that pursuing the headline targets would ultimately help reduce GHG emissions.

The targets and the RTS policies show a clear commitment to alternative modes of transportation. The RTS indicates that the road network (which is also the responsibility of TransLink) is considered to be mostly complete and says, "In 30 years, regional automobile traffic is targeted to be at today's levels" (TL-RTS 2013, p. 10). This is a strong statement for an urbanized area in North America that is projected to gain an additional 1 million residents by 2040. TransLink intends to serve the population increase through investments in multi-modal transportation options. To ensure that transit investments are leveraged, TransLink relies on local decision-makers to permit higher density and mixed-uses near rapid transit stops. The RGS provides relevant accountability between the local land use decisions and the transportation decisions at TransLink. This is manifested in the RTS as follows:

> It is often said that the best transportation plan is a good land use plan, and for good reason: the location of jobs and housing fundamentally determines where and how much people, goods and services need to travel. Ultimately, land use has as great an impact on transportation outcomes as most transportation decisions.
>
> (TL-RTS 2013, p. 9)

Here, the RGS provides a regional vision of urban centers connected by rapid transit. This vision connects land use to transportation decisions in a clear manner. The vision of urban centers connected by transit has been part of the regional discourse since 1996 when the Livable Region Strategic Plan (MV-LRSP 1996, p. 30) was adopted. Throughout the years, the broad lines contained in the 1996 plan have been studied in more detail by TransLink and have ultimately been implemented. The LGA and legislation governing TransLink have supported the role of the RGS in ensuring accountability.

By provincial law, the purpose of TransLink is to support the implementation of the RGS (BC-SCBCTAA 1998-Part 1-Division 1-Section 3). The purpose of TransLink as a transportation authority is described as follows by law:

> to provide a regional transportation system that (a)moves people and goods, and (b)supports (i)the RGS, (ii)provincial and regional environmental objectives, including air quality and greenhouse gas emission reduction objectives, and (iii) the economic development of the transportation service region.
>
> (BC-SCBCTAA 1998-Part 1-Division 1-Section 3)

Based on this legislative requirement, the regional transportation system needs to support the RGS as well as provincial GHG reduction objectives. The legislation creates formal interdependencies between TransLink, British Columbia, and Metro Vancouver. These formal interdependencies are reinforced through another requirement around the investment strategy of TransLink. The investment strategy needs to "set out the relationship between the major actions planned by the authority and (i) the RGS, [...and others]" (BC-SCBCTAA 1998-Part 9-Section 201b). This means that the investments in transportation need to support the development patterns described in the RGS. Since the vision in the RGS entails transit-connected urban centers, the spatial policies around urban centers framework have been a central feature of rapid transit rail planning and investments at TransLink.

Accordingly, the RTS references the urban centers framework as set out in the RGS in multiple locations. The following excerpts provide an example on how policy items from the RGS are transferred into the RTS. Metro Vancouver includes the following statement in the RGS: TransLink is to "prepare and implement strategic transportation plans that support focused growth in Urban Centres and Frequent Transit Development Areas" (MV-RGS 2011, p. 52). In response, TransLink included in its own RTS the following language:

> TransLink is also mandated to support these regional land use objectives, including policies to focus growth in Urban Centres, Frequent Transit Development Areas and along the Frequent Transit Network within a compact urban area clearly defined by the Urban Containment Boundary. [...] Through investing, managing and partnering to deliver the regional transportation system, TransLink can reinforce these regional land use objectives.
>
> (TL-RTS 2013, p. 25)

TransLink's rapid transit investments are primarily targeted at connecting the designated urban centers. This is evident in multiple planning documents for new rapid transit lines. The following quote from the RTS demonstrates the relevance of aligning land use and transit decisions through a commitment to urban centers, as spatial policies which structure the metropolitan area:

> A core issue is the desire of local government authorities, TransLink and developers for greater certainty on both land use and [transit] investment commitments. [...] The closer the cooperation, the greater the potential for success. It is particularly critical when TransLink is making decisions about major capital projects that it can rely on its partners to conceive and follow through on policies that promote complete and compact communities. When these commitments are in place, it's easier for TransLink to be confident about how it sets priorities within a limited budget.
>
> (TL-RTS 2013, p. 9)

This quote underscores the relevance of coordinated action between local governments who are in charge of rezoning and the transit provider who invests in a new system. Metro Vancouver provides a viable coordination service to both sets of stakeholders by developing the RGS. However, the quote does point to an issue that came up during the interviews – while TransLink is formally committed to the RGS by provincial law, communities are committed to the RGS in a manner that involves more leeway at the local level. While many communities do re-designate land use within the urban centers in accordance with the RGS during the RCS process, there seemed to be frustration at TransLink with a few communities that have not re-designated uses as promptly. TransLink is trying to address the time lapse through partnership agreements.

During the interviews it appeared that TransLink was concerned that its transit investment would not be matched in a timely manner in some communities with a local commitment to densifying and diversifying uses in the urban centers. In the RTS, TransLink has an action item to "Establish mechanisms such as partnership agreements and joint planning to provide greater certainty around expected and agreed-upon land use, policies and investments" (TL-RTS 2013, p. 25). More recently, TransLink has begun to enter into partnership agreements with communities once funding has been committed to a rapid transit project. The partnership agreements are intended to ensure that appropriate land use changes occur to support the transit investment as well as to ensure the municipality considers questions of affordability. Within the Mayors' Vision, the partnership agreements are prefaced with the following text:

> The objectives of these [transit] lines are to shape land use; shape travel demand; increase ridership; and reduce emissions. As a result, the business case depends upon the concurrent implementation of land-use policies, and other supporting actions such as transit priority measures, parking management and walking and cycling investments that optimize the potential for the lines' success. Achieving these objectives requires partnerships.
>
> (TL-Mayors' Vision 2014, p. 12).

While TransLink would have liked to include more specific requirements, the actual partnership agreement ended up being more about committing the municipality to a process to work on changing land uses around the station areas to optimize the transit investment.

An underlying challenge with aligning land use and transit action is that Metro Vancouver can only verify if the centers are designated in the OCP but cannot enforce a land use re-designation. Some communities, such as Coquitlam, very proactively developed neighborhood plans and increased densities for their urban centers and are now seeing a great deal of new development. Other communities have not been as proactive. The partnership agreements are in place to expedite the local conversation around re-designating land uses around station areas in urban centers. Prior to diving into detail on the local decision-making, the subsequent section turns to the decision-making within TransLink on determining routes for new rapid transit lines.

Conducting multiple accounts evaluations to determine preferred corridor alignment

Building new transit is a very political process in British Columbia and involves both mayors and provincial decision-makers. In the past there have been several points of conflict, over which corridors to fund and implement. One expert indicated the relationship between the Province and the mayors in the region is still largely "driven by politics." There have been extensive studies on the conflicts around financing existing rapid transit lines and the political tensions throughout the years (Krawchenko 2012, Brunet-Jailly & Arcand 2017). This section briefly reflects on TransLink's considerations when selecting a specific corridor alignment. It is notable that despite much political conflict between the mayors and the Province over prioritizing corridors for funding, ultimately, all corridors focus on connecting the urban centers – the conflicts are more about timing and which suburbs are connected next to the network. Higher costs are justified if more urban centers are connected.

Based on the 1996 Livable Regions Strategic Plan, TransLink had been advancing multiple planning studies for each corridor, including multiple-account assessments. When developing new rapid transit, existing and future land uses are crucial factors. Transit investments can shape future land use, but they also need to serve existing land uses. Two of the most recent rapid transit investments are a good example to illustrate TransLink's approach and philosophy: While the Surrey Corridor will connect the City of Surrey and attempts to shift and shape travel demand (Surrey RTAA 2013, p. 3), the investments in the Broadway Corridor in the City of Vancouver respond to current travel demand. An expert at TransLink compared both projects:

> You get into the 'what comes first question' with billion dollar investments. Broadway is responding to the immediate need for higher capacity transit. Hundreds of people get on buses that run every 90 seconds. So subway is needed to deal with capacity issues. Whereas in Surrey,

> we've been working with Surrey and Metro Vancouver to grow demand in those corridors. So we are incrementally increasing services to start to foster the demand. In the last few years we've introduced B-Line Service [(Bus Rapid Transit)] to grow demand and spur development decisions that help complement [the rapid transit investment].
>
> (VAN-R-TR expert)

When TransLink studies the particular alignment of a transit corridor, one factor is the redevelopment potential along the route. To determine the final alignment of a transit corridor, TransLink analyzes several alternative routes in collaboration with the community. This analysis includes various options for route alignment and technology (Bus rapid transit, light rail, skytrain). To select an alignment, TransLink conducts a Multiple Accounts Evaluation that considers cost and deliverability as well as social, community, land use, and environmental benefits. According to TransLink, the urban centers are prime locations due to their redevelopment potential. For instance, for the Coquitlam Corridor: rather than favoring a cheaper alignment along the highway where land was readily available, a corridor was prioritized that connected more urban centers, thus creating more prime redevelopment potential. Reflecting on connecting the urban centers, one expert indicated that the process has been very successful:

> Not because [the urban centers] are dots on a map but [rather] the region, as in local municipalities, has been very successful in focusing development in those centers. Transit is most successful in places with more people, jobs and activities - so there is more reason to travel to and from there. So that's a good reason to invest in transit servicing the urban centers.
>
> (VAN-R-TR expert)

The commitment to urban centers is supported by an organizational arrangement within TransLink. All of the mayors that are also adopting the RGS at Metro Vancouver are part of the "Mayors' Council" inside of TransLink. Within TransLink, the "Mayors' Council" represents the municipalities in the region in the internal decision-making structure. Among other things, the Mayors' Council approves a ten-Year Investment Plan and a ten-year Vision, called the Mayors' Vision (2014). The Mayors' Vision is a long-term investment strategy which identifies funding priorities for the region as well as potential new funding mechanisms.

Having the Mayors' Vision was especially beneficial in 2016 when a new Federal Budget was adopted. The newly elected federal government made more transit funding available through the Canada Public Transit Infrastructure Fund (PTIF 2020). PTIF increased the share of federal funds from 30% to up to 50% for infrastructure projects (TL-Phase 1, 2017, p. 37; PTIF 2020). The federal objective of PTIF was to help "to improve commutes, cut air pollution, strengthen communities and grow Canada's economy." (PTIF 2020). The money was then allocated to the provinces which further allocated it to the regions. When additional federal funding came along, having the ten-year vision (and all the supporting plans for each project) in place allowed clear communication about the rapid transit infrastructure needs in the Metro Vancouver region. With this new federal funding available, several transit projects were advanced to connect urban centers as envisioned in the RGS.

As most corridors from the 1996 plan had been built by 2011, the RGS (2011) included the three remaining corridors as priorities for transit development (p. 51). Priority 1 was the Coquitlam Corridor which connects several urban centers to the City of Coquitlam. The Coquitlam Corridor opened as the Evergreen Line in 2016. The second priority included the Surrey Corridor and the Broadway Corridors. The Surrey Corridor will connect the urban center in the City of Surrey to other urban centers further out in the metropolitan area (MV-RGS 2011, p. 51). The Broadway Corridor will replace an overcrowded rapid transit bus line within the City of Vancouver. The Surrey and Broadway Corridors are good examples of the two approaches TransLink has taken to transit development.

Thus, the planning system supports the regional vision of transit-connected urban centers by committing the implementing entities to the RGS. Provincial law makes TransLink responsible for implementing the RGS. The municipalities are bound to pursue the redevelopment of urban centers as they self-designate them within the OCP and RCS. Furthermore, communities' adoption of the RGS reinforces the linkage between the regional and local visions. By legislatively defining these integrating mechanisms, provincial law sets the framework by creating formal interdependencies among various decision-making centers. There is a clear separation of powers among the entities involved – the provincial law sets a procedural framework, the region develops the vision, TransLink plans, builds and invests in the transit system, and the municipalities re-designate land uses. The RGS ties together the efforts of all the actors involved. In North America, regional strategies are frequently self-regulated; however, the Metro Vancouver region is in a somewhat unique position since the RGS has clearly structured integrating mechanisms by provincial law. I explore the relevance of the integrating mechanisms for local decision-making further in the next section.

Local decision-making: planning for the urban centers

One component of implementing low-carbon development patterns is the local decision to increase densities and diversify uses around transit. This section discusses the local decision-making for several transit stop locations in Coquitlam and Surrey in the Metro Vancouver region. Both communities created neighborhood plans with land use designations for the station areas. I interviewed planners in the communities about the challenges and opportunities of changing the land uses around the station areas.

Communities in the Metro Vancouver region have experienced a building boom around their transit stops in the past decade. Planners attributed the building boom partly to a shift in the real estate market. Starting around 2010, the Vancouver property market witnessed a doubling in real estate values, particularly in areas around new transit stops or areas designated in community plans for higher-density developments. In some communities, people sold their single-family homes for up to three times the value. Developers were buying up residential property because of the anticipated new value of the re-designated land. This trend occurred across the region. Below, I review the experiences in three communities and how their transit stops came about as well as how they aligned decisions about location and land use.

I asked the experts what factors were enabling the current building boom – particularly referring to the spatial policies in the RGS. The experts pointed out that the urban centers designation had been in place for decades and some station area plans were already 15 years old and had to be redone. They repeatedly said that the real estate boom had only begun in the last five to ten years. Practitioners speculated that several factors may have contributed to the building boom, including speculation around off-shore investments. Positive experiences in suburbs such as Metrotown in Burnaby as well as low interest rates may have also contributed to the building boom.

A city's active commitment to an urban center was a factor in the redevelopment around the station areas as was its embrace of land use changes through a neighborhood planning process. The three areas all share a commonality in that their cities did a market-analysis for the redevelopment potential around the station areas. The cities also engaged the neighborhoods in a planning process for the proposed changes in land use designations. Having the city proactively re-designate land made it easier for a developer to apply for rezoning. My interview subjects frequently cited the example of the first SkyTrain in Vancouver. At the time in 1985, the city of Vancouver actively opposed the line. To this day, none of the station areas have seen the same redevelopment that the newer lines have.

Nowadays, through the designation of urban centers as part of the RCS and OCP, the cities have more active involvement in the alignment of the newer lines. One planner said building the SkyTrain made a big difference in transforming the land markets. The expert pointed to another factor in the boom: the location choice for the urban centers. Many of the urban centers in Metro Vancouver had been designated near indoor malls that were surrounded by acres of surface parking lots, as well as multi-family dwellings within 500 meters of the transit stop. All the experts I interviewed agreed that it is generally easier to rezone an area that is primarily rental based than an area with high home ownership. So the re-designation of land within the urban centers in Metro Vancouver was set up for quicker success – there was less resistance to the land's re-designation and less land assembly needed. The planners though were painfully aware of the downside of rezoning high density rental areas. It leads to higher displacement of lower income renters because the new high-rise residential buildings are all higher priced rental apartments or condominiums.

With all the planning work in place, the communities were ready when the real estate market finally shifted. A planner explained that after 2010, the Metro Vancouver region saw real estate investments, both domestic and international, from investors looking for security. With historically low interest rates, investing in the real estate market made sense for higher returns. One local planner explained:

> We have a lot of people that are baby-boomers with equity that are looking for places to put the money. With more purchasers in the market than there is supply, prices were going up. As prices were going up, more professional developers moved into the market.

While it is hard to discern what actually caused the shift in land markets, the interviews revealed that the region's long-term planning efforts positioned it favorably for when investment opportunities came along. I tell the stories of the individual communities below.

City of Coquitlam: informed land use re-designation at Burquitlam-Lougheed station

The City of Coquitlam is located on the fringe of the Metro Vancouver region in the northeast corner of the region. In the RGS, the City of Coquitlam has a designated urban center and a designated FTDA. Coquitlam was projected to grow from 129,000 residents in 2011 to 224,000 residents by 2041 (MV-RGS 2011, p. 68). In 2016, when the Evergreen SkyTrain opened to connect the city to downtown Vancouver, Coquitlam had 139,284 (Canadian Census). Since the opening of the SkyTrain, Coquitlam has authorized 7,200 new housing units for development in its designated urban center and FTDA. For the chapter, I analyzed the FTDA called Burquitlam-Lougheed station in greater detail. This section briefly reviews the planning history of the station area and goes into more detail on the various land use actions by the City of Coquitlam to foster redevelopment there.

Extending transit northeast from Vancouver to Coquitlam had been in the making for more than a decade. The transit line to Coquitlam was supposed to be built in 2002, but funding was suddenly withdrawn by the province over a conflict with the region's mayors (expert interview, Krawchenko 2012). Prior to the withdrawal, Coquitlam had prepared a neighborhood study for the Burquitlam-Lougheed FTDA (VAN-L-COC expert interview). Without the construction of the transit station, not much of the envisioned redevelopment actually occurred. With shifting provincial politics, the Evergreen Line was eventually opened in 2016. While construction of the stations was underway, Coquitlam adopted transit-oriented development policies to guide any development proposals while they worked on a new vision for the neighborhood (COQ-TDS 2012). One planner remembered:

> The construction of the Evergreen Line started before we started the planning process and the line opened for service six months before we finalized the plan. Therefore all the development pressure started

> before the plan was ready. The council was very development friendly, so they wanted to say 'yes' to the development application before the plan was ready. We were processing development applications under old rules while trying to make them fit with what we thought the new rules would be. [We were] not stopping development or placing moratoriums. [The Plan] Project team and [the development application] file managers met frequently to make sure they lined up.
>
> (VAN-L-COC expert)

The new neighborhood plan for the Burquitlam-Lougheed FTDA was adopted in 2017. The planning document described the plan's vision for the neighborhood as follows: "Burquitlam-Lougheed is a complete community made up of a collection of distinctive neighbourhoods. These range from active neighbourhood centres and streets in the core, to quieter, outlying, lower-residential areas." (COQ-BLNP 2017, p. 8). To achieve this vision and diversify land uses, the city drew three concentric circles around the station area based on policies in its Transit-Oriented-Development Strategy (COQ-TDS 2012). It proposed placing the highest density, shops, offices, and apartments right next to the SkyTrain station. The city envisioned townhomes and apartments within a 5 minute walk of the stop and single family homes and 3–4plexes within a 10–15 minute walk (COQ-BLNP 2017, p. 9). One local planner remembered that a core question during plan development was "how far into the neighborhood will the density increase go?" At the time of the planning process, land assemblers were already approaching homeowners to purchase their land. One planner remembered this about the debate on the planning process:

> Traditionally residents say 'leave us alone, we don't want our neighborhood to change'. [But] this [planning] process was occurring at the same time where the greater Vancouver property market was seeing double increases in values. [...] Residents approached us [saying] that they wanted more change and higher densities than we were proposing. It was all about personal monetary value. But it worked in our favor, groups of neighbors signed petitions: Your densities aren't going high enough.
>
> (VAN-L-COC expert)

Through the land re-designation process, the value of the land drastically changed. This meant that property owners were not selling their homes in a private transaction, but rather selling their land for its value to commercial real estate brokers. During the neighborhood engagement process, the city addressed several concerns from the residents. A planner familiar with the process explained that some residents were concerned about how far the new towers would be from the station. Renters wanted to know what would happen if an old apartment was demolished. The City of Coquitlam took pride in its housing affordability strategy that included assistance to relocate if an old rental property was demolished.

To determine the densities and permissible uses in the neighborhood, Coquitlam also solicited the services of a global real estate services company which prepared a market analysis. A key concern of the community was to ensure "locally appropriate growth." In terms of diversity of uses, the report indicated that there was no market for regional scale employment in Coquitlam. In alignment with the recommendations, the neighborhood plan focused more on re-designating land for local office space and services targeted at the local community. The report indicated that downtown Vancouver has long been a more attractive location for regional scale employment. But the City of Coquitlam has been very successful in terms of residential development. The community planned for up to 10,000 new units by 2041, but had already issued permits for 7,200 new units in 2018.

Zoning and land use designations are organized in a fairly flexible manner. Coquitlam allows ample room for negotiation between a developer and the city. The Coquitlam city council adopted a new land use designations map. Each land use designation contains several zoning categories from which a developer can choose. One expert explained:

> When an applicant comes forward, they apply for a rezoning and development permit at the same time. The applicant can choose from the list of zones within the land use designation for a property. The approval is granted by city council (incl. public hearing).
>
> (VAN-L-COC expert)

For example, the land use designation for the area right around the station is 'Transit Village Commercial' (Figure 4.3). Within that designation a developer can choose between commercial or two types of high density apartment residential. A developer then applies with the city and they negotiate on form and character of the development. Furthermore, developers can get density bonuses.

In 2018, multiple developments were being built in the Burquitlam-Lougheed FTDA. Despite conflicts between the City of Coquitlam, Metro Vancouver, and TransLink in the past two decades over the adoption of the RGS and transit funding, the integrating mechanisms around the RGS have supported coordination and conflict resolution to the extent that local land use efforts align with transit investments. As evidenced by the 2002 Burquitlam-Lougheed Plan, the city has long planned for this station site. TransLink did consider multiple routes for its investment but ultimately selected the more expensive alignment that ensured connecting the locally-designated centers. The redevelopment potential around the station areas and subsequent increase in ridership were definitely factors in TransLink's decision. Next, I will elaborate on the transit planning process in the City of Surrey.

Neighbohrood meets new development near the Burquitlam-Lougheed transit station at the corner of Como Lake Avenue and Claremont Street.

New development adjacent to Burquitlam-Lougheed transit station at the corner of Clarke Road and Como Lake Avenue.

Figure 4.3 Pictures of redevelopment near Burquitlam-Lougheed FTDA.
Source: Own pictures.

City of Surrey: working through transit alignment options

The City of Surrey is one of the larger cities in the Metro Vancouver region with a population of 517,887 in 2016 (Canadian Census). Metro Vancouver projected in 2011 that the City of Surrey will grow to 770,000 by 2041 (MV-RGS 2011, p. 68). Surrey's downtown serves as a hub for transit south of the Fraser River. Accordingly, Surrey Metro Center is designated as one of the two largest urban centers in the RGS (MV-RGS 2011, p. 19f.).

In 2006 and 2007, TransLink studied possible alignments for rapid transit to connect the municipalities south of the Fraser River (TL-SOFATP 2007). The transit plan envisioned downtown Surrey as the hub of transit services to other communities. The South of the Fraser River Study suggested connecting the various regional town centers and municipal town centers by rapid transit (TL-SOFATP 2007, p. 46; TL-SOFATP 2007–Phase 2, p. 9). The study identified two general alignments relevant to the City of Surrey: They are (1) the Newton-Guildford Line, which connects the Surrey City Center to two smaller municipal centers, and (2) the line connecting Langley Town Center to the Surrey City Center along Fraser Highway[4] (Figure 4.4).

A more detailed analysis of the two routes discussed above was then conducted as part of the Surrey Rapid Transit Alternatives Analysis (Surrey RTAA 2012). Twelve possible combinations of the general alignment, with various modes of transportation (bus, light rail, SkyTrain), were evaluated as part of a "multiple accounts analysis." The 12 options included 2 bus-rapid

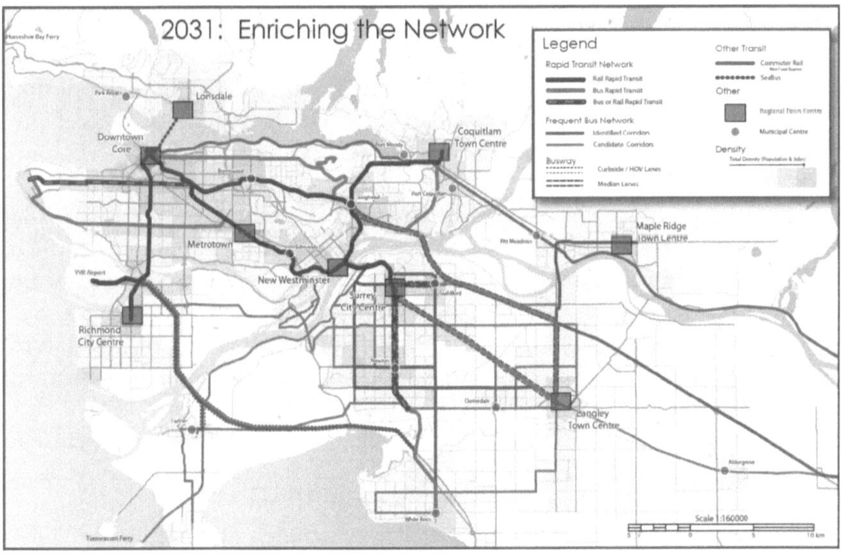

Figure 4.4 Current and future transit network.
Source: TL-SOFATP 2007, p. 48.

transit options, 6 light-rail options, and 4 rail-rapid transit options (Surrey RTAA 2012, p. xi). Performance under several criteria ("accounts") was analyzed for each option (Surrey RTAA 2012, p. viii): transportation, financial, environment, urban development, economic development, social/community, and deliverability. The evaluation was conducted by TransLink in close collaboration with the municipality. When the study was completed, there was no decision on a final alignment and technology but rather the decision was delayed to a later point (RTAA 2013, p. 10).

A couple years later, TransLink confirmed two general alignments as regional priorities in the RTS (TL-RTS 2013, p. 13). both alignments were two of three transit priorities in TransLink's Mayors' Vision (TL-Mayors' Vision 2014, p. III). The Mayors' Vision preferred light rail for both corridors. At the request of the province, TransLink reassessed both alignments. The Newton-Guildford Line was initially prioritized because it performed better in the multiple accounts assessment (TL-Memo 2017). Based on the map, the Newton-Guildford Line would have served denser locations within the City of Surrey (Figure 4.4).

Once the route and technology were chosen, the next challenge was to gather funding for the project. Funding was committed to the "Newton-Gilford-Line" in 2016 when the federal and provincial governments were looking to invest in transit projects to reduce GHG emissions. In fact, the transit project in Surrey was part of the provincial climate action strategy (BC-CAP 2016, p. 21). The initial plan was to first construct the Newton-Guildford Line and to then construct the second priority - the SkyTrain along Fraser Highway into Langley Township. In the meantime, a Bus Rapid Transit was supposed to operate along Fraser Highway to slowly build demand for transit along the corridor. The preliminary design for the Newton-Guildford Line was completed in mid-2018 and TransLink was preparing to authorize funds for construction when a local election changed Surrey's leadership.[5] The newly elected council won on a platform opposing the Newton-Guildford Line in favor of the secondary priority, a SkyTrain along Fraser Highway. With the transit project being financed by 1/3 local funds, the city withdrew.

Curiously enough, the Mayors' Board at TransLink, the province, and the federal government supported this shift in local preference in 2018. It should be highlighted that at this point, both corridors were equally valid options. However, with shifting local political priorities, TransLink had been able to work out an alternative to developing the Newton-Guildford Line as BRT, and reprioritizing funds towards the SkyTrain. Interestingly, the Surrey mayor argued in front of the TransLink Mayors' Council that the technology shift was also in the provincial and federal interest because it invested in a regional infrastructure connecting one additional city (Chan, Dec. 13, 2018). The investment will include funds to develop a new business case for the SkyTrain extension to the City of Langley (TL-SkyTrain 2020).

As the SkyTrain extension is more costly than the Newton-Guildford Line LRT, the senior-level governments are working on funding the project, but face challenges due to COVID-19 (Chan, Sept. 3, 2020). While construction could have commenced in 2018 for the light rail connecting Surrey Downtown to the town centers of Guildford and Newton, the local political leadership opted for the SkyTrain along Fraser Highway.

Land use changes in the City of Surrey

Surrey's downtown will serve as the hub of rapid transit south of the Fraser River because it already has access to the regional SkyTrain network. Currently, the SkyTrain Expo-Line connects Surrey downtown (King George Station) to Vancouver downtown. As discussed above, the plan envisions that the King George Station will serve as the hub for further transit development south of the Fraser River. This section briefly discusses changes in land uses around the King George station as well as the general approach of the City of Surrey to land use development. For context, the City of Surrey is not built out and contains a large share of land outside of the Urban Containment Boundary which is in the Agricultural Land Reserve. While there is greenfield development within the City of Surrey, this greenfield development is within the urban containment area. The strategic approach of densifying to protect open spaces is therefore essential to the City of Surrey to ensure it maintains its land development potential. The subsequent section first discusses the redevelopment around the King George Station and afterwards reviews the general approach to permitting new developments.

Surrey has had a SkyTrain station in its downtown since 1994, but redevelopment did not take place around the station until the last eight to nine years (expert interview; see Figure 4.5). Experts from the city suggested that the change in land values across the region was one factor, but another may have been the city's changes to land use designations. The City of Surrey, similarly to the City of Coquitlam, hired a market analysis firm to determine if the densities in the areas along the SkyTrain were appropriate. From the study, the city learned that some densities were too low to spur market interest. After the market study was completed, the recommended changes in density were then formalized into policies in the OCP and a town center plan was prepared. The experts indicated that some parcels had not yet been redeveloped because some property owners speculated that prices would continue to rise.

While downtown Surrey has a town center plan, much of the other zoning throughout Surrey has not been updated since the 1980s (expert interview). Therefore, many rezonings are done at the request of developers based on the land use designations map which is part of the OCP. The land use designations map in the OCP contains several broad designations such as

View of City Hall and Civic Plaza in the City of Surrey near the Skytrain station Surrey Central Station.

View of Skytrain station from City Hall with new development adjacent to the station.

Figure 4.5 Pictures from Surrey City Hall near Surrey Central Station.
Source: Own pictures.

"urban," "suburban," "rural," and "commercial." Each land use designation has specific permissible densities. For instance, the urban designation permits 37 units per hectare (15 units per acre). Within regionally designated urban centers, densities are permissible up to 72 units per hectare (30 units per acre) (Surrey-OCP 2013, p. 45). The experts explained that spot zoning is very common in the city wherein a developer comes forward with a proposal and the city adopts the zoning accordingly. One local planner explained the type of new development that is most common in Surrey:

> Townhomes are no problem - we could cover all of Surrey in townhomes. We have a lot of small and medium sized developers. It has only been recently that we've seen more sophisticated developers that can do a mixed use tower, who can put the financing together, who can navigate the many moving pieces. We've only recently seen those Vancouver developers come out here.
>
> (VAN-L-SUR1 expert)

Even townhome developments are denser than suburban development. The local planners explained that they were intentionally working with the city council to increase the densities for new developments throughout Surrey in order to be able to justify transit services in the future. The interviews showed that TransLink had been communicating that there needed to be certain minimum densities for transit access. Furthermore, the detailed design study for the Newton-Guildford Line included an effort to re-designate the land use densities along the corridor (see Figure 4.6). The planners I interviewed echoed the feedback about that experience from the City of Coquitlam: namely, property owners in single-family residential areas are quite happy with the increase in permissible densities given their chance to sell their homes for a much higher value when they are ready to move out.

The local planners indicated that much of the actual land use changes depend on the development applications and the elected officials who approve the application. It appeared that the prospect of constructing the Newton-Guildford Line had spurred much development interest along the corridor. However, some of the proposals did not meet the densities expected for a light-rail corridor, and the city had to require higher densities. For instance, townhomes were proposed in locations suitable for four-story apartment buildings.

Another aspect of the transit-land use relationship is the issue of providing transit once densities have increased. Most infill and new developments in the City of Surrey were primarily townhomes, single family houses, or coach houses. The city has been permitting property owners to add coach houses on their properties, which increases the overall density of the city. However, there is a related infrastructure challenge – because the areas are largely unserved by transit, residents generally still have two cars per

The Newton-Guildford Line was planned along this corridor on 104th Avenue (picture taken at the corner with 144th Street).

Townhomes on 144th Street and 103 Avenue in proximity to initially planned Newton-Guildford Line.

Figure 4.6 Pictures along the corridor for the Newton-Guildford Line.
Source: Own pictures.

household which leads to problems with parking and sufficient infrastructure. An expert of the City of Surrey said:

> Planning does all their LU planning and makes assumptions about commercial and high-density based on an idea that transit will come. It's been a huge challenge. The region doesn't have a lot of power over funding transit. The mayors do sit on the Mayors' council but we are relying on the province to pass legislation to fund transit.
>
> (VAN-L-SUR1 expert)

This underscores one of the challenges in a governance arrangement with functionally separated powers. Each decision-making center needs to participate in order to achieve a shared vision. Conflicts over technology, timing, funding, and route alignment are likely to occur and place a strain on the relationships. Faced with these challenges, it has been helpful to have an overarching regional vision as part of the RGS. Overall, the Metro Vancouver region is very strong in developing a clear regional spatial vision which is translated into land use and transit actions at the local and regional levels through a myriad of integrating mechanisms. But, ultimately the transit component hinges on senior-level governments funding transit projects. In that sense, the increased interest of senior-level governments in funding rapid transit projects to reduce emissions was a window of opportunity to implement plans which had long been in the making. Within that window of opportunity, the provincial government even accommodated a repurposing of funds towards a different kind of transit project – emphasizing local control as the City of Surrey itself is most impacted by the transit investment.

Notes

1. For the evolution of both of the agencies and recurring conflicts over prioritizing and funding transit routes (see Krawchenko 2012).
2. The non-urban areas include three land use designations: (1) rural, (2) agricultural, and (3) conservation and recreation (MV-RGS 2011, p. 9f.). The urban land use designations include: (1) general urban, (2) industrial, and (3) mixed employment (MV-RGS 2011, p. 9f.).
3. A common critique on growth boundaries in the United States (oftentimes referencing Portland) is the affordability problem. Metro Vancouver is very cognizant of this issue and strives to ensure "diverse and affordable housing choices" (Strategy 4.1) (MV-RGS 2011, p. 45; see also MV-CCAP 2010, p. 4). Metro Vancouver also has a separate Affordable Housing Strategy.
4. Fraser Highway is not an interstate highway but rather a principal arterial with regular intersections and sidewalks.
5. The interviews were conducted while the Newton-Guildford Line was still being planned for.

5 Ensuring plan consistency in the Puget Sound region

The Puget Sound region (Washington State, USA) is an example of an overlapping planning system where each level of government creates rules-in-use for low-carbon development patterns. Planning documents at multiple levels of government have equal standing in promoting low-carbon development patterns. This chapter explores the rules-in-use around the Regional Growth Strategy (RGS) in the Puget Sound region (Washington State, USA) and outlines approaches for self-regulation to work collaboratively on low-carbon development patterns at the regional level. The chapter highlights policies and opportunities that foster plan consistency between local and regional entities. The discussion provides an example of how state law can encourage plan consistency and coordinated decision-making across levels and sectors of government.

Encouraging low-carbon development patterns as part of growth management in Washington State

Growth management in Washington State

Washington State's planning system is designed to foster self-regulated collaboration among regional, county, and local stakeholders. All three levels of government are involved in creating low-carbon development patterns. The local level is the primary implementing entity for changes in densities and mix of uses. The regional and county levels are involved in directing growth to the urbanized area. And lastly, the transit provider Sound Transit is responsible for the rapid transit network, including funding and alignment decisions. While the state's Growth Management Act creates a broad framework for coordination across the three levels of government, it leaves many procedural details to self-regulated efforts. Nevertheless, requiring to coordinate and ensure plan consistency is uncommon the United States where all land use authority is predominantly exercised at the local level.

In the United States, land use planning and zoning are a jealously protected right of local governments (expert interviews; see also Deangelo & Harvey 1998, p. 120).[1] Most of the 50 states in the United States have delegated

DOI: 10.4324/9781003268505-6

all land use authority to local governments by adopting a model law, the Standard State Zoning Enabling Act (SSZEA) in the 1920s (see also Stephens & Wikstrom 2000, p. 51). The SSZEA delegated all zoning rights to cities but did not create a planning law (Kaiser & Godschalk 1995, p. 126; Meck 2006, p. 589). The US Department of Commerce issued the SSZEA in 1924 and most US states subsequently adopted it. A second model law was issued in 1928, the Standard City Planning Enabling Act (SCPEA). Section IV of the SCPEA would have established regional planning commissions and regional plans however, the SCPEA was not as widely adopted as the SSZEA. So, most states had a legal framework for zoning but no framework for planning across levels of government (Kaiser & Godschalk 1995, p. 126).

In the early 1970s, there were several attempts to create planning legislation at the federal level but none succeeded. Subsequently, in most states in the United States, any sized community can control land use: "legally fragment[ing] entire metropolitan areas into hundreds or even more than a thousand local governments" (Kantor 2013, p. 830). Many local governments create their own legal framework for zoning. The rationale in assigning regulatory powers to the local level is that the local level can better respond to local needs (Hooghe & Marks 2003, p. 234; Homsy & Warner 2015, p. 49; see also Downs 1997; Altshuler et al. 1999; Stephens & Wikstrom 2000, p. 18; Kantor 2013, p. 830). Local autonomy and competition are deeply ingrained in the US culture, which contributes to a perception that legislative rules from the senior-level government are inappropriate (Hardinghaus 2004).

Nevertheless, due to environmental concerns and the negative externalities of suburbanization, some states began to revise their zoning enabling legislation and enact more comprehensive land-use planning laws starting in the 1960s (Popper 1988, p. 99; Kayden 2001, p. 46; Birch 2005, p. 333; Abbott 2006, p. 86; Daniels 2009, p. 187). These states are sometimes referred to as growth management or smart growth states (Gale 1992; Bollens 1993). States that follow a growth management approach include Hawaii (1961), Vermont (1970), California (1972), Oregon (1973), Florida (1985), New Jersey (1986), Maine (1988), Rhode Island (1988), Georgia (1989), Washington State (1990), Maryland (1992), Tennessee (1998), Colorado (2000), and Arizona (1998) (see Gale 1992, p. 427; Abbott 2006, p. 86; Diller 2015, p. 23). Each state's legislation differs significantly, including on questions about what levels of government must prepare plans, what levels have oversight (state or regional), and how the review, comment, or approval procedures are designed (Gale 1992, p. 435; Bollens 1993; Kaiser & Godschalk 1995, p. 143). But even in smart growth states, land-use planning and zoning are commonly conducted at the local level, while the senior level reserves some oversight and permitting power for specific spatial policies (Kayden 2001, p. 46).

As a growth management state, Washington State decided to establish a framework for joint planning across levels of government in order to direct growth to the urbanized area. However, in the spirit of home-rule, Washington State primarily defines desirable outcomes but leaves many specifics up to self-regulation. Several authors have argued that the emphasis on independent actors is deeply rooted in the American political ethos (Hardinghaus 2004, p. 152; Krawchenko 2012, p. 118; expert interviews); a core value for land development in the United States is the ownership of land by its citizens and decentralized self-governance of that land by small communities (Hardinghaus 2004, p. 75). For self-governed communities, it is essential to be able to make their own rules (home-rule) and to have their own funding sources (right to raise and lower a variety of taxes at the local level). As a growth management state, Washington State creates a framework for counties to be more involved in land use governance.

Regional planning established under federal laws

In addition to state planning enabling legislations, US federal laws add another layer of complexity to metropolitan governance. The federal government creates several funding programs in the transportation, housing, and environmental sectors which have an impact on spatial development patterns within metropolitan regions without necessarily intentionally trying to alter development patterns (Popper 1988; Stephens & Wikstrom 2000; Kayden 2001, p. 44; Birch 2005, p. 333; Whittemore 2012). For the federal transportation program, a share of the federal dollars is directly allocated to Metropolitan Planning Organizations (MPOs) that prepare long-range transportation plans. For federal programs in economic development, regional districts are encouraged to use Comprehensive Economic Development Strategies to promote regional priorities that the federal government uses to assess the merits of individual project applications. Lastly, Areawide Planning Agencies are responsible for regional water plans. Having special districts for specific sectors is common across the United States (Kantor 2013, p. 830). The organizations are often governed as councils of governments with boards composed of local government representatives (Wachs & Dill 1999; Altshuler et al. 1999, p. 111).

Frequently, the governance structures in metropolitan areas are truly polycentric, as decision-makers are oftentimes formally independent but may choose to cooperate toward a common goal. Washington State sets integration requirements for the local/county land use decision-making and makes coordination across counties on growth management optional. The implications of these more self-regulated rules-in-use will become clearer as I present more details about the Puget Sound region.

State level considering and encouraging low-carbon development patterns

The emphasis on self-regulation can also be observed for climate governance in Washington State: Washington State provides guidance rather than requirements. For example, in 2008 and 2009, the state legislature adopted emissions reduction targets for state agencies (SoW-61st legislature 2009, SoW-60th legislature 2008, see also RCW 70.235.020, 050 and 060). Several state agencies were also instructed to study and engage with communities in an effort to reduce emissions (Executive orders by Gregoire 2009; Inslee 2014). Several cross-departmental working groups prepared reports suggesting initiatives the state could take to foster climate actions (SoW-CAP 2008; SoW-CTED 2008; SoW-Leading 2008).[2] The reports discuss low-carbon development patterns but none of the recommendations resulted in changes to the Growth Management Act.

The reports suggest low-carbon development patterns as ways to reduce vehicle miles traveled and related emissions (SoW-CAP 2008; SoW-CTED 2008; SoW-Leading 2008). One report discusses changes to the Growth Management Act to promote compact transit-connected communities (SoW-CAP 2008, p. 56). However, the same report concludes that the current purpose of planning under the Growth Management Act sufficiently addresses the need for low-carbon development patterns (SoW-CAP 2008, p. 56). The "Planning for Climate Change" report also suggests requiring governments to include GHG reduction targets in their comprehensive plans (SoW-CTED 2008, p. 9).

Although the reports made specific recommendations on changes to the legislation, they were never included in legislative updates to the Growth Management Act. One expert involved explained that politics over who has jurisdiction made it challenging to update the Growth Management Act. Given the strong feelings about local land-use rights, the state-level government limits itself to providing information on low-carbon development patterns rather than pursuing changes to the planning legislation. The Department of Commerce now provides information around growth management related to climate action and honors communities with an award program (WS-DoC, no date). The historically strong role of the local level in land use decisions clearly influenced the state's climate agenda and efforts. Generally, the state level is more about "serving" the local level than steering through incentives or dictating from above.

Though the state legislature intends to foster VMT reductions, it must rely on the local, county, and regional levels to implement them. The state supports local requests and assists with information on how to implement low-carbon development patterns. However, the state is not an active player when it comes to framing the local climate agenda or fostering low-carbon development patterns. While the various reports at the state level point to the need to integrate land use and transportation decision-making and increase efforts to foster compact urban development, none of these recommendations have been promoted by lawmakers. Within the overlapping planning system, the state level delegates many policy issues to the regional, county and local level. Subsequently, I discuss the role of the regional level.

Regional growth strategy in the Puget Sound region

Self-regulated regional growth management

Low-carbon development patterns are central to Puget Sound's RGS. This section provides a deep dive into the self-regulated aspect of this RGS. Overall, the planning law in Washington State lays the groundwork for collective action between the local, county, and regional levels. Although the local level primarily governs land uses and zoning, the Washington State Growth Management Act creates opportunities that foster integrated decision-making: the state law requires the counties to draft countywide planning policies and permits multicounty planning policies in continuously urbanized areas such as the Puget Sound region. Figure 5.1 and this section provide an overview of the integrating mechanisms and actors within the Puget Sound region.

The Puget Sound Regional Council (PSRC) is the region's MPO. Geographically, PSRC covers the counties of King, Kitsap, Pierce, and Snohomish as well as the 86 local jurisdictions contained therein (PSRC-Plan Review 2014, p. v). PSRC is primarily responsible for planning the regional transportation system and ensuring cooperation between the state and local jurisdictions on transportation issues (USC 23 Sec 134; RCW 47.80.010). Additionally, PSRC prepares the RGS based on an intergovernmental agreement (1993) of the counties and largest cities represented on PSRC board. This means that the RGS is regulated by planning documents created at the regional level, unlike the other two regions which are state-regulated. The Puget Sound region has leveraged several provisions within state law to ensure that the RGS is more than a guiding document for local governments.

The Washington State Growth Management Act creates three integration requirements that establish the context for coordinating across multiple levels of government to address questions of territorial development in the Puget Sound region. The integration requirements are (1) the plan consistency requirements, (2) the permission to regulate consistency through multicounty and countywide planning policies, and (3) PSRC's certification of the transportation element of local comprehensive plans and Sound Transit plans. PSRC and King County use these three integration requirements to establish a review process of local comprehensive plans and Sound Transit plans that affect development patterns. PSRC has established the RGS as a guiding document with some bearing on local land use questions by leveraging the state legislative guidance on multicounty planning policies. Figure 5.1 gives a broad overview on the actors and integrating mechanisms. This chapter reviews how PSRC applies the state legislation to create integrating mechanisms for the RGS.

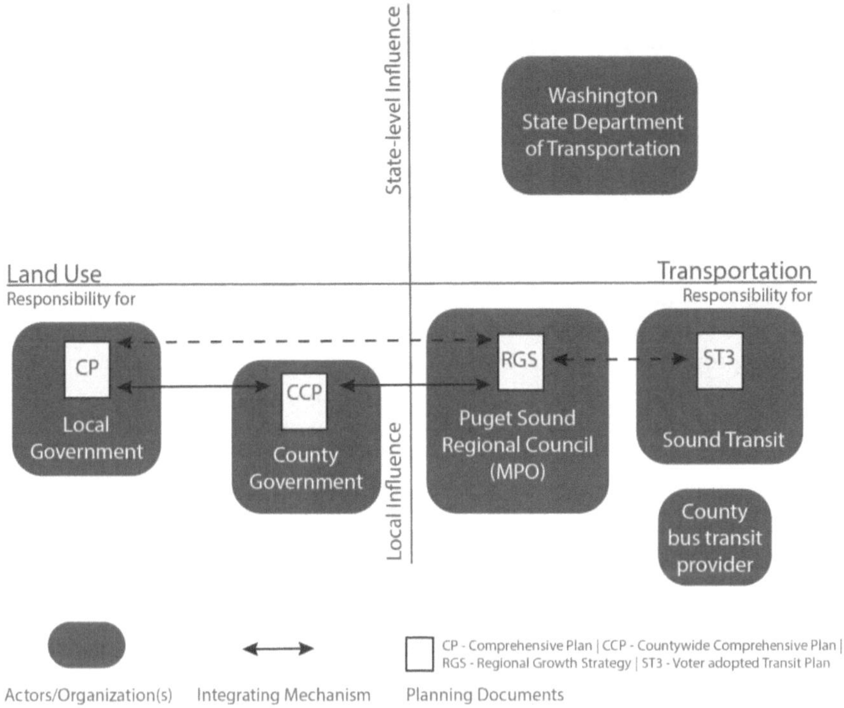

Figure 5.1 Responsibilities in land use and transportation in the Puget Sound region.
Source: Own illustration.

Plan consistency requirements and countywide planning policies

The central integrating mechanism for coordinated land use decisions is a state requirement for plan consistency and coordination among local and county comprehensive plans (RCW 36.70A.100). By requiring consistency between local and county comprehensive plans, Washington State is one of the few growth management states that embeds local zoning into a larger planning context. Local zoning and budget decisions must conform to the local comprehensive plan (RCW 36.70A.120). The local comprehensive plan then needs to be consistent with county comprehensive plans (RCW 36.70A.100[3]; RCW 36.70A.210(7)). Based on this chain of consistency requirements, the county comprehensive plan can have some bearing on local land use decisions.

To ensure consistency, counties are authorized to draft countywide planning policies in collaboration with their communities (RCW 36.70A.210(2)). Among other things, the countywide planning policies regulate how the consistency requirement is actually implemented (RCW 36.70A.210(3)a).

State law defines the countywide planning policies as a "written policy statement or statements used solely for establishing a countywide framework from which county and city comprehensive plans are developed and adopted" (RCW 36.70A.210(1)). Therefore the countywide planning policies and county comprehensive plan provide general directives for local plans and zoning (KC-Comp Plan 2012, p. I-4). To some extent, the countywide planning policies replace a more detailed state legislative framework for planning.

The state legislators adopted this system in the 1990s in an effort to "manage urban growth [... and] reduce sprawl" (PSRC-Vision 2009, p. 2; see also RCW 36.70A.020). Nevertheless, they were careful to highlight that nothing in the law "alter[s] the land-use powers of cities" (RCW 36.70A.210(1)). One expert at the state level explained that the diversity of local preferences in Washington State means that lawmakers have enabled joint planning but do not legally require as many specifics, including how consistency is implemented. In fact, there is a wide variety in countywide planning policies across the state based on county leadership. Each county creates its own countywide planning policies to serve as a legal framework for county comprehensive plans and local comprehensive plans.

Multicounty planning policies as part of the RGS

The Puget Sound region is a special case since its contiguous urbanized area includes several counties and Washington State permits the use of multicounty planning policies to regulate how consistency is established in continuously urbanized areas. Under the Washington State Growth Management Act, multiple counties can jointly create multicounty planning policies which follow the same requirements as countywide planning policies (RCW 36.70A.210 (7)). This means that the multicounty planning policies establish the integrating mechanisms and spatial policies in the Puget Sound region, which are then further elaborated by countywide planning policies (RCW 36.70A.210(3)). The following section in state law describes the responsibility for setting spatial policies on a variety of issues:

> (3) A countywide planning policy shall at a minimum, address the following: (a) Policies to implement RCW 36.70A.110 [Consistency Requirement]; (b) Policies for promotion of contiguous and orderly development and provision of urban services to such development; (c) Policies for siting public capital facilities of a countywide or statewide nature, including transportation facilities of statewide significance as defined in RCW 47.06.140; (d) Policies for countywide transportation facilities and strategies; (e) Policies that consider the need for affordable housing, such as housing for all economic segments of the population and parameters for its distribution; (f) Policies for joint county and city planning within urban growth areas; (g) Policies for countywide economic development and employment, which must include consideration of the

> future development of commercial and industrial facilities; and (h) An analysis of the fiscal impact.
>
> (RCW 36.70A.210(3))

Since the multicounty and the countywide planning policies can contain spatial policies and integrating mechanisms, PSRC and King County decided to include them in the RGS as well as in the King County comprehensive plan (PSRC-Interlocal Agreement 1993, p. 10; PSRC-Vision 2009 pursuant to RCW 36.70A.210(3) and (7)). While formally there is no RGS under Washington State law, PSRC[4] leverages the requirements for multicounty planning policies to self-organize an RGS that has some bearing on local decision-making. The role of the multicounty planning policies is described in the RGS as follows:

> Under the Growth Management Act, multicounty planning policies provide a common regionwide framework for countywide and local planning in the central Puget Sound region. The unified structure established by the multicounty policies has both practical and substantive effects on city and county comprehensive plans. The multicounty policies provide a mechanism for achieving consistency among cities and counties on regional planning matters. They also guide a number of regional processes, including the Regional Council's policy and plan review process, [and others].
>
> (PSRC-Vision 2009, p. 29f)

While there is a consistency requirement and clear direction on what multi-county planning policies can regulate, there is no state direction on enforcement. This has let to considerable conflicts between the municipalities, counties and PSRC. local governments have contested whether there is an actual legal requirement for local comprehensive plans to comply with multicounty planning policies or countywide planning policies.[5] The state actually discussed creating enforcement mechanisms to foster low-carbon development patterns. Yet, it was not included as the currently self-regulated approach was deemed sufficient.

Certification of the transportation element in local comprehensive plans

To self-regulate the enforcement of the RGS, PSRC is leveraging its transportation responsibilities. In addition to the requirements of the Growth Management Act, PSRC is also governed by federal and state transportation laws. The state transportation law authorizes PSRC to certify the consistency of the transportation element of local comprehensive plans with the regional transportation plan (WAC 468-86-150). PSRC leverages the requirement to also review the land use sections in local comprehensive plans. PSRC also derives its authority from its responsibilities as a regional transportation authority (RTPO) under state law. The state requires that the transportation element of a local comprehensive plan be consistent with the regional long-range transportation plan (PSRC-Interlocal Agreement 1993, p. 11; PSRC Policy 2003, PSRC-Plan Review 2014; WAC 468-86-150). One point of contention during the approval process of local comprehensive plans has been over whether PSRC has the authority to certify land use policies in local comprehensive plans as well.

State law requires the regional transportation planning organizations to create guidelines and principles for transportation planning. The guidelines and principles

> shall address at a minimum the relationship between transportation systems and the following factors: Concentration of economic activity, residential density, development corridors and urban design that, where appropriate, supports high capacity transit, [...], development patterns that promote pedestrian and nonmotorized transportation.
>
> (RCW 47.80.026)

As PSRC's multicounty planning policies also serve as the guidelines and principles for transportation planning, PSRC can include development patterns and land use issues in its review process. By working with the PSRC board, PSRC negotiated with its members so that it can also certify parts of the land use components in local comprehensive plans, as they pertain to concentration of economic activity and residential density (expert interviews).

PSRC also attached a financial incentive to the certification process. PSRC leverages its role as the federally designated MPO to only allow jurisdictions with certified plans to be eligible to apply for funding for transportation projects (PSRC-Vision 2009, pp. 29f). While PSRC board members had agreed to consider land use aspects for the certification, conflicts arose once specific local comprehensive plans were not certified. Within this self-regulated context, enforcing the development patterns and spatial policies within the RGS has been very contentious; communities frequently claimed that PSRC was overstepping its authority. To resolve conflicts around the Growth Management Act, the state legislation created the Growth Management Hearings Board – a quasi-judicial entity that hears conflicts arising from the Growth Management Act.

To summarize, state legislation requires consistency in local and county comprehensive plans. The state law delegates the responsibility to determine how consistency is established to the county and region levels (RCW 36.70A.100; RCW 36.70A.210; RCW 36.70A.210(7)). The regional and county levels have created multicounty and countywide planning policies to guide integrated decision-making (RCW 36.70A.210(3)a). These policies are included in the RGS and in the county comprehensive plan. Together, the multi-county and the countywide planning policies can govern territorial development within the Puget Sound region by providing a framework for local policy-making. Enforcing this consistency has been somewhat contentious. To conclude, the countywide and multicounty planning policies define the integrating procedures as well as the spatial policies in the Puget Sound region. The state law does not define any integrating mechanisms other than requiring integrated decision-making through the plan consistency requirement.

Relevance of low-carbon development patterns in climate efforts at the regional and county levels

Through the multicounty and countywide planning policies, PSRC and King County can define broad visions for the territorial development of the Puget Sound region. PSRC and King County leverage this ability for their climate efforts by clearly linking their climate agendas to the spatial policies in the RGS and in the King County Comprehensive Plan. The subsequent sections describe to what extent low-carbon development patterns are a part of these climate agendas.

PSRC's climate agenda places low-carbon development patterns front and center to reduce transportation emissions in the region (PSRC-GHG Strategy, p. 4). A strategy to reduce emissions is to focus new development in regional growth centers served by rapid transit (PSRC-GHG Strategy 2018, p. 3; PSRC-Vision 2009, p. 13). The centers are characterized by denser, mixed-use pedestrian-oriented developments with access to reliable transit (PSRC-Vision 2009, p. 14). Encouraging low-carbon development patterns is estimated to reduce emissions by 6% (PSRC-GHG Strategy 2018, p. 4). Vision 2040 stresses the importance of continuing this approach to address climate change (PSRC-Vision 2009, p. 15). Yet, PSRC relies on actions at the county level, the local level, and by the rapid transit provider Sound Transit to implement low-carbon development patterns.

King County – the largest county in the Puget Sound region – also emphasizes low-carbon development patterns in its climate action strategy. King County is a leader in climate actions and growth management within the Puget Sound region and is very active in pursuing climate actions across various county agencies. An organizational structure supports continued cross-departmental debate.[6] King County's Strategic Climate Action Plan (KC-SCAP 2015) lists land use and transportation commitments as its primary goals. One expert explained that the SCAP focuses on actions in areas that the county can influence. This includes spatial policies for the urban growth area as well as the bus transit services within the county. Particularly, the county responsibility for urban containment is highlighted as a key element of climate mitigation. The spatial policies at play are subsequently explored in more detail. It is noteworthy, that while low-carbon development patterns are on the climate agendas of both PSRC and King County, the actual spatial policies have not significantly changed to pursue reductions in GHG emissions.

Spatial policies and accompanying integrating mechanism in the Puget Sound region

This section reviews the spatial policies set out in the RGS and by King County. Given the emphasis on self-regulation in the planning system, each spatial policy is accompanied by its own integrating mechanism. Therefore, this section reviews the integrating procedures in conjunction with the respective spatial policies. This is distinctly different from the other two regions. The other two are characterized by legislatively defined integrating mechanisms that evolve around the RGS. A unique characteristic of the Puget Sound region is that integrating procedures are particular to each spatial policy rather than to full planning documents.

The RGS prepared by PSRC contains several spatial policies to direct growth. At the heart of growth management in Washington State is the designation of the urban growth area and the direction of growth thereto. This is achieved by permitting the counties to draw an urban growth boundary around the urban growth area in conjunction with a growth targeting process for communities. This county responsibility is guided by the multi-county planning policies in the RGS which are supposed to impose coherence between the four counties. Besides the state required spatial policy to designate an urban growth area, PSRC included regional growth centers as a spatial policy approach in its RGS Hence, PSRC created a separate set of procedures around designating regional growth centers – municipalities can apply to become a regional growth center. One characteristic of the overlapping planning system is many overlapping responsibilities without clear functional distinctions. The subsequent sections review the spatial policies and affiliated integrating mechanisms individually.

Defining the urban growth area and drawing a growth boundary

The Washington State Growth Management Act (1990) makes counties responsible for designating urban growth areas. An urban growth area is characterized as follows by state law "(1) … within [the urban growth area], urban growth shall be encouraged and outside of [the urban growth area] growth can occur only if it is not urban in nature." (RCW 36.70A.110 (1)). The urban growth area is characterized by "adequate existing public facility and service capacities to serve such development" (RCW 36.70A.110 (3)). Accordingly, in the 1990s all counties designated an urban growth area within their comprehensive plans and adopted countywide planning policies for the urban growth areas.

An underpinning concept of the urban growth area is the designation of three types of land: urban land, rural land, and resource lands. The urban land is the "Urban Growth Area" (*Siedlungsbereich*) which, in King County, is characterized by housing, commercial, and industrial developments in a variety of densities (KC-CPP 2012, p. 18, policy DP-2). The rural lands primarily serve agricultural uses and the resource lands include forests, the Cascade Mountains, timber production and mining (KC-CPP 2012, pp. 29 and 30, policy DP-45, DP-46, DP-52). Some of the growth boundary is along the unincorporated area of King County – which means that the county, rather than the communities, is directly working with property owners on rezoning requests. If conflicts over the boundary do arise, the state has created the Growth Management Hearing Board, a court specializing in land use questions within Washington State. Otherwise, the urban growth area is reviewed at least every ten years during the amendment process of the King County comprehensive plan (KC-CPP 2012, p. 22, policies DP-14 ff.).

Each county developed its own set of policies around designating the urban growth area and defining spatial policies for it. When the growth areas were initially drawn, some counties included larger portions of agriculturally used lands while others did not. The responsibility for maintaining the urban growth area boundary is specifically emphasized in King County's SCAP as a relevant spatial policy to reduce emissions (KC-SCAP 2015, p. 40).

King County attributes emissions savings to its consequent directing of new growth into the urban growth area. One target in the SCAP is to ensure that "97 percent of new residential construction occurs within the UGA" in King County (KC-SCAP 2015, p. 42). King County estimates that due to the designated urban growth area, 7% of GHG emissions are avoided in the county annually (KC-SCAP 2015, p. 44). The respective section in the SCAP reads as follows:

> Since 1994, when King County's Growth Management Act (GMA) boundaries were established, new residential construction has been focused within defined urban growth areas. As a result, since 2011, less than two percent of new residential construction has occurred in the rural area, exceeding the new target of maintaining 97 percent of new residential growth within the urban growth boundary. This shift has helped decrease total vehicle miles traveled and associated GHG emissions in King County.
>
> (KC-SCAP 2015, p. 44)

Nevertheless, the planners I interviewed did point out that there is development pressure along the edges of the urban growth area. One planner at the county level referenced efforts by King County to purchase the land or easements on the land adjacent to the urban growth area to alleviate some of the pressure.

The designation of the urban growth area is the strongest spatial policy within the Growth Management Act. PSRC and King County have included other spatial policies in the multicounty and countywide planning policies. These other spatial policies address questions about the quantitative location of new population and employment growth within the urban growth areas. PSRC, in coordination with the counties, created a community classification called "regional geographies" which serves as the basis for the allocation of growth targets by the counties.

Allocating growth targets using "Regional Geographies"

Regional geographies are used to allocate growth targets for future population and employment growth to the 89 communities within the region. All the communities are, by definition, a part of the urban growth area.[7] The regional geographies have been a self-regulated process at PSRC since first being introduced in the RGS "Vision 2040." Previously each county used a separate process to allocate its growth targets. In an effort to provide a coherent framework, PSRC introduced the regional geographies to provide a context for the assumptions about which cities are desirable for more growth. The relevant section within Vision 2040 reads as follows:

> VISION 2040 provides guidance for the distribution of growth to regional geographies, which are defined by the idea that different types of cities and unincorporated areas will play distinct roles in the region's future. Cities, towns, and neighborhoods of various sizes and characters will continue to offer a wide choice of living options.
>
> (PSRC-Vision 2009, p. 16)

The regional geographies classify communities within the urban growth area into four primary categories: metropolitan cities, core cities, large cities, and small cities (Figure 5.2). The majority of the growth is envisioned for metropolitan cities. There are five designated metropolitan cities which are expected to absorb a large portion of the projected future employment (42%) and population growth (32%; PSRC-Vision 2009, p. 20). Each county contains one metropolitan city, with King County having two designated metropolitan cities. Besides the metropolitan cities, further growth is projected in the second highest ranking communities, called "core cities." Core cities are supposed to be the backbone of the multi-modal transportation system.

The core cities are envisioned to accommodate 22% of the population and 29% of the employment growth in the region (PSRC-Vision 2009, p. 21). The third tier of communities are called large cities which are supposed to accommodate 14% of the population growth and 12% of the employment growth in the region (PSRC-Vision 2009, p. 22). Lastly, small cities are envisioned to accommodate 8% of the population and 6% of the employment growth in the region (PSRC-Vision 2009, p. 23).

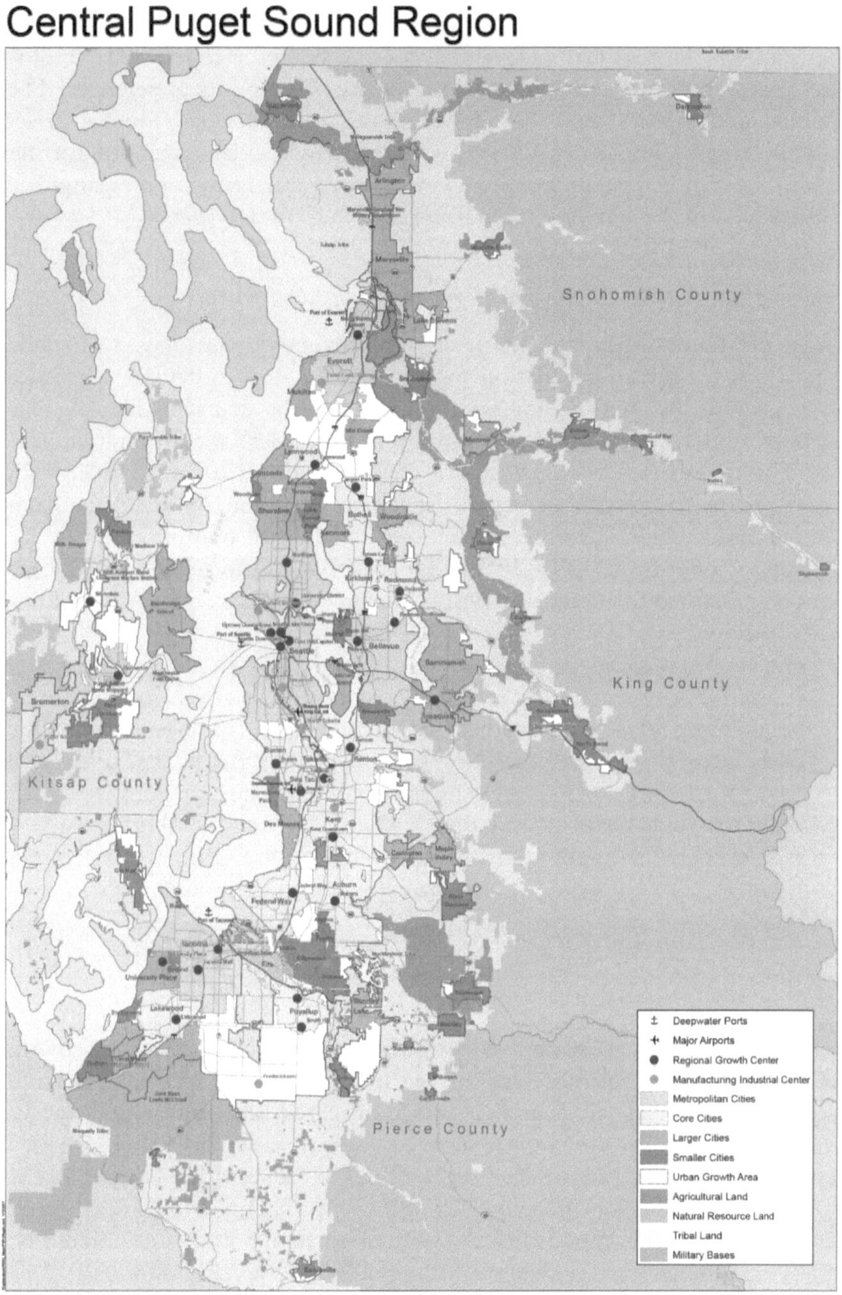

Figure 5.2 Map showing regional geographies and urban centers designated by PSRC.

Source: PSRC-Reference Map 2018.

My interviews made apparent that cities like to keep growing for financial reasons. At the same time, some cities do not like to see any growth. Within this context, the regional geographies are considered a framework to allocate some growth to each type of community based on its preferences. The regional geographies are then applied during the counties' process to set growth targets. The King County Comprehensive Plan does not further address the regional geographies; however, the regional geographies language is referenced in the numeric table assigning the growth targets.

Assigning growth targets to regional geographies at the county level

Under the Growth Management Act, comprehensive plans have to include projections for future population growth (RCW 36.70A.070(1)). The state issues growth assumptions for each county and the counties then allocate those growth assumptions to the communities through a collaborative process. This negotiation between the counties and cities is informed by PSRC's growth assumptions for each regional geography. Vision 2040 and the King County countywide planning policies stress that each community receives a "fair share" of growth (KC-CPP 2012, p. 5; PSRC-Vision 2009, p. 47). One planner explained the determination of the growth targets for each community as follows:

> If [each city was planning for its own growth], all cities combined may be planning for 2 million rather than the expected 1 million people. One of the great things with the Growth Management Act [...is that] they all have to use some form of the state number. They have to work with each other to decide how to split it up. [...] The city categories [regional geographies] help them split up the population growth. During the last round, we set the growth expectations, the counties did their targets which were more or less aligned with us.
>
> (SEA-R-LU1 expert)

Each community uses the growth targets to make decisions on transportation and other infrastructure services needed to support population growth. State laws say communities have "to ensure that the land use element [and] capital facilities plan element [...] are coordinated and consistent" (RCW 70A.070(3)). This requirement is supposed to ensure horizontal consistency between land use and transportation decisions at the local and county levels.

Accordingly, King County uses the growth projections to forecast travel demand (KC-Comp Plan 2013, pp. 7–10). This state policy is elaborated on by a King County countywide planning policy which reads as follows:

> DP-13 All jurisdictions shall plan to accommodate housing and employment targets. This includes: Adopting comprehensive plans and zoning regulations that provide capacity for residential, commercial, and

> industrial uses that is sufficient to meet 20-year growth needs and is consistent with the desired growth pattern described in VISION 2040.
>
> (KC-CPP 2012, p. 20)

This policy applies the growth projections to the zoning regulations within the community. Accordingly, communities have to zone sufficient capacity to accommodate the projected growth. One of the county planners described this process as central to meeting the consistency requirements. In short, the counties allocate growth targets to the community through a collaborative process. That allocation process is informed by PSRC's regional geographies classification and Washington State's growth target for King County. The growth targets are intended to be used in the local comprehensive planning and zoning processes to ensure sufficient capacities to absorb future growth.

Including the growth targets in the local comprehensive plan

Once the growth targets have been negotiated at the county level, they still have to be applied during the local comprehensive planning process. Based on the county targets, the local level actually decides on its own targets. One county planner said:

> And so the target is a statement of the city as this is our policy. This is how we want to grow. This is how big we want to grow in the future. And it's decided on a regional level, but each jurisdiction says what their future is.
>
> (SEA-KC-LU1 expert)

During the last round of growth targeting and updates of local comprehensive plans, most communities adopted the agreed growth targets, but some came up with their own. Most conflicts in King County arose when communities on the fringes were planning compact and complete communities away from the new transit infrastructure under construction. These communities were exceeding their growth targets by 500%–700%. They were trying to be climate conscious by building denser and mixed-use retail developments, but they would not have been connected to the regional rapid transit system, meaning people would still rely on cars. This underscores the importance of integrating transit and land use decisions – an increase in housing densities without transit access on the fringes of urbanized areas might mean an increase in VMT and thus in transportation emissions.

Enforcing the growth targets has been a challenge for PSRC and King County because the integrating procedures are not clearly defined in state law. As described above, PSRC has the legislative authority to certify the transportation element of local comprehensive plans based on its own guidelines which include the growth targets. This has created some tensions. In cases of conflicts over a contentious topic, the lack of clarity of the legislation may fuel power struggles between the different levels of government, yet it also provides regional flexibility and adaptability.

Designation of regional growth centers

Another set of spatial policies in the RGS includes the designation of growth centers. At the time I conducted the interviews, PSRC was responsible for designating regional growth centers and the counties designated countywide centers. Accordingly, PSRC has policies for regional growth centers and King County has more specific policies for countywide growth centers *(SEA-KC-LU1 expert)*. Initially, each of the four counties within PSRC had its own approach to designating regional growth centers. In 2003, in an effort to harmonize the county approaches, PSRC developed numeric thresholds describing what qualifies as a center for the region (expert interview). The subsequent section first discusses the policies in the RGS followed by a discussion of the countywide policies in King County.

Regional Growth Centers are defined in Vision 2040 as follows:

> The development of centers lies at the heart of VISION 2040 […]. Centers are characterized by compact, pedestrian-oriented development with a mix of uses. Centers provide proximity to a diverse collection of services, shopping, recreation, and jobs, as well as a variety of attractive and well-designed residences. They are locations identified to take a greater proportion of future population and employment in order to curb sprawl […]. Major regional investments for transportation and other infrastructure should be prioritized for these locations.
>
> (PSRC-Vision 2009, p. 47f)

PSRC identifies two types of regional growth centers – (1) metro growth centers and (2) urban growth centers. While the metro growth centers are larger and denser agglomerations of employment and housing, the urban growth centers are primarily considered to be downtowns in suburban cities and neighborhood centers in metropolitan cities (PSRC-RC Frame 2018, p. 6; PSRC-Vision 2009 – Appendix E1, p. E-10). The urban growth centers are introduced to encourage all of the region's cities to develop a compact location within the community (PSRC-Vision 2009–Appendix E1, p. E-10).

Ultimately, communities apply to PSRC to have a location designated as a regional growth center. PSRC self-regulates the application process for regional growth centers (PSRC-Vision 2009, p. 48, Policies MPP-DP-6). Essentially, the application process is the integrating mechanism which ensures that the local, county, and regional levels work towards advancing the same regional growth centers. The specific spatial policies used for the growth center designations include existing densities, planned densities, mix of uses, a minimum size, existing and planned transit access, market potential, and evidence of a regional role (PSRC-RC Frame 2018, p. 5f.). Another aspect of the integrating mechanisms is that communities are also asked to prepare a subarea plan for the regional growth center prior to designation (PSRC-RC Frame 2018, p. 5). Lastly, communities are asked to demonstrate local investments in the urban center to prove the local commitment (PSRC-RC Frame 2018, p. 4).

The spatial policies on regional growth centers are closely connected to the regional geographies classification as well as the growth targeting process. During the growth targeting process, communities can justify higher growth numbers if they have designated regional growth centers (expert interview, PSRC-Vision 2009, p. 48, Policies MPP-DP-5). Eventually, the regional growth centers are envisioned to be connected through rapid transit as part of a regional network. To further incentivize planning for regional growth centers, the multicounty planning policies prioritize regional growth centers for transportation and economic development funding controlled by PSRC (PSRC-Vision 2009, p. 48, Policies MP-DP-7).

Countywide growth centers

In addition to the regional growth centers, King County also designates countywide growth centers – part of an overlapping planning system involves that several levels of government perform a functionally similar task. A functional separation of powers would mean that one level would draft the policies, another level would designate, and yet another level of government would apply to be designated. Currently, King County has designated growth centers almost entirely identical to the centers designated by PSRC. This has evolved historically, as the county would ask PSRC to recognize countywide growth centers as regional growth centers (expert interview). However, this might change with the next scheduled policy update of countywide planning policies in 2023/2024 (PSRC-RC-Frame 2018, p. 15).

King County prioritizes its designated centers for investments based on a countywide planning policy (KC-Comp Plan 2012, pp. 2–6, policy U-108). The countywide planning policies are consistent with the Vision 2040 policy request for counties to prioritize the regional growth centers. Echoing Vision 2040, the countywide planning policies define regional growth centers as locations of concentrated housing and employment growth (KC-CPP 2012, p. 25, Policy DP-29). King Counties planners took pride in the fact that their policies raised the bar for local governments because the county policies were more stringent that PSRCs.

To qualify as a center, an area needs to have existing or planned high capacity transit access and meet certain criteria *(KC-CPP 2012, p. 25, Policy DP-30)*.The spatial policies (DP-31(a) and (b)(i–iii)) establish the criteria reads as follows (KC-CPP 2012, p. 25, Policy DP-31):

> a) Encompasses an area up to one and a half square miles; and b) Has adopted zoning regulations and infrastructure plans that are adequate to accommodate: i) A minimum of 15,000 jobs within one-half mile of an

> existing or planned high-capacity transit station; ii) At a minimum, an average of 50 employees per gross acre within the Urban Center; and iii) At a minimum, an average of 15 housing units per gross acre within the Urban Center.
>
> (KC-CPP 2012, p. 25, Policy DP-31)

This set of spatial policies is consistent with PSRC policies. The countywide spatial policy uses guidance provided by Vision 2040. In Vision 2040, PSRC states that a transit station needs 20,000–25,000 activity units within a square mile to support ridership. According to Vision 2040, this equals about 30–50 activity units per acre (PSRC-Vision 2009, p. 48). By setting a minimum of 50 employees per gross acre and 15 housing units, King County exceeds this guidance and ensures its planning policies are consistent with Vision 2040.

The self-regulated integrating mechanism used by PSRC and King County is an application process. Cities apply for an area to be a designated growth center. Part of the integrating mechanism is the policy that the city has to adopt zoning regulation and infrastructure plans for the new urban center (DP-31(b)). This directly connects the spatial policies and the integrating mechanisms. Through this combination, the county can guide local land use decisions and encourage rezoning.

The countywide planning policies also make more specific policy requests to be finalized at the local level; communities are required to adopt a map and policies that promote quality of life in the county growth centers. This includes that county growth centers should have "a broad mix of land uses that foster both daytime and nighttime activities and opportunities for social interaction" (KC-CPP 2012, p. 25, Policy DP-32). Through these policies, King County essentially encourages communities to increase the densities and the mix of uses within their county growth centers, which are, in turn, ideally served by high-capacity transit. One county planner explained:

> So we don't necessarily mandate rezoning, but there's a lot of the criteria that points to higher densities and growth next to transit, which may result, depending on the center, in some changes on that front.
>
> (SEA-R-LU3 expert)

To summarize, PSRC and King County create a self-regulated framework for designating regional growth centers and thereby create a set of consistent spatial policies to describe the character of regional growth centers. Communities that meet these spatial policies can apply to have a center designated as a regional growth center. By using the spatial policies as criteria during an application process, PSRC and King County can guide local decisions on densities and the mix of uses. The self-regulated context creates a situation in which PSRC and King County perform the same governance functions twice: regulation and designating centers. Since King County policies have to be consistent with PSRC policies, the countywide centers are mostly identical with the regional growth centers. As indicated above, there is an ongoing attempt to change the process by having the counties designate smaller centers (as a second tier). It will be interesting to see how this situation changes with the next revision of the countywide planning policies. To conclude, in contrast to the other two regions, spatial policies in the Puget Sound region overlap to ensure that each entity maintains its independence.

Transit implementation: unilateral transit decisions in a negotiated setting

Successfully implementing low-carbon development patterns depends on ensuring a spatial match between the location of regional growth centers (higher densities and mixed uses) and the investment in rapid transit infrastructure. From a climate perspective, a crucial question is to what extent the designated regional growth centers in the RGS are actually connected by rapid transit. The agency responsible for rapid transit is called Sound Transit. Besides Sound Transit, each county operates its own countywide bus services. Furthermore, the road network is governed by the Washington State Department of Transportation, PSRC, counties and cities (RCW 81.112.070 & RCW 81.112.080). In other words, the overlapping planning system is mirrored in transportation governance.

At the regional level, Sound Transit and PSRC are the two primary regional organizations concerned with transportation questions in the region. PSRC has the more general responsibilities of preparing the RGS and a regional transportation plan as well as allocating federal transportation dollars to local road projects. Sound Transit has the more specialized responsibility of planning and developing the rapid transit network within the designated urban area. Sound Transit operates in three of the four counties included in PSRC, namely Snohomish County, King County, and Pierce County. All three are represented on the Sound Transit board of directors by locally elected officials (ST 2020). Sound Transit's efforts to build new rapid transit are funded through a regional tax approved by the voters in the tri-county region. Building and operating the rapid transit system is Sound Transit's primary responsibility. While PSRC includes a very generalized alignment of the rapid transit route in its RGS, Sound Transit's System Plan ultimately guides the transit investment authorized by the voters (Figure 5.3).

As part of the overlapping planning system, Sound Transit's decision-making is mostly independent of PSRCs RGS. In the absence of state legislated integrating mechanisms, the transit provider can make independent decisions about the alignment of new rapid transit lines that are only vaguely connected to the development patterns described in the RGS. Sound Transit does coordinate and negotiate with the local level government about the alignment of the rapid transit corridor, but this coordination and negotiation has not consistently supported the spatial vision of transit-connected urban centers as described in the RGS. The subsequent sections examine the self-regulated efforts over the past decade to ensure that spatial policies in the RGS are factored into the transit decision-making processes.

Though the general idea of connecting regional centers is reflected in the Sound Transit System Plan, that does not mean that the rapid transit system will necessarily connect all of the regional centers designated by PSRC or the counties. State law loosely connects Sound Transit's long-term strategy to the transportation plan prepared by PSRC through a certification of plan consistency process. The subsequent section discusses the degree of dependency in decision-making between both organizations based on state laws and self-regulated efforts.

Funding the transit network

Transit funding in the United States is commonly delegated to the local, county, or regional level. The federal and state governments tend not to provide significant funding for transit as there is no direct revenue source (Hess & Lombardi 2005). The state and federal government collect the gas tax, but the proceeds are usually strictly reserved to be spent on the vehicular road network (Lloyd 2019). At the federal level, there is one exception with the TIGER funding which is competitively awarded across the United States for projects of national significance (TIGER 2020). Therefore, funding rapid transit is usually a regionally-organized and state authorized effort (RCW 81.104.010).

In the Puget Sound region, voters ultimately approve financing rapid transit with the use of sales tax and property taxes authorized for transit projects. Washington State law establishes Sound Transit as an agency that derives its funding for constructing the rapid transit system from voter approved ballots (RCW 81.112.030). With each ballot, voters approve funding for a specific phase of the rapid transit system plan.

By a simple majority, voters approve the revenue sources and the phasing of rapid transit construction (RCW 81.112.030). The first round of funding and projects, called Sound Move, was approved in 1996. Unfortunately, those projects were not completed on time or on budget, so it was a hard sell for Sound Transit to convince voters a second round of funding was needed in 2008 (expert interview). But it succeeded: ST2 was passed in 2008 and Sound Transit made improvements to ensure completion on time and on budget (expert interviews). Projects funded by the first two measures, Light Rail and Bus Rapid transit, have been largely completed (ST3-History 2018).

In 2016, voters approved a third round of funding to expand the transit system with ballot measure ST3 (ST3-History 2018). ST3 included funding for 62 miles of new light rail financed by a less than 0.5% increase in Motor Vehicle Excise Tax as well as sales and use taxes. Voters also approved a property tax increase of $0.25 annually per $1,000 of assessed property value (ST3-Tax 2018). New stations are scheduled to open between 2021 and 2035 (ST3-Expansion 2018). The approved funding is challenged almost annually by new ballot measures trying to oppose the tax increases. In 2016, several advocacy coalitions which had previously opposed the measures supported Sound Transit's ballot initiatives (expert interviews). A possible explanation for the support may be that Washington State does not have an income tax. One expert explained that it makes voters more amenable to having other more specialized taxes for specific purposes. Nevertheless, Sound Transit is under constant pressure to complete the transit projects on time and on budget. This may have implications for the selection of preferred alternatives when deciding on corridor alignment. To connect the urban centers in the Vancouver region, TransLink needed to select alternatives that were costlier in the short-term but more promising (in terms of increased ridership due to land use changes) in the long-term. Making such an argument is harder for Sound Transit due to the cost pressure (see Chapter 8 for a comparison). The cost pressure Sound Transit is facing, needs to be kept in mind when considering to what extent its investments help implement the regional vision.

Determining the preferred alternative for corridor alignment

Once the general corridor alignment in the Sound Transit System Plan is adopted and voters approve the funding, Sound Transit's planning division develops corridor studies to assess alternatives for each corridor alignment. The voter approved System Plan is schematic and only shows the general location and direction of a corridor (it looks more or less like a transit map). The more detailed corridor studies determine the property-specific alignment of rail infrastructure and stations. The Board of Sound Transit selects the preferred alignment which is then studied in more detail. Once the detailed design is finalized, construction can start (expert interview).

Sound Transit works with the municipalities throughout all of these phases. The collaboration with the communities was fine-tuned throughout the years. Conflicts that arose during the ST1 planning phases were addressed by restructuring planning procedures during ST2 and ST3. Particularly communities such as Tukwila that were founded by ST1 did not see their designated urban centers connected (more details below). One such change was to focus on land use questions and consider transit-oriented development potential as early as the corridor study (ST3-TODP 2014, p. 7). Prior to discussing the challenges in Tukwila (founded with ST1) and Shoreline (founded with ST2), subsequently the current approach for ST3-founded communities is briefly described.

With ST3 funding, Sound Transit changed its processes to ensure more community engagement and place a higher emphasis on the regional centers. For ST3 funded projects, the regional centers and land uses are included as evaluation criteria for the preferred alignment. The criteria are as follows:

> Consider regional connectivity to and between centers; potential to create or support transit communities; potential to support economic development; and service to transit-dependent markets.
>
> (ST3-TODP 2014, p. 9)

Furthermore, the following criteria are described to assess the transit-oriented development potential along the considered corridor alignments:

> Land uses: quantify land most likely to redevelop and/or support transit (commercial, multi-family, or mixed use zones). Quantify land least likely to redevelop (parks and recreation, right-of-way, or institutional). Demographics: existing and future population and employment within the project area, potential corridors and potential station areas. High need populations: existing poverty, minority, and zero-car ownership populations in potential corridors and station areas. [...] Activity centers: assess activity centers based on regional and local adopted plans, policies, and key employment, recreational, and housing centers.
>
> (ST3-TODP 2014, p. 9)

In addition to considering the designated regional centers, Sound Transit engages with communities to identify suitable areas within the community to support transit-oriented development. This may include the regional centers but can also include other areas within the community. One challenge of having a non-binding RGS is that each entity essentially works independently on determining what location is preferable. While Sound Transit considers the regional centers designated by PSRC and King County, it also has its own preferences as to which locations may be most suitable for redevelopment. Sound Transit looks at existing concentrations of employment and housing to determine station locations.

The focus on locations with concentrated employment and housing can be traced back to the state legislation of the 1990s, which formulated a content requirement for the interlocal agreements between Sound Transit and municipalities:

> (3) [...] Agreements shall also include plans for concentrated employment centers, mixed-use development, and housing densities that support high capacity transportation systems.
>
> (RCW 81.104.080)

This certainly includes regional growth centers, but it can also include other locations. The legislation does not address if the locations consist of current high density or future high density. Since the RGS and its spatial policies are not part of the state legislation, the legislature cannot point to the spatial policies in the RGS on regional centers. Ultimately, Sound Transit has to redo the work already done to develop the RGS – namely to engage communities in a process of identifying preferable locations for rapid transit access in the community. My research shows that there was ultimately a power struggle over which party gets to determine the location to be served by rapid transit.

There also seemed frustration at PSRC with Sound Transit not connecting all of the regional growth centers. After ST1 was mostly completed, PSRC launched the Growing Transit Communities planning process which was intended to some extent to facilitate a land use revision at the local level for transit stations. This was a two-year planning effort funded under the Obama administration's Sustainable Communities Initiative that created a transit-oriented development strategy for the region. The strategy contains new transit corridors and stations, and identifies needed land use changes along the corridors (PSRC-Growing Transit Communities 2013). Communities are committed to implementing the Growing Transit Communities effort through a Regional Compact – a voluntary memorandum of understanding among participating communities.

More recently, Sound Transit has also made efforts to demonstrate and foster consistency with the RGS. First of all, Sound Transit committed itself to ensure plan consistency with the state, local, and regional growth strategies (ST3-Resolution R2012-24, 2012, p. 34). Second, in its recent System Plan, Sound Transit explains how it will achieve the goals of the RGS (ST3-Appendix D 2016; ST3-System Plan 2016, p. 2). Sound Transit also adopted its own Transit-Oriented Development Policy in December 2012 (ST3-Resolution R2012-24, 2012; see 8.4.3 for details). Usually, the land uses within about half a mile of a rapid transit station are included in transit-oriented development considerations (ST3-Appendix D, p. D-8). In the policy, Sound Transit commits to consider opportunities for Transit-Oriented-Development through the various design phases of a transportation project (ST3-Appendix D 2016, p. D-9). The policy also sets out more details on defining Transit-Oriented-Development and how Sound Transit is pursuing it.

The Transit-Oriented Development Policy and subsequently adopted program have informed how Sound Transit works with communities in the various design phases for the transit lines, including the selection of a preferred corridor alignment. Practically speaking, Sound Transit engages municipalities in the multiple planning phases of the rapid transit projects. Cities can review the transit system plan before it is put before the voters. The impacted cities are part of a steering committee that provides input to the alignment decision process. As the project advances towards the detailed designs, Sound Transit works with cities individually to determine questions of right-of-ways and station placements. Sound Transit has continuously worked on improving its procedures and learning from mistakes that were made during ST1 (local case Tukwila below) and ST2 (local case Shoreline below). The two local case negotiations in Tukwila and Shoreline presented below were conducted under "old" procedures and not the new procedures adopted with ST3 funding.

As discussed above, Sound Transit faces enormous pressure to deliver on time and on budget, which means the decision-making is heavily cost-driven. Sound Transit chose to align the rapid transit along the interstate highway for projects in ST1 and ST2 because it could easily obtain right-of-way from the state government. One expert remembered:

> So it's generally cheaper for us to go along the highway because we can negotiate something called an airspace lease with WSDOT. So it's basically a permanent easement to run the light rail through their property. We have to pay for it but it's not in cash. We pay for it in other ways by planting trees in other places, that kind of thing. So there's a positive way to do that. But, you know, it's already a large piece of property that's owned and operated for transportation purposes. So you don't have to buy a lot of individual properties.
>
> (SEA-R-TR expert)

Placing the alignment along the interstate highway brings with it the difficult challenge of rezoning single-family neighborhoods (see City of Shoreline section). Other options include using existing rail tracks, but those are privately owned and permits to run passenger service on them are generally expensive. Sound Transit would also be permitted to purchase properties for a new right-of-way; however, one expert explained that a property owner who does not want to sell could potentially damage Sound Transit's reputation.

While Sound Transit seemed to genuinely want to work with the communities to find a win-win-solution, the cost pressure was apparent during the interviews. Experts I interviewed indicated that cost pressures can lead to a different decision from the locally preferred alternative. To some extent, many assumed that land uses would change once the transit investment was in place. Multiple transit stops going north from Seattle towards Lynnwood currently serve single-family neighborhoods, with a few exceptions. One transit stop serves a mall called Northgate Station. Redevelopment at Northgate was already taking place in 2018 as the station was being built. The subsequent stops at 130th and 145th street are in the City of Seattle and had not been rezoned at the time of the interviews. The two stops in the City of Shoreline have been rezoned. The City of Lynnwood is trying to redevelop the area around its station (expert interview). Only time will tell which stations will see the desired redevelopment.

As Sound Transit has learned from ST1 and ST2, the subsequently presented local stories from the City of Tukwila and the City of Shoreline underscore the need to work in collaboration with the local government and to strive for mutually agreeable solutions when it comes to corridor alignment.

Local decision-making: negotiating the transit alignment

PSRC's RGS clearly articulates a vision to achieve low-carbon development patterns in the Puget Sound region. In order to implement this vision, PSRC relies on Sound Transit and the communities. More specifically, the transit provider's efforts need to spatially align with a community's efforts to prioritize locations for higher-densities and mixed-uses. In the other two regions, the regional planning organization serves as the arbitrator of both implementing parties (local governments and transit providers). In the RGS, agreed upon development patterns are written down. The planning system in the Puget Sound region does not have legislatively-defined integrating mechanisms to hold the decision-making centers accountable to the spatial policies in the RGS to the same extent as in the other two regions. Sound Transit is a (mostly) independent agency of PSRC. For the most part, the communities and Sound Transit negotiate the preferred corridor alignment without the involvement of PSRC and with only marginal reference to the RGS. One can argue that Sound Transit's corridor alignment decisions are driven by financial considerations rather than spatial development considerations. The subsequent section examines the implications for the local level.

City of Tukwila: a city dedicated to its urban center and a cost-conscious transit provider

The City of Tukwila is located to the south of the City of Seattle and to the east of Seattle-Tacoma International Airport. The RGS classifies Tukwila as a core city with a designated regional growth center (PSRC-Vision 2009). King County projects the city will gain 4,850 new housing units and 15,500 new jobs between 2006 and 2031 (KC-CPP 2012, p. 20).[8] The daytime population is estimated to be about ten times higher than the residential population because Tukwila has several major retail centers and industrial land (TUK-Comp 2015, pp. 2–4). The City of Tukwila was connected to the Sound Transit system through the first round of voter approved transit funding. At the time, there were no best practices in place for planning and building a new rapid transit system in the region. When the alignment negotiations began, Sound Transit and the City of Tukwila clashed over the location of the rapid transit station.

In the 2000s, Sound Transit and the City of Tukwila discussed several alignments before Sound Transit made a decision on the preferred location. Building the Tukwila International Boulevard (TIB) station was a compromise that ensured a fast connection to the airport and avoided a costly crossing of the highway into the designated regional growth center of Tukwila. The city wanted to connect to its designated urban center but the cost prevented it. Furthermore, the city opposed another alternative that would have operated the rapid transit as light rail along a major road. The subsequent section reviews the implications of choosing a transit stop location different from the one preferred by the local government. Sound Transit has since made many revisions to its procedures for determining transit stop locations to better accommodate local-level governments.

The TIB station opened in 2009 and is the first stop on the route from Seattle-Tacoma International Airport to downtown Seattle (Figure 5.3). The TIB station is located on the western edge of the City of Tukwila, about 2 miles west of the designated regional growth center. The regional growth center is a large retail agglomeration (malls and strip malls) directly adjacent

Tukwila International Boulevard Station - Looking across Southcenter Boulevard towards the rapid transit station.

View from Tukwila International Boulevard Station - Park'n Ride and strip malls across Southcenter Boulevard

Figure 5.3 Pictures of Tukwila International Boulevard Station.
Source: Own pictures.

to the highway cloverleaf of I-5 and I-450. The multiple large highway interchanges proved costly to any attempts at aligning land use and transit decisions. Hence, a different location was selected for the transit station.

As the TIB station has been in-service for over ten years, there have not been many changes in development patterns around it. Locals thought the location was less than ideal (expert interviews). The City of Tukwila would have liked to see its designated regional growth center connected to the rapid transit system and had been planning for a high-density, mixed-use, regional growth center area since the mid-1990s (TUK-Comp 2015, pp. 10–12f.). In fact, the city asked PSRC to designate the "Southcenter area" as a regional center in 1995 and created a neighborhood plan in 2002. The City of Tukwila has been investing in its designated regional growth center and permitting higher density developments (Figure 5.4). The city also invested in new streetscaping and a bridge for easier connection to the Amtrak-served Sounder Commuter rail station close by (see Figure 5.4). The city also built a bus terminal for better access to the Southcenter area.

While the City of Tukwila has been focused on its designated regional growth center for the past two decades, the area around the TIB station has not seen the same type of activity. The area around TIB is characterized by car-oriented strip-malls constructed in the 1950s, high crime rates, and low-income multi-family housing (expert interview). After the TIB station opened, there was not much city activity or development interest around it. In 2015, the City of Tukwila designated the area as a local center and started a visioning process (TUK-Comp 2015, pp. 8–2). In March 2020, 11 years after the station opened, the city was working on revising the zoning code and restricting some car-oriented uses (TUK-TIB 2020).

The experience of the city underscores the importance of connecting locally prioritized areas to the regional rapid transit network. Tukwila has been committed to its designated urban center but not to the TIB station in the same extent. At the time the station location was selected, there were intense negotiations between Sound Transit and the city. Already over budget and afraid to lose voter support, Sound Transit decided to place the station at TIB and prioritize connecting the Seattle-Tacoma International Airport. For Sound Transit costs would have multiplied if they had connected to Tukwila's designated regional growth center due to the highway crossings. Unfortunately, an earlier decision to run the transit alignment along the west side of the highway had ripple effects on the City of Tukwila's options. Given the circumstances, Sound Transit's decisions was cost driven rather than development pattern driven.

In terms of the rules-in-use, Sound Transit and the City of Tukwila are constituted by state law as independent decision-makers for land use and transit. These two decision-making centers negotiated a compromise. The spatial policies in the RGS and King County's comprehensive plan did not play a role in this negotiation.

Throughout the interviews, I got a strong sense that culturally no one government agency can tell another one what to do (a distinct feature of an

Pedestrian bridge across Green River connecting designated regional growth center to Amtrak transit station in the City of Tukwila.

New development near bus transit stop on Andover Park Way in the designated regional growth center in the City of Tukwila.

Figure 5.4 Pictures of South Center in Tukwila (designated regional growth center).
Source: Own pictures.

overlapping planning system). Each entity establishes its own regulations, which do have to be consistent with others, but the entity remains mostly independent. Hence, Sound Transit makes the final decision over the alignment even if it is not ideal from a local land use perspective and does not fit within the RGS. These are common power struggles over priorities and authority in metropolitan regions.

Improvements at Sound Transit since ST1

Since the investments of ST1, Sound Transit has made significant improvements to its process for involving the community in the decisions on station placements. The process was fairly new when I conducted my interviews. With the adoption of its Transit-Oriented-Development Program, Sound Transit started to differentiate between "Agency Transit-Oriented-Development" and "Community Transit-Oriented-Development." Agency Transit-Oriented-Development refers to surplus property that Sound Transit will develop for affordable housing in accordance with state requirements on parcels adjacent to the transit stop. Community Transit-Oriented-Development refers to encouraging development within a ½ mile radius in collaboration with the community (ST3-Resolution R2012-24, 2012, p. 34).

In 2015, Washington State authorized Sound Transit to lead the redevelopment efforts on property adjacent to a transit station (ST3-Appendix D, p. D-9; RCW 81.112.350(1)(b)(i)). An expert at Sound Transit explained:

> We typically buy more property than you need for the final station because you have to stage the construction around. And so you end up with surplus property after you're done. The way we used to do that is you'd buy the smallest amount of property necessary. Build your station and you'd have these little awkward slivers of property left over. And you try to sell them but nobody wants them because they're just not practical. [...] So now we've recognized that's not a smart way to do it. So we're gonna do a couple of things. One, we're going to think about as we construct the station, what the future Transit-Oriented-Development opportunities are at that station site. And so when you're doing the station planning, you're also doing Transit-Oriented-Development planning. [...] So it's all thought through ahead of time. And so and in fact, here's where it really gets good, is that your building of this station and the building of the Transit-Oriented-Development happens at the same time.
>
> (SEA-R-TR expert)

Sound Transit has started to purchase larger plots of land for the construction of the transit station. Once the station is finished the surplus land will be developed by Sound Transit, the community, and a developer.

The Tukwila case suggests that, ideally, a new transit line would serve a location the community has prioritized. It is also possible for a transit provider to influence the redevelopment of individual parcels in proximity to the transit stop and encourage new development; but as the City of Shoreline case shows, the alignment of the rapid transit line (preferred alternative) is a crucial decision because rezoning single-family neighborhoods for higher density and mix of uses is a political challenge.

City of Shoreline: the Herculean effort of re-designating land in a single-family neighborhood

The City of Shoreline is located to the north of the City of Seattle along the I-5 corridor. The City of Shoreline is designated as a "Large City" in PSRC's RGS (PSRC-Vision 2009, p. 22). As a designated larger city, Shoreline is projected to gain 5,000 new housing units and 5,000 new jobs between 2006 and 2031 based on the King County growth projections (KC-CPP 2012, p. 20). The City of Shoreline aspires to concentrate the new growth near transit (SHO-CAP 2013, p. 6). This section takes a deep dive into the challenges of rezoning single-family neighborhoods to accommodate new transit investment. I briefly review the negotiations between Sound Transit and the City of Shoreline regarding the corridor alignment and discuss the efforts to rezone around the future light rail stations.

Sound Transit is currently working on constructing two new light rail transit stops in the City of Shoreline which are projected to open in 2024. The City of Shoreline and Sound Transit negotiated these transit stops after voters approved ST2. During the scoping process for the Environmental Impact Statement,[9] the city and transit provider discussed two corridor alignment options for the Lynwood Link Extension through the City of Shoreline (ST-Scope 2011, p. 2). The first option was to have the new rapid transit on Aurora Avenue (State Route 99) which serves the designated town center in the City of Shoreline (SHO-Center Plan 2011). Aurora Avenue is characterized by its existing retail development and has a large right of way. The City of Shoreline would like to see more retail, grocery, services and restaurants in its town center along the corridor (SHO-Center Plan 2011, p. 9, policy TC-5). But because this option was not prioritized for rapid transit light rail, Aurora Avenue is now served by Bus Rapid Transit through King County Metro (SHO-Center Plan 2011, p. 4; SHO-Comp Plan 2012, p. 57, policy T31). The second, and ultimately prioritized, option was to have the new light rail aligned along I-5 where right-of-way could be obtained cheaply from the state government.

The final decision for the I-5 alignment was influenced by multiple local and transit-provider concerns. The City of Shoreline was hesitant about the Aurora alignment because the road had just been under construction for several years which had impacted businesses along the way. Furthermore, prior to entering the City of Shoreline, the light rail was already aligned with the interstate. With local concerns and Sound Transit's cost pressures, the highway alignment was ultimately chosen (ST-Scope 2011; ST-EIS 2015, p. S-4).

Committing to the interstate alignment meant that redevelopment would need to be in predominantly single-family neighborhoods. The single-family neighborhoods put the City of Shoreline in a tough position with some of the Sound Transit board members. At the time, one official on the Sound Transit Board questioned the need for transit stops in the City of Shoreline at all (expert interview). The board member proposed an amendment to eliminate the two stops in the City of Shoreline due to the low ridership prospects in single-family neighborhoods. This amendment was later withdrawn as council members in the City of Shoreline were able to influence other Sound Transit board members. The experts I interviewed emphasized the crucial role the individual leadership of the council member who later became the mayor played in the negotiations.

To assure Sound Transit that the City of Shoreline was committed to changing land uses around the future transit stops, the city adopted a policy to initiate the preparation of two neighborhood plans for the future transit stops on 145th and 185th Street (SHO-Framework Policy 2012). The neighborhood plans were to guide land use decisions around the station areas. The policy states the following:

> The station area is "defined as the ½ mile walk-shed from a light rail station. This area will always be evaluated for multi-family residential housing choices that support light rail transit service (R-18 and greater), non-residential uses, non-motorized transportation improvements and traffic and parking mitigation. Areas within a ¼ mile walk-shed of a station will be evaluated for multi-family residential housing choices that support light rail transit service (R-48 or greater). Planning for station areas includes evaluating land uses, transportation and parking issues associated with the development of a light rail station. Station area planning incorporates both the station area and the study area".
>
> (SHO-Framework Policy 2012, p. 1)

Based on the policy framework, the City of Shoreline embarked on a neighborhood planning process to identify new land uses and later rezone around the two future stations (SHO-145th Street Plan 2016; SHO-185th Street Plan 2015). The experts I interviewed highlighted the challenges with re-designating land in a predominantly single-family neighborhood. In fact, rezoning single-family neighborhoods frequently faced neighborhood opposition throughout the region.

Several interviewees held up the neighborhood planning efforts in Shoreline as a success story in the Puget Sound region. The leadership of the city council and mayor were able to plan for higher densities and a mix of uses in a predominantly single-family neighborhood. Local leadership was able to reframe the conversation by pointing out that the actual changes to the built

New development on 185th Street at the corner of Densmore Avenue North in predominantly single-family neighborhood. The transit stop will be located 0.7 miles away near the highway interchange.

House in single-family neighborhood along 6th Ave NE - The house is about 0.4 miles from the new transit stop at 145th street. This neighborhood was mostly opposed to the rezoning efforts by the City of Shoreline.

Figure 5.5 Pictures of neighborhoods around future transit stations in the City of Shoreline.

Source: Own illustration.

environment would not happen for another 10–15 years (which means kids could finish school in the neighborhood). Furthermore, the zoning changes would mean that families could sell their homes at much higher values when they are ready to move out. These were the key arguments used to ultimately pass the neighborhood plans in 2016. Since then, some areas have seen redevelopment while others have not (Figure 5.5). During the time of the planning process, people opposed to the stops frequently threatened that the council members would be voted out of office – but that did not happen at the next election (expert interviews).

Around the future transit stations, the City of Shoreline created three land use designations. The three land use designations are called "station area 1," which is immediately adjacent to the station, "station area 2," which is a transition zone, and "station area 3" which includes the neighborhoods further away. On December 30, 2015, the City of Shoreline adopted new land use policies for the three zones with Ordinance 730.

The opposition is still active and as recently as 2018, the city council was persuaded to adopt a 20% tree retention policy for the properties around the station. While the plan had already accounted for additional parks and street trees, 20% tree retention on properties means that the overall density of the neighborhood will be lower and 70-foot tall buildings less likely. This is one paradox of climate mitigation: more trees are good, but higher densities with access to retail around transit stations are helpful in reducing the overall carbon footprint of a neighborhood.

The Shoreline case presents an example of the efforts the city had to put into the planning process around rezoning the station areas in predominantly single-family neighborhoods. However, given the challenges and many persistent battles around rezoning a single-family neighborhood, this may be a unique example, rather than what happens in the majority of cases. If the city did not rezone, developers would still have the option to apply for zoning amendments to individual properties. This is frequently met by neighborhood opposition and can be very costly for a developer to obtain the needed permits (expert interview). In Vancouver and Stuttgart, local governments would rather refrain from rezoning single-family neighborhoods and instead ensure that transit alignment serves areas more likely to be rezoned. Experts in the Puget Sound region posed these issues as a chicken and egg question – what comes first, land use or transportation. My research in the three regions suggests that ideally land use and development pattern considerations come first, followed by transit investment, and lastly rezoning decisions.

Notes

1 The strong emphasis on local land use regulations originates from the constitutional rights of cities. In many US states, including Washington State, municipalities have powers granted to them by state governments, but they do not possess inherent (constitutionally granted) powers by themselves (PCLD 2011, p. 225). Through zoning enabling legislation, many states have granted

municipalities legislative-like powers for zoning (PCLD 2011, p. 255). This is frequently referred to as home-rule for land use and zoning. Home-rule enables cities to be fairly independent actors in land use questions. For instance, most US cities create their own zoning bylaws, including zoning categories and procedures.

2 The Washington State climate legislation included benchmarks to reduce vehicle miles traveled (VMT) across the state (RCW 47.01.440; SoW-60th legislature; WSDOT-Sustainability 2016, p. 3). To achieve these benchmarks, the climate legislation directly charged various departments with developing best practices and tools for implementing the VMT reductions (RCW 47.01.440; SoW-60th legislature, p. 17). Accordingly, in 2008 the Department of Ecology together with the Department of Community, Trade, and Economic Development produced two reports: "Leading the Way on Climate Change" (SoW-Leading 2008) followed by "Growing Washington's Economy in a Carbon Constrained World" (SoW-CAP 2008). Additionally, the Department of Community, Trade, and Economic Development issued the report "Planning for Climate Change" (SoW-CTED 2008) to the state legislature.

3 The specific section reads as follows:

> The comprehensive plan of each county or city that is adopted pursuant to RCW 36.70A.040 shall be coordinated with, and consistent with, the comprehensive plans adopted pursuant to RCW 36.70A.040 of other counties or cities with which the county or city has, in part, common borders or related regional issues.
>
> (RCW 36.70A.100)

4 In the Puget Sound region, PSRC is responsible for the multicounty planning policies. Therefore, PSRC has more responsibilities than MPOs commonly have within the United States, which are usually responsible for transportation issues.

5 During the time of the interviews in 2018, several law suits were still pending and additionally an effort was underway to revisit the provisions in the Growth Management Act.

6 A cross-departmental team of staffers meets every other week to discuss issues and progress. Each second meeting the staffers report to the Climate Leadership Team, which is composed of the directors of all major agencies in the county. One expert indicated that it helps bring the climate agenda into everything they do and to expedite certain needs.

7 The agricultural and resource lands are part of unincorporated King County, meaning they are not part of a municipality.

8 In its comprehensive plan, the City of Tukwila forecasts 27,670 new jobs by 2030 (TUK-Comp 2015, pp. 13–14). The inconsistency with the King County Plan was addressed within the Comprehensive Plan: "The City will revise the employment forecast and land use assumptions in the Transportation Element for consistency with land use-related elements and adopted growth targets during the next scheduled Transportation Demand Model update in 2016" (TUK-Comp 2015, pp. 13–14).

9 As an agency designated under state law, Sound Transit is required to comply with the State Environmental Protection Act (SEPA). Furthermore, Sound Transit planned to apply for additional federal funding for the light rail project and would therefore need to comply with the National Environmental Protection Act (NEPA) (ST-Board Motion 2012, p. 4). The NEPA and SEPA requirements both include the preparation of an Environmental Impact Statement.

6 Nesting plans in the Stuttgart region

A European example of rules-in-use for implementing low-carbon development patterns provides an interesting contrast to the North American models. This chapter presents the rules-in-use in a nested planning system where decision-making becomes incrementally more specific with each respective level of government. The discussion demonstrates how federal law supports a system for negotiations between the local and regional levels on policy objectives and implementation; a system geared towards resolving conflicts and balancing various interests when implementing low-carbon development patterns.

Germany's nested planning system intentionally involves all levels of government in land use governance as decisions get incrementally more specific. In a nested system, each level of government fills in more detail on policies defined at a higher level. Though the local level ultimately makes decisions on diversifying uses and increasing densities, those decisions are shaped by federal, state, and regional policies on the direction of growth. The planning system's nested structure creates a hierarchy of plans that gets incrementally more specific on questions of sustainable development patterns. The spatial policies in the state and regional plans have legal implications for sectoral decisions on the alignment of rapid transit projects. This section reviews the nested structure of policy-making in Germany and spatial policies.

The German planning system consists of nested decision-making, where each level of government inserts more details for a particular question or issue. The nested planning system originated from the idea that there are decisions that directly impact the population within a community but that certain decisions also impact a larger geographic footprint (Falk 2006). As part of the "principle of subsidiarity," decision-makers strive to take "decisions as closely as possible to the community directly affected." (Wilson & Piper 2010, p. 93; see also Benz 2009, p. 27f; Fürst 2010, p. 52; GG Art. 30 and Art. 83). German researchers distinguish between responsibilities at the local level (örtliche Aufgaben) and responsibilities that are larger than local concerns (überörtliche Aufgaben)[1] (Hendler 2005, p. 878; Falk 2006; BW-Drucksache 18/10883, p. 37). In this system, zoning is the community's responsibility.

DOI: 10.4324/9781003268505-7

Yet, there is regional and statewide interest in a coherent legal framework, environmental protection, and infrastructure investments (Sinz 2005; Falk 2006, p. 147; GG-Art. 28 Abs. 2; G-BauGB-§1 Abs. 4; Stark 2009, p. 49; Fürst 2010, p. 86). Hence, decision-making is functionally separated between regulatory tasks (federal, state, region) and implementation tasks (local level). I explain the specific separation of powers in spatial planning in Germany below.

Nested spatial planning system in Germany

Spatial planning in Germany is considered a shared responsibility among all levels of government. Each level has distinct and clearly defined powers (CEC 1997, p. 40; ARL 2005, p. 895ff.; Schmidt & Buehler 2007, p. 57). The primary role of the federal legislature is to provide a coherent legal framework for planning across the country to ensure legal consistency and predictability for property owners (Goppel 2005, p. 562; Schmidt & Buehler 2007, p. 57; Stark 2009, p. 44; GG-74(1)18). Federal laws are then filled in by state laws and regional policies, becoming incrementally more specific. The local level administers zoning and building permits and determines suitable sites for (re)development. Lastly, the county level reviews local plans' compliance with federal, state, and regional regulatory frameworks. Generally speaking, communities are free to zone as long as the decisions fit within the law and regional policies (G-BauGB §6). Therefore, local decisions are nested within statewide and regional policy frameworks. The following section provides more detail on the responsibilities of each level of government.

Federal and state planning laws

Several federal laws are particularly important to planning in Germany. First, the Federal Spatial Planning Law (G-ROG) defines minimum requirements for statewide and regional comprehensive planning. The provisions in the Federal Spatial Planning Law set the context for implementing low-carbon development patterns in Germany. The second law is the Federal Zoning Law (*G-BauGB*), which outlines zoning classifications and procedures for the local level. Third, various sectoral laws connect decisions on spatially impactful projects (e.g. highways) to spatial plans. Fourth, all laws are supported by an administrative law (*Verwaltungsfachgesetz*) empowering the executive actors, including public administrators at the local level to ensure due process for property owners across Germany.

The federal laws are made more specific by state laws. For instance, while the federal law describes the purpose of regional planning, the state laws regulate the organizational structures of regional planning organizations (*Regionalplanungsverbände*). Since 2006, German states' spatial laws can deviate from the federal government's (GG §74(1)31; G-ROB 2011, 141). However, none of the German states has developed regulations that drastically deviate from the federal spatial planning law. Most experts describe the state law of Baden-Württemberg, as well as the federal legislation, as "ground rules of the game" that hold all actors accountable to certain substantive and procedural standards. The state and federal laws regulate the following aspects of spatial planning: content categories of plans (G-ROG §13(5), BW-LplG §11), procedures for creating, approving, and implementing plans (BW-LplG §12–§14) and procedures to ensure alignment of plans across levels and sectors of government (G-ROG §15 and §19, VwVfG §§72–78, BW-LplG §14). The regulations apply to the administration of Regional Growth Strategies (RGSs), local plans, and sectoral plans.

In addition to specifying the legislative framework for planning and zoning, the state level also prepares a statewide development plan (*Landesentwicklungspläne*). The state development plans do not directly address zoning on a property-by-property basis, but instead outline more general spatial development patterns and policies for the state as a whole (Stark 2009, p. 45). For instance, the statewide development plan defines rural (*Ländliche Räume*) and urbanized areas (*Verdichtungsräume*) across the state, and it also identifies priority transportation corridors. The statewide development plan is intended to help coordinate land use developments with state infrastructure investments by developing a comprehensive vision that balances the various spatial needs of communities and sectoral agencies[2] (Kaiser & Godschalk 1995, p. 124; Sinz 2005, p. 863). Only the local zoning map is binding on property owners. While the state development plan has fairly broad objectives and policies, the regional level further specifies and applies them to specific geographies.

Regional planning organizations

The regional level creates specific spatial policies for development patterns in metropolitan areas and provides a place for coordination among local, state, and various sectoral agencies on the spatial development of the region (Schmitz 2005, p. 965; Fürst 2009).[3] The regional level is usually not its own layer of government but rather organized as a functional layer. Regional planning organizations are frequently councils of government in which communities come together to plan (Schmitz 2005, p. 965; Falk 2006, p. 97; Schmidt & Buehler, 2007, p. 59; Fürst 2010). However, there is a wide variety of specific organizational structures across Germany (Breu, Priebs, & Tönnes 2015). For instance, a few states have chosen to maintain state control of regional planning (Schmitz 2005, p. 965; Falk 2006, p. 97; Schmidt & Buehler, 2007, 59; Fürst 2010). In Baden-Württemberg, voters elect the board of the Verband Region Stuttgart (VRS, regional planning organization) as a regional parliament with 80 regionally elected officials (BW-GVRS §8 und §12). Despite its difference in organizational structures, the VRS fulfils the regional planning function commonly done at the regional level across Germany. Federal and state law task the regional level with preparing an RGS – a legally-binding document in Germany that includes spatial policies and generalized maps for a metropolitan region.

Local right to self-administration

The local level is the point of implementation of regional and statewide plans and policies (Fürst 2010, p. 84; Expert interview; BMVBW 2001, p. 5; Stark 2009, p. 48). Only the local level can issue building permits and zoning maps detailing uses and conditions for individual properties (G-BauGB §10 Abs. 1; Fürst 2010). At the local level, the local land use designations map (*Flächennutzungsplan*) is the primary tool that drives community development. In contrast to Seattle and Vancouver, usually the local governments in Germany do not write their own zoning policies because there is a federal zoning law (G-BauGB). Yet, cities do zone the land. This is a primary feature of the nested governance arrangement: the federal zoning categories are applied based on regional policies, to a map created by local governments. The subsequent discussion will examine this process as it pertains to creating low-carbon development patterns in the Stuttgart region.

Two federal principles protect the rights of cities from overreach by senior-levels of government: the constitutional rights of cities and the principle of subsidiarity. Cities have a constitutional right to local self-administration (*Recht auf lokale Selbstverwaltung*; §28(2) GG; also translated as the "right to govern all affairs of local significance" by Deangelo & Harvey 1998, p. 120). Local self-administration in planning means that local governments are free to apply existing federally-defined zoning categories to a map of the city. The city then administers building permits based on the procedures defined under federal and state laws (expert interview). Furthermore, the local level has to follow several regional policies on desirable locations for new development. For instance, the regional level can influence densities as well as the location of rapid transit. Other tasks such as ensuring a mix of uses around a transit stop are considered a strictly local task. As one regional planner said:

> The mix of uses is not a responsibility of regional planning. Mixing uses is strictly an urban planning responsibility. Urban planning [local level] has to ensure that services are available to residents.
>
> (STU-R-LU expert)

Despite the legal requirements set by senior-level governments, the local constitutional right to self-administration also ensures that communities have a right to participate in the planning process at higher levels and challenge unduly burdensome regional and state policies in courts. The rationale for the German approach is that local land use (and zoning) decisions impact the service provision for infrastructure (transportation, water, and sewer) and need for protection of open spaces in the region. Therefore, there is a heightened need for coordination on spatial development patterns. Based on the constitutional right to self-administration, the local, regional, and state-levels are interdependent since the local level is the implementing level while the state and region are regulating entities.

As spatial planning involves governmental actors at multiple levels of government, the federal law creates an integrating mechanism called principle of reciprocity (*Gegenstromprinzip*). The principle of reciprocity promotes a balance of statewide and local interests (G-ROG §1(3)). While planning requires coordination and conflict resolution, the principle of reciprocity preserves the rights and interests of each level of government in land development. Essentially, as a mechanism, it creates interdependencies across levels of government in land use and sectoral decision-making. The principle is based on Section 3 of §1 G-ROG and reads as follows:

> §1(3) – „The development, regulation and stewardship of the parts of the German territory shall fit in with the existing conditions and future needs of the entire territory; the development, regulation and stewardship of the entire territory shall fit in with the existing conditions and future needs of the parts of the German territory."

The principle of reciprocity essentially requires that planning for small territories (e.g. local governments) needs to account for planning in larger territories (e.g. region or state) and vice versa. By giving both perspectives (local and above-local) relevance, the principle of reciprocity is supposed to prevent top-down planning as well as incrementalism (expert interview). Practically, representatives of each level of government take part in planning for projects that may impact their interests (Peine 1998, p. 173; Fürst 2010; G-ROG §9). Furthermore, the state can only regulate to the extent that statewide interests are involved; at the same time making sure that local and statewide interests are balanced (BW-LplG §2(2); Peine 1998, p. 171; Fürst 2010, p. 88; G-ROG 2017, §1(3); expert interview). If one level has not been able to properly participate or believes its rights are infringed, it can challenge the spatial plan in court.

Low-carbon development patterns – business as usual in Stuttgart under federal and state laws?

One might wonder what influence federal and state climate objectives have on planning for low-carbon developed patterns at the regional and local levels in a nested planning system. While the climate agendas at the federal and state levels include recommendations for low-carbon development patterns, much of the efforts at the senior levels are spent on fostering renewable energies, building energy efficiency, and investing in new transportation technologies (G-Klimaschutzplan 2050, p. 29; §5 in BW-Drucksache 15/3842). While the nested planning system offers opportunities similar to British Columbia, the federal government of Germany and state government of Baden-Württemberg prioritized actions in the energy sector by creating voluntary incentives for communities (G-Klimaschutzplan 2050, p. 77). During my interviews with practitioners in the Stuttgart region, it became abundantly clear that low-carbon development patterns were considered business as usual – I will explain further after briefly reviewing the energy-focused approach to climate actions.

Similar to British Columbia, the state of Baden-Württemberg engaged its local governments through a climate mitigation compact (Klimaschutzpakt; BW-Klimaschutzpakt 2018). The state government negotiated the compact with several local government unions. 220 communities and counties in Baden-Württemberg had signed the compact by 2018 (BW-Klimaschutzpakt 2018, p. 9). The climate compact emphasizes the action areas, including participation in the European Energy Award (EEA 2020) and municipal corporate climate actions (*Vorbildfunktion der Kommunalverwaltung*; BW-Klimaschutzpakt 2018, p. 2). A primary objective of the compact is to encourage more communities to identify climate actions at the local level either by creating a climate action plan or through participation in a European certification program (BW-Klimaschutzpakt 2018, p. 4). The compact does not specifically mention low-carbon development patterns.

I learned from the interviews that communities and counties in the Stuttgart region were responsive to the incentives set by senior-level governments. Communities took advantage of the opportunity to receive funding for hiring local climate managers, for preparing climate action plans, or for participation in the certification program.[4] The climate managers were actively working to implement the action items in the local and county climate action plans. Many of the climate managers were not urban planners by profession but were from professional backgrounds more suited to the energy focus set by the senior-level governments. One possible explanation for the focus on the energy sector is that the state department (*Ministerium*) responsible for creating the climate action plans is also the department responsible for the energy sector. The experts at the state level indicated that the plans were developed in close collaboration with other departments, but that energy was closest to their area of expertise (STUT-S-CL).

While the local governments were responsive to the federal and state climate agendas and incentives, low-carbon development patterns played a minor role in Germany's overall climate mitigation strategy.[5] The federal and state climate action plans mention low-carbon development patterns in the context of reducing transportation emissions. Key concepts of low-carbon development patterns include integrated urban development (*integrierte Stadtentwicklung*) and promoting a city of short distances (*Stadt der kurzen Wege*) (G-Klimaschutzplan 2050, p. 55).

At the state level, Baden-Württemberg promotes "development patterns that avoid increasing transportation demand" (*verkehrsvermeidende Siedlungs- und Verkehrsplanung*; BW-IEKK 2014, p. 101). The state estimates that if one-quarter of all households had a 20% shorter commute after their next move, the transportation sector could reduce its emissions by 1% within a five-year timeframe (BW-IEKK 2014, p. 102). Therefore, the climate action plan of Baden-Württemberg recommends making "city and region of short distances" a priority for development patterns across the state (action item 65).[6] This includes the need to "concentrate development in communities with access to rapid transit"[7] as well as to "reduce new development on greenfields and to support infill development"[8] (BW-IEKK 2014, p. 102).

While the federal and statewide climate action plans do contain land use recommendations (less than 5% of all recommendations), the recommended low-carbon development patterns have traditionally been part of spatial planning policies in Germany. During the interviews, practitioners argued that policies on compact and complete communities along transit corridors have been routinely considered in planning in Germany for several decades. That might be a reason why the planners I interviewed focused more on the energy sector than on re-envisioning development patterns.

Even the changes to the federal planning law were focused on actions fostering renewable energies. When the federal government did include climate mitigation and adaptation as a purpose of planning in the federal zoning law (*Baugesetzbuch*-G-BauGB) and federal planning enabling legislation (*Raumordnungsgesetz*-G-ROG 2017; G-Gesetz zur Förderung 2011), the section in the federal planning enabling legislation read as follows:

> The spatial needs of climate mitigation have to be taken into account - this includes actions to mitigate climate change as well as actions to adapt to climate change. Thereby, the spatial preconditions for renewable energies, the frugal use of energy and for carbon sinks are to be created.
>
> (G-ROG §2(2)6 Satz 7 und 8)

Subsequently, the state law on climate authorizes regional planning organizations to determine locations for wind energy plants and other energy-related facilities (BW-Drucksache 15/3842-Artikel 2-§11; BW-IEKK 2014, p. 145). That might explain why the climate mitigation efforts in spatial planning have focused on finding sites for renewable energy facilities. In fact, this has shaped the agendas for the regional planning organizations in thinking about and conceptualizing climate mitigation.

Regional perspective on low-carbon development pattern

Climate mitigation and adaptation are clearly on the agenda of the regional planning organization VRS. For example, VRS joined the Covenant of Mayors for Climate and Energy as a supporter in 2009 (VRS 2009). Furthermore, VRS has been actively participating in several federally funded research projects and international exchanges with other metropolitan regions on climate issues (VRS-WIV 11617, pp. 2 and 5). VRS also included climate mitigation and adaptation as a regional policy principle in its RGS (VRS-Regionalplan 2009, p. 3- principle 1.1.3; VRS-RTP 2018, p. 11). However, echoing federal and state guidance, VRS's climate efforts have focused more on renewable energy and climate adaptation rather than revisiting the development patterns of the region to reduce GHG emissions.

When asked about the climate focus, one expert at the regional level explained:

> Compact and complete communities is a concept that's been around long before climate mitigation was an issue. [...]. There are multiple reasons for developing compact and complete communities, including the protection of resources [...]. Therefore, the climate mitigation discourse did not change a lot for us regarding development patterns. What really changed for us was the new responsibility to find sites for renewable energy.
>
> (STU-R-LU expert)

There was a consistent understanding among all the experts I interviewed in the region that "low-carbon development patterns" as described in Chapter 1 have been the purpose of planning in Germany all along, pointing to the spatial policies in the federal and state legislations which authorize the more specific regional spatial policies.

Based on federal law, the purpose of spatial planning has, for many years, included the avoidance of additional traffic, the prioritization of infill development, and the stewardship of open spaces (G-ROG §2(2)3; G-ROG §2(2)6; G-ROG §1(1)). Furthermore, the Baden-Württemberg statewide development plan from the year 2002 included policy requirements on "low-carbon development pattern" – long before the statewide climate action strategy (BW-IEKK 2014) was adopted. For instance, the state development plan includes the following policy for the regional and local levels:

> 2.2.3.2 "[...] New development is to be prioritized along primary development corridors and focused in areas with access to public transit, particularly rapid transit".
>
> (BW-LEP 2002, p. 16-requirement 2.2.3)

This policy statement clearly directs new growth to locations along the rapid transit corridors. This is further supported by another statewide policy which takes the pressure off of developing greenfields:

> 2.2.3.1 "The use of greenfields for urban development is to be limited to the least amount necessary. Urban development is to be prioritized on sites in the exiting urbanized area, including brownfields, infill sites, and greenfields reserved for development".
>
> (BW-LEP 2002, p. 16-requirement 2.2.3)

This means that requirements in the statewide development plan do support suggested land use measures in the climate action plans. The structure of the German planning system makes these state requirements legislatively-binding for planning at the regional and local levels.

VRS does link its spatial policies to its climate efforts in several documents. One VRS board memo indicates that vehicle miles traveled are being reduced by leveraging the ability in the RGS to designate (*ausweisen*) primary development corridors (*Festlegung von Entwicklungsachsen*) as well as preferred locations for housing and retail (*Verortung von Wohnbau- und Gewerbeschwerpunkten*) (VRS-WIV 11617, p. 5). However, much of the board memo focused on VRS's role in mobility and energy. Furthermore, for its climate adaptation efforts, VRS also emphasizes several spatial policies in its RGS, including policies to protect open spaces that bring fresh air into the communities and policies to direct development to easily accessible locations (VRS-Klimaatlas 2008, p. 5; VRS-Regionalplan 2009, p. 10; VRS-Klima 2016). While VRS takes pride in their climate adaptation and climate energy efforts, low-carbon development patterns have not been the primary strategic focus.

In fact, the concepts of increasing densities and diversifying uses as described in Chapter 1 were challenged during discussions with a regional expert. Several experts highlighted the double-edged sword of increasing densities in the Stuttgart region:

> Increasing densities may not be possible because of the topographic conditions - we need to preserve the open spaces to ensure that fresh air can get into the city, especially during the hot summers. Increasing densities in already dense areas is a challenge.
>
> (STU-R-LU expert)

Furthermore, regarding the mix of uses, the experts highlighted that mixing small scale retail and housing is a local responsibility. The regional level takes a coarser view on uses including housing in general, large scale retail and industrial uses. The regional expert viewed mixing housing and industrial uses particularly critically. The expert's concerns included industrial emissions and freight access to industrial sites conflicting with residential neighborhood priorities. He explained:

> When we mix housing and industrial the conflicts intensify. We don't end up with shorter distances. [...] Basically, it gets harder to have good housing or good industrial uses. However, both should be accessible [by transit].
>
> (STU-R-LU expert)

Therefore, from a regional perspective, housing and jobs should be located along the rapid transit network to and from job agglomerations. Rather than having cities of short distances, the regional expert was advocating for a region of short distances. Yet, mixed-uses in terms of office, retail, multi-family and single-family housing were clearly welcomed but seen as a local responsibility.

My interviews and research show that the existing spatial policies had not been re-examined from a climate perspective but rather were deemed sufficient to foster a reduction in vehicle miles traveled. Federal law and spatial policies in the RGS do support polycentric development patterns of transit-connected municipalities. This means that there has not been an assessment of ways to leverage the existing spatial policies to further reduce VMT. Among the interviewed experts, there seemed to be a sense that the existing policies already promote the development patterns advocated in climate action agendas.

To conclude, the German planning system, with its legislatively-defined integrating mechanisms, places the regional level in a position to promote low-carbon development patterns across metropolitan regions. The experts in the Stuttgart region argued that several of the existing spatial policies in the RGS do, in fact, support low-carbon development patterns: The existing policies allow regional planning organizations to engage communities in conversations about low-carbon development patterns. The subsequent chapter examines the regional spatial policies the Stuttgart region. Each region in Germany creates its unique set of spatial policies that is guided by federal principle and statewide spatial policies.

Spatial policies in the Stuttgart region to support low-carbon development patterns

Regional planning in the Stuttgart region

This section provides a deep dive into the role of the regional level within the nested German planning system. Under German federal law, a primary purpose in spatial planning is the coordination of conflicting interests for the use of land at various levels and sectors of government. To facilitate this coordination among multiple actors, federal law intentionally positions the RGS and associated integrating mechanisms to facilitate conflict resolution. Of the three regions I analyzed, the German planning system is the most extensive in terms of substantive and procedural legal requirements for regional planning. This section examines the various federal and state requirements shaping the interdependencies among decision-making centers when implementing low-carbon development patterns.

Regional planning in Germany is governed by the Federal Spatial Planning Law. The law defines the purpose of regional and statewide planning as balancing the various interests in the use of land across Germany (BMVBW

2001, p. 5; Sinz 2005, p. 867). The relevant section of the Federal Spatial Planning Law reads as follows:

> §1(1)"The territory of Germany as well as its parts (Teilräume) are to be developed, regulated and stewarded **through spatial plans,** collaboration on spatial issues, and through coordination of spatially-impactful plans and projects (raumbedeutsamer Planungen und Maßnahmen). Thereby, (1) various needs and expectations for the use of the territory are to be coordinated (and aligned) and conflicts are to be balanced at the respective level of government; and (2) future uses and functions of the territory are to be included".
>
> (G-ROG §1(1), own translation, highlights by author).

From this statement, state and regional agencies derive their responsibility to prepare spatial plans which then guide development patterns (Höhnberg 1998, p. 223). Spatial plans include statewide development plans and RGSs. By federal law, spatial plans have to be comprehensive (*zusammenfassend*), sectorally integrated (*fachübergreifend*) and include an area larger than one municipality (Hendler 2005, p 878; G-ROG 2017, §3(7); BW-Drucksache 18/10883, p. 37). As plans at each level of government are prepared at a specific scale[9] (Stark 2009, p. 48), the RGS is required to provide more detail on policies contained in the statewide development plans as well as to be considerate of local plans (G-ROG §13(2)). Within the hierarchy of plans, the mapped component of the RGS broadly outlines the urbanized areas (cities, villages, townships, etc.), protected open spaces and priority infrastructure corridors (§13(5) ROG).

Besides regional planning, VRS is also responsible for open space planning (*Landschaftsrahmenplan*), transportation planning, waste management, economic development, and tourism marketing (BW-GVRS §3(1)(1)-(7)). VRS prepares the RGS in collaboration with communities and the state government (G-ROG §7 and 13). The RGS contains maps and policies regarding the urban area, open spaces, and infrastructure in the region. Once finalized, the state government approves the RGS (Fürst 2010, p. 71). The RGS then applies to planning in 178 local jurisdictions in five counties. Additionally, VRS prepares the regional long-range transportation plan and administers the transit services across the region.

Figure 6.1 shows the responsibilities of VRS in land use and transportation governance for the region. VRS coordinates the development patterns of the region between the state and local levels. The RGS serves as the central element of integrated decision-making across levels and sectors of government on development patterns. The spatial policies in the RGS are linked to implementing planning documents through integrating mechanisms.

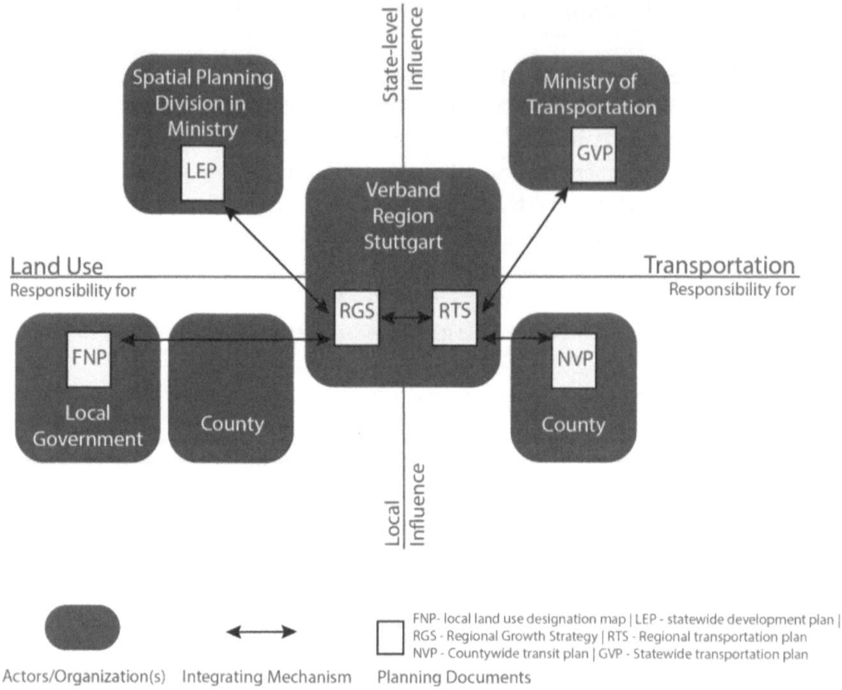

Figure 6.1 Responsibilities in land use and transportation in the Stuttgart region.
Source: Own illustration.

Legislatively-binding RGS with binding and guiding policy statements

Once adopted, an RGS is legislatively-binding to other governmental agencies but not to property owners. Only the local level is permitted to create zoning maps. Hence, maps at the regional level have fuzzy boundaries which are then negotiated between the local and regional levels. This negotiation is shaped by the spatial policies in the RGS which apply to all of the municipalities in the region (BW-LplG §11 (1) und (2)). However, not all policies in the RGS are strictly legislatively-binding. Federal law creates two types of policy statements which can be included in spatial plans allowing ample regional discretion. The policy statements speak to the extent of how legislatively-binding a policy actually is – some policy statements are binding requirements (*Ziele*) while others are only guiding principles (*Grundsatz*); G-ROG §3(2) and (3), BW-LplG §4, G-BauGB §1(4)). Furthermore, RGSs usually contain statewide policies (*Nachrichtliche Übernahme*) as well as suggested policies (*Vorschlag*; VRS-Regionalplan 2008, p. XI). Policy requirements and guiding principles have different bearings on the decisions by local governments and sectoral agencies. Because policies that are required are also legislatively-binding for subsequent decision-makers, the regional planning organization in the

Stuttgart region prefers to regulate issues as requirements rather than guiding principles. This is not common across Germany and depends on the political power structure within the board of regional planning organizations. The expert I interviewed said:

> Our RGS contains only a few principles (Grundsätze) on less relevant issues. We would have liked to have no principles at all. We agreed with our regionally elected board that the objective is to use requirements that send clear signals to the communities. Principles can be deemed not relevant for the issue at hand by a community. Particularly when we talk about protecting open spaces or ensuring minimum densities, it is crucial to have requirements rather than principles.
>
> (STU-R-LU expert; own translation)

The regional expert did highlight that not all regional planning organizations in Germany emphasize planning with requirements. Particularly in regions with boards of locally elected officials, it is more common to work with principles.

To demonstrate the relevance of the RGS, one regional planner gave the following example about the protection of open spaces in the Stuttgart region: The City of Stuttgart has struggled with good air circulation due to its topography. It relies, to some extent, on the suburbs to maintain certain open spaces to ensure fresh air can circulate in the city. The properties with open spaces, however, would be highly lucrative to developers if they were allowed to be developed. From a regional perspective, the public interest in securing good air circulation outweighs the individual property owners' concerns. The regional planner said it would be a lot harder to protect the open spaces if the local level was the only one charged with it. The planner said: "There are a few things in regional planning that need to be regulated rather than negotiated" (STU-R-LU expert, own translation).

A legislatively-binding RGS has a different character than a guiding RGS. The RGS is primarily a regulatory instrument which weighs and protects the various rights to the use of land. This is frequently called passive coordination (*negativ Koordination*) in the German planning research. Passive coordination is defined as ensuring that a project by one set of actors does not negatively impact the objectives of a project by another set of actors (Fürst 2014, p. 452). In contrast, proactive coordination means that actors actively work together to reach a common goal with a societal benefit or win-win-situation (*Mehrwert*) for all involved (Fürst 2014, p. 452). By protecting the rights of various actors and setting out a shared regional vision, the RGS does not specify the actions to be taken. In fact, the RGS cannot mandate that a community develop a certain location. But the RGS can restrict areas from being developed for reasons defined in state, federal, and EU laws – this includes environmental protection and agricultural lands.

The German planning views the purpose of the RGS as protecting certain areas with a use to society and ensuring efficient use of public investments. One of the interviewed experts stressed the special character of the RGS:

> An RGS is usually not implemented but rather applied. Many policies in the RGS are restricting certain developments in certain areas. Therefore, I wouldn't talk about active implementation which would imply actions and financial means. The success of a RGS - particularly with regards to climate adaptation - is when something doesn't get built in an undesirable location, e.g. a flood zone. The RGS can have this impact because it is being applied during local and sectoral planning procedures.
>
> (STU-R-LU expert)

Ultimately, the RGS is a legal document that regulates the location of the urbanized areas, open spaces, and infrastructure corridors on a non-parcel-specific basis. Furthermore, the RGS defines some spatial policies for development within the urbanized areas. The next section describes the integrating mechanisms that connect the policies in the RGS to local and sectoral implementation decisions and discusses the specific spatial policies in more detail.

Approval of local land use designations maps

The RGS provides the policies for the development of a local land use designations map. Unlike in North America, German cities do not prepare comprehensive plans containing policies; rather, cities issue a land use designations map. The local land use designations map (FNP) indicates what areas the city would like to develop in the future. A community can then zone the identified areas of the city (see Hirt 2007, 2012, 2013 for a discussion of differences in zoning between the countries). The local land use designations map is regulated by the federal law on zoning and by the policies in the RGS. Usually, either the county or state district confirms that a local land use designations map complies with the law (G-BauGB §6(1)). As one expert explained:

> It is ultimately up to the local governments to decide where they want to develop – their decision is only limited by existing state and federal law which for instance includes protected areas for environmental reasons mapped in the RGS."
>
> (Interview county official)

Therefore, the local implementation decisions are nested within a context of state and federal laws and regional policies.

The approval process itself is structured by a set of legislatively-defined procedures in federal and state laws (Fürst 2010, p. 137). In Baden-Württemberg, administrators at the county or state level complete the review using a checklist prepared by the state – they check if the local political decision aligns with state and regional policies (manifested in laws and the RGS; expert interview). The regional level can comment in the review process but the counties conduct the ultimate review.

Based on the land use designations map, communities zone land within the urban area of the community. During the zoning process, cities must still follow the policies marked as requirements within the RGS. The section in the federal zoning law reads as follows: "Zoning maps (B-Pläne) are to be adjusted to the requirements in the RGS" (G-BauGB §1(4)). A planner at the regional level explained:

> Based on the federal zoning law, communities have to adjust their zoning maps to the requirements (Ziele) in the RGS. This also means that a zoning code which is out of compliance has to be proactively adjusted to ensure conformity with the regional requirements. [...] Therefore we concentrated on creating requirements rather than principles during the development of the current RGS. We can go to court if a community is out-of-compliance with its zoning map.
>
> (STU-R-LU expert)

Though senior levels have the ability to deny land use designations maps or sue in courts about zoning decisions, the preferred solution is to find compromises before conflicts occur (expert interviews). Since the regional level does not have implementation or enforcement powers, there has been a focus on building consensus when preparing the RGS. This leads to regional planning organizations that strive to create win-win-situations, balance interests, and be the initiator of joint projects and collaborations among its members (Fürst 2010, p. 238). Within this context, the RGS and the affiliated procedures are the central mechanism for spatial development pattern negotiations. Connecting local zoning decisions to the requirements in the RGS levels the playing field to ensure that local and regional interests are considered when developments are pursued.

Academic planning researchers credit the extensive set of legal rules with ensuring at least passive coordination among actors, although more proactive coordination is desirable (Fürst 2014).

The regional planning organization board's willingness to litigate is another factor that determines whether non-conforming local decisions will be taken to court. The interviewed planner did point out that this is a political decision, which other regions in Germany might not make since the boards are composed of locally elected officials. The Stuttgart region prides itself on being willing to enforce the RGS through the court system, if needed. Another challenge with this approach is that some communities had many Greenfields approved for development in the 1990s. Since they already have Greenfields in their local land use designation map, the regional planning organization cannot influence the subsequent zoning decisions.

Spatially significant actions by sectoral agencies

Sectoral agencies also have to account for the policies in the RGS for any spatially significant actions (G-ROG 2017, §4). Spatially significant actions (*Raumbedeutsame Planungen und Maßnahmen*) include any plans, regulations, policies, projects, and funding for projects that "take up territory/space or impact spatial development patterns" (own translation, G-ROG §3(6)). Sectoral agencies are required by federal law to comply with the requirements and give due consideration to the principles set out in a spatial plan for an area (Fürst 2010, p. 158; G-FStrG §16; G-ROG §4 (1) and (3)). While sectoral agencies must comply with regional and statewide plans, there are procedures for variances because sectoral plans (and local zoning codes) have strong autonomy in the German constitution (GG §65; G-ROG §14 and §15). Through a set of legislatively-defined procedures, multiple entities coordinate on the development of sectoral projects to ensure alignment with spatial policies (Fürst 2010, p. 137).

State-regulated spatial policies specified in the RGS

Part of the German planning system is a set of spatial policies at the state and regional levels that structure the territorial development. The spatial policies assign certain rights and attach certain requirements to development considerations at the local level. The subsequent section discusses a subset of the spatial policies most relevant for creating compact and complete transit-connected communities. In the Stuttgart region, many of these spatial policies are legislatively-binding; this includes a classification of communities, density requirements, a prioritization of corridors, the protection of open spaces, and direction of large retail to certain communities.

Federal guidance on development patterns

The federal law describes what type of general development patterns should be pursued by spatial planning at the state and regional levels. The respective section in the federal law reads as follows:

> §1(2) The responsibilities of §1(1) [purpose of planning] are to be executed to achieve a sustainable development of the German territory and its parts, that balances the social and economic needs for the use of land with the ecological functions of that land; and that contributes to long-lasting and well-balanced development patterns (dauerhaften, großräumig ausgewogenen Ordnung) that ensure equal living conditions in all part of the German territory (gleichwertigen Lebensverhältnissen in den Teilräumen).
>
> (G-ROG §1(2), own translation)

The paragraph sets a vision for sustainable development patterns that are considerate of economic, social, and ecological needs – because those activities take up land. The idea is to balance the various uses within a territory larger than one municipality; some areas are designated for ecosystem functions, while other areas are more suitable for economic activities (e.g. factories, etc.). This broad federal vision is supported by a set of federal spatial development principles that ought to be considered when preparing spatial plans (G-ROG §2; Runkel 2005, p. 1317). The principles at the federal level are intentionally abstract to allow discretionary decision-making at the state, regional, and local levels (Stark 2009, p. 44). Furthermore, states and regions are free to add to the list of principles.

The federal principles can be conflicting – for instance, they prioritize both economic development and environmental protection. Therefore, the responsibility at the regional and local levels is then to balance the different needs with regard to the specific available land and conditions (Runkel 2005; Fürst 2010). This means land in desirable locations for economic development (e.g. access to existing infrastructure) is indicated as such in regional and local plans; so is land that needs to be protected due to its rich soil for agriculture; and land with strong biological ecosystems needs to be protected for its environmental value. Yet, only the local level is permitted to draw parcel-specific boundaries. Consequently, one area of the region and city may be designated for environmental protection whereas another area may be prioritized for economic development. Through the principles, the federal government sets an agenda which indicates what factors ought to be considered when preparing spatial plans. Therefore, the principles (and subsequent state and regional policies) have to be taken into account for planned sectoral projects (Peine 1998, p. 179; Runkel 2005, p. 1315; Stark 2009, p. 46; Fürst, 2010, p. 189).

Pursued spatial vision: a polycentric region

The vision for spatial development in the Stuttgart region is to concentrate existing and new development in communities along primary development corridors (VRS Regionalplan 2009, p. 8-principle 1.4.2.6). The primary development corridors are all served by rapid transit and radiate outwards from the center of the city. While communities adjacent to the corridors are prioritized for new development, the spaces in between the corridors are prioritized for protecting open spaces (agriculture, naturally sensitive areas, and parks). This development pattern is required by the state. The state requirement reads as follows:

> To ensure balanced development patterns and to avoid sprawl, new development is to be concentrated in communities classified as a central place (first through third tier) and along the primary development corridors.

> In-between the corridors sufficient open space needs to be preserved. [...] To avoid a continuously settled area [bandartige Siedlungsstruktur] along the primary development corridors, urbanized area is to alter with open spaces along the primary development corridors.
>
> (BW-LEP 2002, p. 23-requirements 2.6.4 and 2.6.4.1)

By directing growth to communities along the primary development corridors, the region and state are pursuing a polycentric development pattern in which jobs and housing are clustered in multiple large and small communities across the region (VRS-Regionalplan 2009, p. 8-principle 1.4.2.1). While development is clustered in some communities, other communities retain open spaces such as agricultural, environmentally sensitive, and recreational land. A planner at the regional level said:

> We are working to maintain and foster the polycentric development patterns in the region. We think that having multiple employment centers across the region creates efficient settlement structures. Therefore we emphasize the development of housing and employment along the rapid transit corridors at the regional level.
>
> (STU-R-LU expert)

By advocating the clustering jobs and housing in multiple denser transit-accessible communities across the region, the RGS recommends reducing transportation demand as distances between destinations within the communities are shorter (VRS-Regionalplan 2009, p. 15). An underlying policy principle is to match development and infrastructure, meaning that new development should occur next to existing infrastructure and new infrastructure should connect underserved existing developments (VRS-Regionalplan 2009, p. 7; principle 1.4.2.4: *Zuordnung von Siedlung und Infrastruktur*). This vision is supported by a set of spatial policy requirements that serve to structure the region. The subsequent section reviews these spatial policies in the RGS and the related sections in federal and state laws that authorize the spatial policies.

Community classification

The heart of regional and statewide planning in Germany is a classification of communities into several tiers (*System der Zentrale Orte*). Each state in Germany creates its own types of communities. Based on the classification, communities have certain rights and responsibilities. This classification is authorized under federal law which specifies that new growth should occur within communities that already have sufficient infrastructure (G-ROG §2(2)2). Sufficient infrastructure includes, for instance, transportation, sewer, and water utilities but also social services such as daycare facilities, hospitals, and schools. Hence, communities are classified based on their current population, jobs, and services. If combined with density requirements or growth targets like in the Stuttgart region, the classification can be used to steer development patterns. The subsequent section gives a brief overview of the theoretical underpinning and the application in the Stuttgart region.

The theoretical underpinning of the community classification is Christaller's theory of central places. The theory of central places describes a hierarchy of communities based on the types of goods and services a community provides for its hinterland (Blair & Caroll 2009, p. 52). The smallest communities provide, for example, grocery stores for their hinterland. The larger communities would also provide clothing stores. The hinterland of the larger community includes the smaller communities (Blair & Caroll 2009, p. 52f.). In Germany, Christaller's theory of central places is applied, to varying extent, by state law to structure territorial developments (BMVBS 2012, p. 40).

In Baden-Württemberg the state-development plan specifies a four-tiered classification system for communities (BW-LEP 2002, p. 20f.). Criteria for the definition of each tier include the current population as well as employment and housing characteristics. Thereby, each tier serves a certain sized population with jobs, services, and housing. Goods and services that cannot be offered in each community are to be concentrated in higher order communities (VRS-Regionalplan 2009, p. 41). For instance, first-tier communities (*Oberzentren*) are defined as a center with several thousand residents in an urbanized area. The majority of jobs, particularly high skilled jobs in a region, are located in the first-tier communities (BW-LEP 2002, p. 21–requirement 2.5.8). Furthermore, the first-tier communities include amenities serving a larger population. The second-tier communities (*Mittelzentren*) include at least 35,000 residents and offer a variety of jobs and housing options (BW-LEP 2002, p. 21–requirement 2.5.9). The lower ranking communities (third tier, *Unterzentren*) primarily function as larger communities in rural areas. All remaining communities (primarily rural villages) are in the fourth tier.

The definitions of community types are vague enough to leave room for interpretation and specification by the lower levels of government. However, the state designates first-tier and second-tier communities while the lower ranking communities (third and fourth tier) are negotiated at the regional level (VRS-Regionalplan 2009, p. 39f; BW-LplG §11(3)). The classification is displayed in a legislatively-binding regional map, called the development pattern map (Figure 6.2). The highest ranking communities (first and second tier) include cities such as the core city of Stuttgart and larger suburban communities with job agglomerations (BW-LplG §7(2)2).[10]

As shown in Figure 6.2, usually, the highest ranking communities (first and second tier) are designated along primary development corridors. The primary development corridors are characterized by certain infrastructure

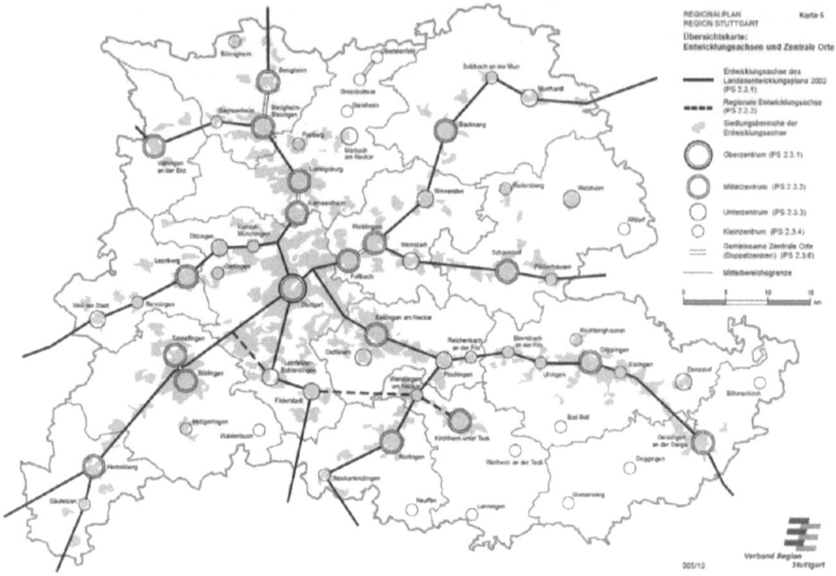

Figure 6.2 Development pattern map showing primary development corridors and community classifications for the Stuttgart region.
Source: VRS-Regionalplan 2009, p. 51.

features (*leistungsfähige Bandinfrastruktur*) such as regular transit, federal and state highways, and large power, water, sewer and telecommunication lines (VRS-Regionalplan, 2009, p. 34; policy 2.2.3-principle). The state government and the regional planning organization designate the primary development corridors. The Stuttgart region intentionally aligned its primary development corridors with the rapid transit network to ensure that new developments occur in proximity to the rapid transit network. Other regions in Baden-Württemberg primarily align their primary development corridors with interstate highways. The primary development corridors guide subsequent infrastructure investments through the integrating procedures. However, just being located along a rapid transit corridor does not guarantee a higher tier (VRS-Regionalplan 2009, p. 42).

Growth percentage of permissible new housing units

The tiers are carefully assigned because being a higher tier grants a community certain rights for new development (housing) which other communities do not have (expert interview). While the communities designated in the first, second, and third tier are permitted to absorb new outside growth, the fourth-tier communities are only permitted to grow for the needs of their existing population and businesses (VRS-Regionalplan 2009, p. 82f.). The regional planner explained:

> For directing growth in the Stuttgart region, the classification of communities into two groups is a crucial spatial policy: Some communities can only grow for the needs of the existing population, which we call Eigenentwicklung. Others have to absorb more growth than they need to support the current population. There is a clear quantitative distinction: We want new development along the transit corridors and little development in non-transit accessible areas.
>
> (STU-R-LU expert)

These fourth-tier communities are called "low-growth-communities" (*Gemeinden beschränkt auf Eigenentwicklung*). The policies in the statewide spatial plan authorize the regional planning organization to determine which communities are low-growth-communities (BW-LEP 2002, p. 25-requirement 3.1.5). The low-growth-communities include primarily rural villages across the region. VRS created a growth target for those communities as a policy principle in its RGS: low-growth-communities are permitted to develop new housing equaling 1% of existing housing units every five years (VRS-Regionalplan 2009, p. 55, policy principle 2.4.0.5.1).[11] In contrast, the first-, second-, and third-tier communities in the urbanized area are permitted to grow 1.5% of existing housing units every five years (VRS-Regionalplan 2009, p. 55, policy principle 2.4.0.4.1). Both policies are guiding but not required. The interviewed regional planner explained:

> Without being permitted to grow at least a little bit, we would see more lawsuits about the RGS. We cannot and should not prevent a community entirely from building any new housing. We need to at least permit a little growth in all communities. [...] It's about allowing the community to have options.
>
> (VRS-R-TR)

Nevertheless, the regional policies are clearly targeted towards promoting more growth in communities along the primary development corridors (first, second and third tier) to ensure that investments in infrastructure are continuously utilized. As more new development is permitted in first-, second-, and third-tier communities, sprawl might remain a challenge in those communities. Therefore, VRS introduced density requirements.

Density requirements

To reduce sprawl (*Flächeninanspruchnahme*), the state and region introduced density requirements. In closer proximity to the rapid transit system, higher densities for housing (*Bruttowohndichte*) are required (VRS-Regionalplan

2009, p. 59f.). The density requirements (*Richtwerte für Siedlungsdichte*)[12] are as follows (VRS-Regionalplan 2009, p. 56-requirement 2.4.0.8):

- First-tier communities (Oberzentren): 90 residents per hectare (~36 residents per acre)
- Second-tier communities (Mittelzentren): 80 residents per hectare (~32 residents per acre)
- Third-tier communities (Unterzentren): 70 residents per hectare (~28 residents per acre)
- Fourth-tier communities: 50 to 60 residents per hectare (~20 to 24 residents per acre)

The density requirements apply to the community at large (BMVBS 2012, p. 21). This allows some flexibility because the community has the option to admit higher and lower densities in various locations as long as the average equals the minimum density requirement (VRS-Regionalplan 2009, p. 59f.).

The minimum densities are enforced during the preparation of the local land use designations map. Based on the minimum density, a community can determine how much new buildable land it needs to open up for new development to service the projected population growth (VRS-Regionalplan 2009, p. 59f.). As the community determines the need for new buildable land, a clear priority is to prioritize infill over greenfield developments (VRS-Regionalplan 2009, p. 55-requirement 2.4.0.6). The regional planner explained:

> Minimum densities are crucial to ensure affordable housing in the region. In most instances, communities overachieve on the minimum densities. [...] The minimum densities are marked as requirements so we can apply them during commenting on local zoning and land use designations maps.
>
> (STU-R-LU expert)

The density requirements and growth targets for fourth-tier communities are an example of the balancing act at play at the regional level. Federal law charges the regional level with a clear responsibility to organize development patterns, but at the same time the local level has the right to self-administration. Therefore, the policies in the RGS require average densities for the community at-large, meaning the density requirements are not location specific which allows for local discretion in zoning. Asked about this approach, a planner at the regional level explained:

> Local autonomy in urban planning is highly regarded in Baden-Württemberg and regional planning should not get involved in too many details of urban planning. We set a framework for the development of the local land use designations map [...] by indicating which communities are

> permitted to grow more]. But how communities want to grow within this framework is within their realm of responsibility.
>
> (STU-R-TR expert)

Working with density requirements is not very common in regional planning – During the development of an RGS, it is hard to get the buy-in from communities. Nevertheless, the urban planners I interviewed indicated that the communities benefiting from the permitted higher growth (first, second and third tier) are in favor of the regional level's involvement. The communities classified as "low-growth communities" show mixed support depending on local political majorities and current population growth.

Preferred locations for higher-density housing (*Schwerpunkte des Wohnungsbaus*)

Besides the density requirements and growth targets for low-growth communities, VRS has two other sets of spatial policies in which it gives more location-specific direction. Generally, communities have the right to determine the locations of new development as long as they comply with the spatial policies in the RGS. For some communities, the RGS identifies "preferred locations for higher-density housing" (*Schwerpunkte des Wohnungsbau*) which are usually in proximity to transit. Regardless of the tier of the community, the RGS permits (and requires) higher minimum density in such locations (90 residents per hectare -36 people per acre; VRS-Regionalplan 2009, p. 56 requirement 2.4.0.8). These preferred locations are identified at parcel level and no other conflicting uses are permissible (VRS-Regionalplan 2009, p. 139ff.-requirement 2.4.4.1). The preferred locations for higher-density housing are negotiated with the communities during the development of the RGS:

> We need the community's commitment to the location otherwise there would be no use in designating the location in the RGS. The community is the implementing entity. We cannot implement the preferred locations. So it would be rather pointless to include a preferred location for housing without having reached a consensus with the community.
>
> (STU-R-TR expert)

Federal law authorizes regional planning to designate locations as preferred locations (*Vorranggebiete*; G-ROG 2017, §7(3)1). Communities are not obliged to build in those locations but no other type of development is permitted there. One regional planner indicated that the "preferred locations for higher-density housing" are a good example for the implementation challenges at the regional level:

> We can only make offers at the regional level to develop certain areas. However, the communities decide if they use the right to develop

> at higher densities in those locations. The community does have to comply with the requirements in the RGS and wouldn't be permitted to develop at a lower density or with a different use. However, there is no obligation to develop anything at all. [...] If we really want to see a 'preferred location develop' we rely on a lot of consulting with the communities.
>
> (STU-R-LU expert)

Occasionally, after a local election, a previously preferred location is not pursued any further by a community. The subsection about local decision-making in the Stuttgart region presents an example of a community developing the preferred location for higher-density housing.

Large retail permissible in designated urban centers

In addition to setting requirements for housing, the region can also set requirements for the location of large retail. One of the purposes of the community classification system is to ensure sufficient services (*Versorgungssicherheit*) across the region (VRS-Regionalplan 2009, p. 42). The concept of "sufficient services" is intentionally vague but has implications for permissible locations for large retailers, large employers, hospitals, universities, and other uses that serve large populations. Particularly, large retailers have to undergo a so-called "spatial compatibility assessment" (G-ROV §1(19)). Thereby, a clear regional objective is to avoid large retail on the fringes to prevent an increase in VMT (VRS-Regionalplan 2009, p. 105). Thereby, climate mitigation is one of multiple reasons for this set of policies, as the subsequent quote shows:

> If large retailers were to locate on the fringes of the urbanized area, vehicle miles travelled would increase. This situation would hinder the objective to reduce carbon emissions. [...] Therefore, it's a responsibility of regional planning to try and prevent such developments.
>
> (VRS-Regionalplan 2009, p. 105)

Accordingly, the RGS contains the following policy requirement concerning large retailers. Large retail projects with more than 800 square meters (~0.2 acres) are only permissible in communities with the status of a central place (first, second and third tier; VRS-Regionalplan 2009, p. 103-requirement 2.4.3.2.2). The communities further limit the location to the designated urban center (*Siedlungs- und Versorgungskern;* VRS-Regionalplan 2009, p. 103-requirement 2.4.3.2.3). The communities suggest the specific location, which is then displayed with a parcel-based boundary in the regional land use designations map (VRS-Regionalplan 2009, p. 103-requirement 2.4.3.2.3(1)). Large retail projects are not permitted outside of these urban centers (VRS-Regionalplan 2009, p. 103-requirement 2.4.3.2.3(2)). However, the RGS intentionally stresses that local grocery stores are still desirable to ensure walkability in all types of communities. Furthermore, rapid transit access is suggested for all large retail projects larger than 25,000 square meters (~6.2 acres) (VRS-Regionalplan 2009, p. 104-principle 2.4.3.2.6).

Open spaces

In addition to policies directing growth to particular communities and locations, the RGS also contains policies on open spaces. The areas in between the primary development corridors (*Achsenzwischenräume*) are to contain open spaces with clustered smaller rural villages (*Dorf*). The open spaces (*Freiraumstruktur*) in the Stuttgart region have a complementary function to the urbanized areas (VRS-Regionalplan 2009, p. 8–principle 1.4.2.6 (G)) and serve several functions that are partly protected under EU, federal, and state law. The functions include: (1) recreational purposes, (2) preservation of natural habitats, agricultural land, and forests, (3) production of fresh water, (4) capture of water during flooding events, and (5) protection of natural resource rich areas (VRS-Regionalplan 2009, p. 149). Based on EU, federal, state, and regional policies, these different areas have an inherent value and function to the people living within the region. For instance, under the German constitution GG §20a natural resources are protected. The interviewed regional planner explained:

> Regional planning can really regulate when it comes to open spaces. Here we can clearly restrict certain uses. A community cannot build in protected open spaces (Grünzüge). [...] Thereby, infill is a clear priority prior to developing greenfields [...]. We really scrutinize if a community wants to build on a greenfield. A community will have to prove that it has no remaining infill or brownfield locations.
>
> (STU-R-LU expert)

In the nested planning system, the state and the regional level map the general areas that are protected under EU, federal, and state laws. However, the parcel specific boundaries are negotiated during the preparation of the local land use designations maps, which means the boundary between urban uses and open spaces is fuzzy in the RGS (VRS-Regionalplan 2009, p. XI). The regional expert explained:

> Certainly, each community has a right to development. Therefore, a central component of preparing the local land use designations map are questions over the locations in which a community can grow. The quantity and the location of new growth is certified in the land use designations map by the county or state. When a community is ready, they can pursue development in those locations.
>
> (STU-R-LU expert)

Within this context, there is still greenfield development in Germany. Not all open spaces are actually protected by law and there is some room for discretionary decision-making when determining parcel-based boundaries. There are also procedural options to create new green space elsewhere. Nevertheless, during the preparation of the local land use designations map each community identifies the current urbanized area (housing, employment, and mixed-uses), the future urbanized area, and protected open spaces. The future urbanized area includes sites for new housing and economic development to meet the projected population growth at the regionally required average densities.

Federal law further emphasizes the protection of the open spaces as designated in local land use designations maps. The federal law creates a clear mandate for the states, regions, and local levels to restrict housing and retail developments in designated open spaces[13] (G-BauGB §35). Developments are not permissible if they are in conflict with a local land use designations map, with a sectoral plan, if they threaten natural resources, or if they unduly burden the public infrastructure (G-BauGB §35(3)). The protection of open spaces is an example of the German planning system's nested structure that becomes incrementally more specific. The federal law defines general rules, the regional level maps general patterns of open spaces, and the local level determines the parcel-based boundaries of open spaces. The local decision is approved by the counties that ensure the local level complies with the federal and regional frameworks. Parcel-specific mapping of policies is a primary responsibility at the local level.

Mapping of policies

Mapping of policies is a central feature of planning at the local and regional levels in Germany. Differentiating between policy setting and mapping as distinct responsibilities at each level is part of the system. Therefore, the regional land use designations map (*Raumnutzungskarte*) in the Stuttgart region is more general than zoning maps (*Bebauungsplan*). The regional land use designations map identifies urban areas in contrast to open spaces. Various policy objectives (e.g. protection of open spaces) are assigned to different areas of the region (expert interview). Furthermore, the regional maps assign rights by setting a community classification, primary development corridors, and affiliated policies as discussed above. The general approach is to first politically define rules that administrators can then easily verify if other decision-makers are in compliance with the rules. According to one expert, mapping policies ensures that rules can be applied unambiguously. The planner explained:

> If a rule is only a policy, no court can prove if the rule was followed. If a policy only states to 'ensure the protection of open spaces', it would be hard to win in court. Therefore, we have to unambiguously clarify to

> which general locations this applies. Otherwise the negotiation with the local level would be impossible. For instance, initially we had said that large retail should be located downtown. [...] As soon as a city had an investor with a random property, downtowns started to have very odd shapes and locations. [...] To avoid this, we asked communities to delineate their downtowns on a map. With a map, it's clear to every property owner which policies and rights apply to their land. This makes the application of the policies so much easier. [...] Lastly, since the compliance of local land use designations maps is enforced by different agencies, they like to have maps rather than to interpret policies. [...] Since the plan is adopted by politicians and represents the political will, the application can be done by administrators.
>
> (STU-R-LU expert)

To summarize, the nested German planning system is focused, by design, on vertical coordination of the use of land. In the Stuttgart region, several spatial policies are applied to not just limit growth in open spaces (restrictive), but to also positively shape the development patterns by indicating locations of desirable growth. The planners are clearly aware that the policies intervene in land markets and impact the value of properties (expert interview). This is generally justified by the federal policies that authorize planning to direct growth for several public purposes (G-ROG §2). This situation gives the planning system more leverage in the direction of growth than governmental agencies would have in a market-led planning system in North America.

Implementation of transit expansion

In-house transit planning at VRS

The nested governance structure in land use planning is echoed in transit planning. The local and regional levels determine the need for transit services, the funding comes from the federal and state governments, and the state government procures transit providers (BW-Mobility 2020; BW-Zielkonzept 2025). The transit is then operated by private companies that bid with the state government for sections of the network. The state of Baden-Württemberg therefore ultimately decides on the frequency and type of transit service offered in a region (BW-Mobility 2020). However, the networks themselves are planned at the county and regional levels and synchronized by the state government across regional and county boundaries. In the Stuttgart region, VRS is responsible for rapid transit while the counties are responsible for the busses serving the rapid transit stations (BW-ÖPNV-Pakt 2014).

The nested governance structure of spatial planning documents is mirrored in transportation planning. There is a federal transportation program for federal routes (*Bundesverkehrswegeplan*), a statewide transportation plan

(*Generalverkehrsplan*), a regional transportation plan (*Regionalverkehrsplan, RTP*), and a countywide transportation plan (*Nahverkehrsplan*). The plans get incrementally more specific; the federal and state transportation plans set a legislatively-binding framework for the RTP and county transportation plans (VRS-RTP 2018, p. 18). The RTP is legislatively-binding for the counties but not for the state or federal government (BW-ÖPNVG §11(2); VRS-RTP 2018, p. 18). The RTP is also utilized to comment on infrastructure projects pursued by the state and federal government (VRS-RTP 2018, p. 12f.).

VRS responsibilities for spatial planning and transportation planning

VRS is in a special position compared to other regional planning organizations in Germany. Besides its responsibilities in spatial planning, VRS has extensive authority for transportation and transit planning (BW-GVRS §1(3)1 and §4) and is responsible for the rapid transit network in the region, including rail lines and express busses (BW-GVRS §4; G-PBefG §8). VRS also prepares the RTP (VRS-RTP 2018) which has a legislatively-binding character for the countywide transportation plans (*Nahverkehrsplan*; BW-ÖPNVG §11). Being responsible for the transit system and the RGS enables VRS to integrate decisions on transportation with decisions on land use in the same organization. The prioritization of corridors is driven by the land use considerations in the RGS.

An agency responsible for both spatial planning and transportation planning is an example of an integrating mechanism. The regional transportation planner explained that within the organization, RGS and RTP are prepared on an alternating schedule. To some degree, the same staffers work on both plans. This helps to establish deep integration between both planning documents. Both plans build upon each other; the RGS informs the land use scenario utilized to assess the performance of different scenarios for the transportation system (VRS-RTP 2018, p. 19). Furthermore, the RTP examines transportation actions proposed in the RGS in more depth (VRS-RTP 2018, p. 12).

Spatial policies in RGS guiding transportation decisions

The connection of spatial planning and transportation planning is further emphasized by state law in Baden-Württemberg. The state government creates legislative principles for transportation planning. These principles establish the nexus between spatial and transit planning (öffentlicher Personennahverkehr). The relevant section in the state transit law (BW-ÖPNVG) reads as follows:

> (1) Planning for transit needs to align (abstimmen) with the principles and requirements of spatial plans [...]. (2) [Spatial] plans should ensure that transit sufficiently connects housing, recreation, and employment, as well as public, social and cultural services. (3) Particularly in the

urbanized area (verdichteter Raum), planning for transit should have priority over planning for single-occupancy vehicles.

(BW-ÖPNVG §3)

Overall, the state directive is to ensure that transit is a viable alternative to single-occupancy vehicle trips (RMK-NVP 2017, p. 13). Thereby, land uses – existing and planned – are somewhat thought of as a priori to transportation decisions. The policies in the RGS concerning community classifications inform transportation decisions at the county and regional levels.

The community classification is one of multiple factors used to prioritize transportation projects in the region (VRS-RTP 2018, p. 76). A policy in the RTP is that the transportation system is supposed to "strengthen the higher tiers in the community classification" (*Teilziel 8: Stärkung der zentralen Orte*; VRS-RTP 2018, p. 39). The community classification informs decisions on the frequency of transit services – with more frequent transit services in higher tiers. One objective is to ensure that second- and third-tier communities are easily accessible for fourth-tier communities (VRS-RTP 2018, p. 39; BW-Zielkonzept 2025, p. 14). As mentioned above, the second- and third-tier communities are located along the rapid transit network. The second- and third-tier communities therefore also serve as regional transit hubs which ensure transit access to downtown Stuttgart from other parts of the region. Broadly speaking, busing connects the fourth-tier communities to the second- and third-tier communities (expert interview). The rapid transit system connects the second- and third-tier communities to the City of Stuttgart (first tier). To some extent, the spatial policies on community classifications help to integrate decisions between land use and transportation decision-makers as they provide a clear structure to the development patterns. The spatial policies can have this integrating character because of the integration between the RTP and RGS.

Relevance of low-carbon development patterns in transit decision-making

Improving the rapid transit system in the Stuttgart region has been on the agenda, even prior to climate mitigation concerns, in an effort to reduce congestion. A central approach has been to work with primary development corridors, where communities are permitted higher densities (STU-R-TR expert). Rather than pursuing the construction of new lines, the levels of government in the Stuttgart region have focused on increasing frequency and ensuring better access to the rapid transit system (bus and park and ride stations). A constraint on new construction of rapid transit in the region is the available right of way and capacities in the tunnels at the main train station. The topography (rolling hills) going into the City of Stuttgart is especially challenging.

In the past ten years, two new rapid transit lines went into operation on the transit freight right-of-way. The two ring lines are the S60 and the S4 (see Figure 6.3). For the S4, improvements to upgrade the existing rail infrastructure for new rapid transit access between the second-tier communities Backnang and Ludwigsburg cost 11 million euros (VRS-S4 2012). Building the S60, which creates a new connection to Böblingen, cost 160 million euros for 14 kilometers of rapid transit (expert interview). A regional transportation planner I interviewed explained that rather than doing a completely new construction project, they were able to upgrade the existing routes and improve the existing station areas along the S4. Both corridors strengthened the access between second-tier communities rather than connecting to downtown Stuttgart.

Investment in the new rapid transit lines was not necessarily an effort to foster low-carbon development patterns. Some stations are intentionally built as park and ride stations, which do not encourage development around them. The regional transportation planner explained the rationale as follows:

> It would be great if someone would also develop next to the station area but unless the development is a high-rise, it would not create as much additional demand for rapid transit as a park and ride station does. [...] Park and ride stations are important for people living in fourth tier communities wanting to take rapid transit into the city of Stuttgart. Furthermore, our park and ride stations usually have a small enough footprint that they do not negatively impact the pedestrian experience

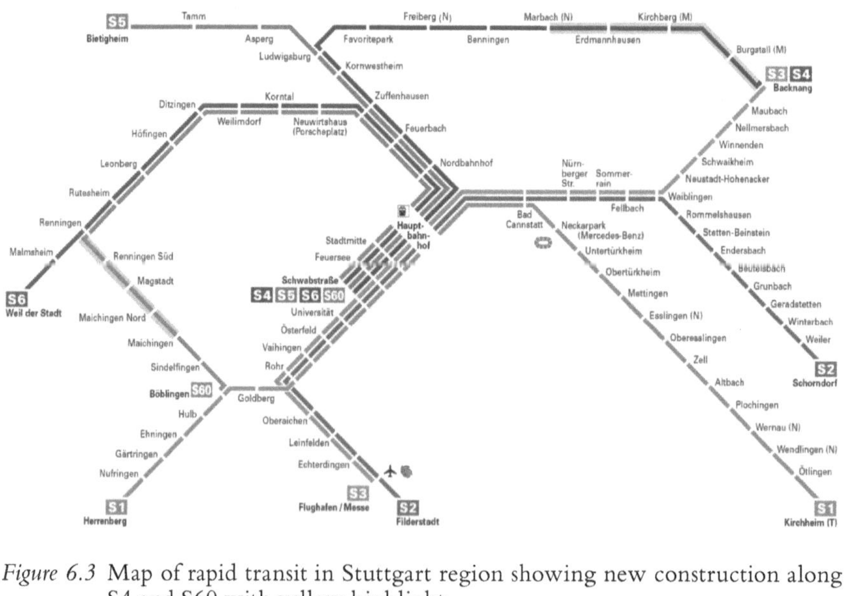

Figure 6.3 Map of rapid transit in Stuttgart region showing new construction along S4 and S60 with yellow highlight.

Source: VRS-S4 2012, p. 2.

> to get to the train station. Therefore, we think that park and ride makes more sense next to the station than a new development.
>
> (STU-R-TR expert)

The reluctance to leverage all new rapid transit stops for low-carbon development finds expression in the debate about re-designating several communities along the S4 rapid transit corridor. During the time of my interviews, experts in the Stuttgart region were debating the re-designation of the S4 corridor as a priority development corridor to permit more growth in its fourth-tier communities. Planners at the local, county, and regional levels explained that the primary intent of the S4 was to help commuters between two second-tier communities rather than to permit new development along the corridor. The conflict around re-designating the S4-corridor as a priority development corridor first arose during the preparation of the RGS. Some communities (Wangen, Erdmannhausen, Kirchberg an der Murr) along the S4 requested a new priority development corridor and a subsequent change in the tier designation of the communities along the corridor (VRS-Regionalplan 2009, p. 309).

Interestingly, the initial request by the community was denied with one of the reasons being climate mitigation concerns (VRS-Regionalplan 2009, p. 309). Planners were concerned that new housing development would increase VMT because of the current lack of services in these communities. The transportation planners are interviewed were very wary of new development in the "wrong" locations because of the traffic implications.

The planners indicated that while permitting more development in the communities along the S4 corridor might possibly increase the number of transit riders, in reality it would cause more people to drive and contribute to the region's existing congestion problems. Hence, re-designation as a priority development corridor was denied. A heated debate over re-designating the S4-corridor as a priority development corridor took place at a VRS board meeting. The board ultimately decided to preserve the current classification status of these communities as fourth tier. Besides the possible increase in traffic, multiple planners mentioned other reasons like the topographic conditions: the rapid transit line runs through the valley while the communities are on top of a hill. The rapid transit lines are therefore on the far edge of the communities. Furthermore, the valley is prone to flooding which makes land in the valley protected as open spaces as designated in the RGS. The communities are also very small at present and do not have the infrastructure necessary to support an increase in population. Lastly, a regional planner explained:

> The communities already do not use the areas they are permitted to develop in their land use designations map. As they already stay below their possibilities, we did not see the necessity to change their community classification. We will discuss this in more detail with the communities

since theoretically they could be a third tier community. But we don't want to set the precedent that just having a rapid transit stop adjacent to the community enables a higher classification.

(STU-R-LU expert)

This example shows the multitude of relevant considerations that factor into the community classifications and designation of primary development corridors. Furthermore, it also gives an insight into how the multitude of spatial policies are relevant for specific locations. In fact, a core responsibility of spatial planning is to balance the multiple conflicting objectives based on the guiding spatial policies in federal and state laws as well as in the RGS.

Transit planners in the Stuttgart region have also focused on improving existing rapid transit. They use transit investment in the Stuttgart region to purchase new vehicles to increase the frequency of transit and to better align bus pick up and drop-offs at the rapid transit stations. Efforts are primarily focused on increasing the service and reliability of the existing lines, adding park and ride stations, and improving the multi-modal infrastructure of the last mile of getting to and from the train stations (BW-ÖPNV-Pakt 2014). A flagship project is improving the signals on the way into the Stuttgart main train station where multiple rail companies operate on the same tracks. The planners hope to increase the rapid transit speeds and allow more train service by optimizing the signals. The Stuttgart region has received 500 million euros in federal and state funds to install the ETCS technology. Any improvements to the rapid transit system primarily rely on available funding programs at the federal and state levels.

Funding the rapid transit network

State and federal programs fund the transportation projects in the Stuttgart region. The various entities responsible for transportation submit their respective projects for funding. Projects are then assessed with a cost-benefit analysis. If a project is awarded funding, multiple levels of government share the costs. According to the regional transportation planner, the region had to come up with 15% of the costs to finance the S60. This was shared between the local governments, the counties, and VRS. The federal government took on 60% of the costs, and the state of Baden-Württemberg 25%. VRS took on half of the 15% for the region and the two involved counties split the other half (STU-R-TR expert). The next section briefly describes the two primary funding programs: a regional fund (*Regionalisierungsmittel*) and funding from the federal Municipal Transportation Financing Act (*Gemeindeverkehrs-finanzierungsgesetz*).

The federal funding is apportioned to the states (G-RegG §5), which use it to operate the transit system, invest in infrastructure, and purchase new vehicles (G-ÖPNV 2020). The state of Baden-Württemberg received 913.7 million euros in 2018, and will receive that amount with an annual 1.8%

increase until 2031 (G-RegG-Anlage 1). Baden-Württemberg also received an additional 16.7 million euros in 2020, which will increase annually to 64.6 million euros by 2031, to fund the rail transit network (G-RegG-Anlage 3).

In January 2020, the federal government authorized a funding program for rail projects with the Municipal Transportation Financing Act. The new funding is targeted at maintenance and improvement projects, including transit stations and rail infrastructure (G-ÖPNV 2020; G-GVFG §2). A special feature of the program is that corridors that were abandoned can be reactivated with the funding (G-ÖPNV 2020; G-GVFG §2). This additional funding was made available to achieve the federal government's climate objectives. Starting in 2021, 1 billion euros in funding was made available for rail infrastructure annually, and it is scheduled to increase to 2 billion in 2025 with an annual increase of 1.8% thereafter (G-ÖPNV 2020; G-GVFG §10). The federal government is paying 75%, rather than the usual 60% for rail projects (G-ÖPNV 2020). By providing additional federal funding for transit projects, the federal government hopes to incentivize more rapid transit projects.

The law also strengthens the nexus between spatial planning and transportation projects. By law, only projects that are in accordance with the requirements (*Ziele*) in the regional and statewide plans (G-GVFG §3(1)a) and the transit plans of the counties can receive funding (G-GVFG §3(1) b). Additionally, projects can only be funded if there has been coordination (*Abstimmung*) with related development efforts at the local level ("*städtebauliche Maßnahmen, die mit ihnen zusammenhängen*"; G-GVFG §6(2)).

I got a sense from the planners I interviewed that accessing funds was not a particular problem. The federal laws provide a stable financing mechanism for transportation projects over the next decade. With already sufficient state and federal funding, regional and local planners did not think a regional tax (as proposed in Vancouver and implemented in Seattle) was necessary. The local share of funding usually comes from a city's budget which is financed through property taxes and general (not transportation specific) apportionments from senior-level governments (STU-R-TR expert).

Local decision-making: increasing densities along transit corridors

Low-carbon development patterns are implemented within a very clearly defined set of laws in Germany. The legislation that grants certain rights and responsibilities to specific actors has been established for almost 40 years. In order to develop a location in a community, there are clear procedural guidelines, zoning categories, and spatial policy requirements from the federal, state, and regional levels that guide local decision-making. The federal zoning law (BauGB) ensures due process for property owners and coherent procedures across the country.

Cities in Germany take a very different role than US or Canadian cities in implementing compact and complete communities. German cities frequently act as developers and land-assemblers themselves, which gives them significantly more leverage over a specific site's uses. Based on federal law, the city can assemble the land and invest in public infrastructure to serve the new development. Cities operate under several federally-defined procedures to ensure due process and avoid takings. For instance, rather than exercise eminent domain, a city engages property owners in a federally-defined land-reassembly process (*Umlegungsverfahren*). A planner explained this practice:

> A challenge in Baden-Württemberg is that by law, each agricultural property gets divided among all inheritors. This has been going on for a few hundred years. [...]. You might have a property that is 500 m long and 5 m wide. For a 10 Hectare (~25 acres) Site, the city might have to contact up to 150 people. [...]. It's a big effort! And then there is a lot of negotiation because one person always doesn't want to sell.
>
> (STU-R-LU expert)

A city approaches property owners to see if they are interested in participating. By participating, the property owner maintains the value of its property but the property may change in (1) size due to changes in (2) land use rights (e.g. higher permitted density and changes in permitted uses) and (3) new access to public infrastructure (water, sewer, streets). Federal law regulates how the city negotiates with property owners and what each party can expect in terms of land values and public infrastructure costs. When the city acts as a land assembler, it can later find a developer to follow the city's vision for an area. Cities select areas for new development while preparing the local land use designations maps. The procedures around preparing and approving the local land use designation maps serve as integrating mechanisms with the spatial policies in the RGS. A city essentially determines appropriate locations for future local growth based on the spatial policies outlined in the RGS. The subsequent section provides more details on the local-regional interaction.

Allmendäcker: building in a regionally-preferred location for higher density housing along new rapid transit line in Sindelfingen/Maichingen

Sindelfingen is a community directly adjacent to the city of Stuttgart. In 2018, Sindelfingen had 64,867 residents (BW statistics 2019). As a second-tier community, Sindelfingen is currently developing a new site for higher-density residential housing near rapid transit called "Allmendäcker." The Allmendäcker site is located on a greenfield in a neighborhood called Maichingen (which was previously its own community until it merged with Sindelfingen). The greenfield is located along the newly constructed rapid transit corridor of the transit line S60. Allmendäcker provides an example of how the spatial policies in the RGS shaped development patterns over time.

The city first included Allmendäcker in its 1984 land use designations map. At the time, a rapid transit line was not being considered at the regional level. The site could not be developed in the 1990s due to RGS requirements to protect open spaces, particularly areas vital for producing fresh water (expert interview). After the 2008 RGS adopted the new rapid transit line and designated the area as "preferred location for higher-density housing," the city decided to finally pursue the Allmendäcker development. The experience shows how policy priorities change over time as the development pressure in the region changes. A local planner said:

> The idea was born in the region and as a city we used the opportunity. Having the rapid transit access was not particularly pursued by the city. The city is ultimately a beneficiary of this situation.
>
> (STU-L-SIN)

Due to the rapid transit access, the 2008 RGS defined Allmendäcker as a "preferred housing location" requiring a minimum density of 90 residents per hectare (36 people per acre). From my interviews with the regional planners, I learned the station was placed very intentionally as there was development potential and proximity to large employers along the S60 corridor.

A major employer in Sindelfingen is the car manufacturer Mercedes-Benz, whose assembly line is adjacent to the downtown Sindelfingen transit stop. The newly constructed S60 transit line connects the downtown Sindelfingen station to the Allmendäcker development site. Allmendäcker was designated a "preferred location for higher-density housing" (*Schwerpunkte des Wohnungsbaus*) in the 2009 RGS (VRS-Regionalplan 2009, p. 74).

The planners discussed several locations for new development in Maichingen when preparing the RGS. Allmendäcker made the most sense due to the transit access. The regional transportation planner explained:

> Another site was considered close to a new recently completed roadway. [...] We wanted to prioritize transit access. [...] The priority housing locations are meant to increase densities where it makes sense from a transportation perspective.
>
> (STU-R-TR expert)

To protect the areas for fresh water, the city and VRS compromised opened parts of the site while allowing others to be preserved as open spaces. The city embraced the concept of "mandatory green space" for enhancing residents' quality of life and included playgrounds and other amenities while ensuring green infrastructure for rainwater storage and treatment. This example illustrates the purpose of planning in Germany: to balance multiple conflicting goals in a growing region. In the 1980s the region saw no need for low-density development of the site, but the construction of the rapid transit line connecting multiple regional employment centers made the site a desirable location for new high-density development. The higher density made it possible to preserve a large portion of open space. The regional planner explained the decision:

> If we don't have enough housing in the region, people will have to live outside the metropolitan area and commute here to work. That is ecologically worse than any site along the rapid transit lines within the region. Sometimes a site isn't developed for localized ecological reasons, however, if you look at it from a regional perspective, another site might be developed that is much worse due to the traffic it creates. You can build a passive house in the wrong location [...] if it means that you just added 50 drivers to the roads. Then one didn't win anything.
>
> (STU-R-LU expert)

The local level government was able to thread the needle of conflicting regional requirements to achieve most of the goals (expert interview). Accordingly, parts of the site are protected green spaces and within the buildable 23.1 hectare (~ 57 acre) of the development site, a mix of 4-story multi-family, duplex, and single family homes. The goal is an overall average density of 45 housing units per acre (Sindelfingen Planungsworkshop 2016). The new development also includes a mixed use area with a daycare, a bakery, and several doctors' offices (see Figure 6.4 for pictures).

Breuninger area: prioritizing a former light industrial site near transit station for redevelopment

The City of Schorndorf is a second-tier community close to the fringe of the Stuttgart region with a population of 39,612 residents in 2018 (BW statistics 2019). The City of Schorndorf decided to redevelop a vacant industrial site near its downtown rapid transit station. The rapid transit line has been in place for several decades. The new development will be located on a former brownfield which had been home to a leather manufacturer for decades until 2008 (Schorndorf-Arcadis 2016, p. 5). The City of Schorndorf is a community reprioritizing infill development after clashing with the regional level over the extent of planned greenfield development.

The conflict with the regional level arose over the land use designations map in the early 2000s (local expert interview). Like many cities in the Stuttgart region, Schorndorf is urbanized but surrounded by greenfields (agricultural land and ecologically sensitive land). In 2005, the city proposed to develop several of the greenfields that were not environmentally protected. After a conflict over the amount of greenfield development in the local map, the city took the region and state permitting agency's advice seriously and refocused

New development „Allmendäcker" adjacent to new rapid transit stop in the City of Sindelfingen (Maichingen) in a preferred location for higher-density housing.

View from transit plattform of the Allmendäcker development.

Figure 6.4 Pictures of redevelopment near new S-60 transit stop in Sindelfingen (Maichingen).

Source: Own pictures.

its efforts on infill development. The supplementary report to the land use designations map includes the following note:

> The City of Schorndorf commits itself to develop only 70% by 2015 of the area indicated in the local land use designations map. This means that only 28 hectares (69 acres) rather than 40.2 hectare (99 acres) of new development will be developed.
>
> (Schorndorf 2015, p. 13)

Since then, according to a local planner, the city council of Schorndorf has prioritized infill over greenfield development. In 2005, the city's historic downtown saw many vacancies and properties ripe for redevelopment. A city official said:

> In the last 10 years, since the policy has been adopted, we have seen a lot of the vacancies disappear and have been able to revitalize our downtown. Because of the reduced supply of greenfield land, the market shifted towards investing into the urbanized area.
>
> (STU-L-SCH expert)

The site next to the train, the "Breuninger Area," had been purchased by Schorndorf and the city put together a request for proposals by developers to redevelop the site based on the city's expectations. The city then selected a winning bid. One expert I spoke to pointed out that the developers in the region are more interested in developing multi-family housing than single-family housing to address market demand. Once the winning bid is selected, the city rezones the site in collaboration with the selected developer. The site and design have been committed for 230 new apartments (Schorndorfer Nachrichten 2019) through a contract (*städtebauliche Verträge*) between developers and the city.

Conversations about the local land use designations map aided the City of Schorndorf's redevelopment efforts. The legislatively-defined procedures for the local land use designations map and the RGS helped create a situation in which the community prioritized infill development. One effect of clear legislatively-defined procedures is that the community often engages with the region and state prior to submitting documents for approval in order to reach mutually agreeable solutions. One expert said:

> We have leverage if we pursue efforts jointly. It gets difficult if one side acts confrontational. Usually, approaching an issue jointly helps us achieve our own goals.
>
> (STU-L-SCH expert)

Another local official highlighted that having clearly defined legal rules at the regional level on protected green spaces and growth targets has alleviated conflicts among local governments and the intensity of competition for residents and businesses. Throughout the interviews, it was apparent that the RGS enabled local planners to engage elected officials in different conversations about new developments.

The nestedness of the German planning system, with all its legal rules, appears to put the regional level actors in a strong position to coordinate development patterns at the regional level. The German system is not top-down because the local level has the ultimate decision on site selection and is vital for the implementation. However, the regional level does frame the local decision with all its spatial policies. In contrast to a market-led planning system, not every site and land parcel in the region is available for development. The available greenfield sites are carefully selected at the local level by applying regional spatial policies to the land use designations map. This means the local community's choice is anchored by the spatial policies at the regional level, which for instance prohibit development on certain open spaces and assign quantitative growth targets in the form of density requirements. The legislatively-binding RGS and the clear enforcement procedures clearly facilitate the integration of decisions.

My research seems to indicate that a clear legal framework allows the local level to be more active in pursuing compact and complete communities. Local expertise in the above examples lay not in developing policy frameworks but in specifically applying the laws and regional policies to locations within the city to develop. The local communities are in an implementing role and not a regulatory one. I suspect that not having to also draft regulation frees staff resources to actively engage in sorting out the details of implementation.

Notes

1 Falk (2006) highlights that these two concepts are embedded in planning in the following German Bundesländer: Bayern, Mecklenburg-Vorpommern, Niedersachsen, Rheinland-Pfalz, Saarland, Sachsen-Anhalt, und Thüringen (p. 154).

2 These include actions in the following sectors: transportation, agricultural, forestry, soils, natural resources, water, air, tourism, spatial development (*Siedlungsentwicklung*), housing, economic development, urban design (*Städtebau*), and the environment (BMVBW 2001, p.5; Sinz 2005, p. 867; Fürst, 2010, pp. 48 and 142f).

3 In some states, regional planning organizations have additional powers. For instance, Nordrhein-Westfalen regional planning organizations get to propose a list of transportation infrastructure priorities for the region (Schmitz 2005, p. 971). The VRS is also responsible for planning the regional transportation system.

4 Multiple municipalities were also preparing Green City Plans in response to the Diesel-Skandal. Here the agenda setting was primarily focused on technology-based solutions. Implementation of the Green City Plan was about accessing federal and state funds.

5 While sprawl is an issue in Germany, it is not nearly at the same extent as metropolitan regions in North America – thus contributing less to the overall

emissions. Siener (2004) indicates that sprawl in Germany is about 10% of the rate in North America.

6 Own translation: *"Stadt bzw. Region der kurze Wege" als Leitbild der Stadt- und Regionalentwicklung*

7 Own translation: " *Konzentration von Siedlungsschwerpunkten an Standorten mit guter Anbindung an den öffentlichen Nahverkehr, insbesondere Schienennahverkehr"*

8 Own translation: " *Reduktion der Ausweisung neuer Siedlungsflächen und Stärkung der Innenentwicklung in Städten und Gemeinden"*

9 Regional maps are prepared at a scale of 1:50.000–1:100.000. The scales read as follows: 1:100.000 means 1 cm on the map equals 100.000 cm (1 km) in reality. Statewide plans are prepared at 1:100.000–1:500.000, RGSs are prepared at 1:50.000–1:100.000, land use designations maps are prepared at 1:5.000–1:50.000, and zoning maps are 1:500–1:5.000 (Fürst 2010, p. 237; Umweltbundesamt 2015).

10 Interviews were conducted in the first-tier community, the City of Stuttgart, and in four second-tier communities, namely, Backnang, Böblingen, Waiblingen, and Schorndorf located in two different counties. I initially approached third-tier communities for interviews. However, it became quickly apparent that the third-tier communities were serviced by the second-tier communities' planning departments. Therefore, I discussed issues pertaining to two third-tier communities in the respective second-tier community interview.

11 Across Germany, multiple states take various approaches to allocate growth to fourth-tier communities. Several states permit a percentage of existing housing units or existing population while other states decide to allocate growth by a permitted percentage of the currently urbanized area of the community (BMVBS 2012, p. 35f.).

12 Density requirements are used in only a handful of states in Germany (BMVBS 2012, p. 21).

13 With a few exceptions for agricultural and energy producing facilities. Another layer of protection for agricultural land is added by the federal agricultural law in which farmers are only permitted to sell their land to other farmers (expert interview).

7 Reflecting on spatial policies as rules-in-use in regional growth strategies

The built form of many cities and regions is shaped by a set of rules-in-use that describes the desirable look or appearance of a location. The rules-in-use address questions about a place such as: will this place be a residential neighborhood or a possibly a mixed-use neighborhood which would include store-fronts for local businesses. Even in many market-led planning systems, cities still adopt zoning codes that contain permissible densities and uses, and set out design requirements for an area. The zoning code might address questions such as how tall can buildings be, how close to the streets can they be, and how many parking spaces need to be provided. While zoning is very specific to individual properties and needs to be regulated locally, spatial policies are not property specific. Spatial policies are frequently used in growth managing states and provinces in North America as well as in spatial planning countries in the European Union. In contrast to zoning, spatial policies are vague and describe desirable development patterns. Spatial policies tend to be written at the county, regional, and state level which all need to leave ample room for interpretation at the local level. But even local comprehensive plans can contain spatial policies that inform the zoning code.

To foster low-carbon development patterns, spatial policies might call for increased densities and diversified uses within a ½ mile of a rapid transit station. This chapter dives into more detail and explores the nuances of spatial policies. The three regions I investigated demonstrate the variety of spatial policies that can be included in a Regional Growth Strategy (RGS) to foster low-carbon development patterns in metropolitan regions. A similarity between all three regions is the explicit commitment at the regional level to build compact and complete communities along transit-corridors in an effort to reduce GHG emissions (Heinen 2018b). The three regions provide different examples of qualitative and quantitative spatial policies that guide growth in metropolitan regions to reduce transportation emissions. The spatial policies utilized across the different regions demonstrate the nuances of limiting growth in certain locations while promoting growth in others.

Spatial policies are substantive rules-in-use which express desirable development patterns for a region. Spatial policies are defined as any public sector policy for managing the location and spatial distribution of development

DOI: 10.4324/9781003268505-8

in an area. Yet, spatial policies are different from zoning. They are neither detailed on uses nor specific on design criteria. Spatial policies are policy instruments relevant for land use and infrastructure decisions. An implementing entity making zoning or infrastructure investment decisions seeks guidance from spatial policies on setting priorities. Spatial policies concern the location and quantity of new growth. They translate visions for a particular area into policy statements that implementing entities then apply. While one might initially think of spatial policies as regulatory approaches, spatial policies can also be combined with incentive-based approaches, the acquisition of land or allocation of infrastructure funding (Bengston et al. 2004). Spatial policies need to be combined with appropriate – meaning culturally and constitutionally permissible – integrating mechanisms that ensure collaboration across levels of government and that protect the rights of the local level (see Chapter 8).

Each region is characterized by a different mix of spatial policies targeted at directing growth.[1] While all three regions share a vision of compact and complete transit connected communities, their respective regional planning organizations employ various spatial policies. Some encourage growth in certain locations while discouraging growth in others. Spatial policies to discourage growth include urban containment boundaries, designated open spaces, and designated urbanized areas. Spatial policies to affirmatively direct growth to certain locations include the designation of urban centers, community classifications, density requirements, and growth targets. All three regions used a mix of spatial policies.

One notable difference between the three regions is the specificity of regulations at the regional level. The British Columbia and Baden-Württemberg planning systems worked with the notions of "statewide significance," "regional significance," and "local significance." Planners in both systems clearly understand which spatial policies are most suited to each level of government. In Germany, for example, the local level determines a location's mix of uses while the regional and state levels are concerned with general development patterns of a larger area. In the German system, regulation becomes more specific with each subordinate level of government, exhibiting elements of both self-regulation and state-regulation.

Finding the appropriate level of detail to be regulated at various levels of government can be a challenge. All three regions take different approaches. It is notable that lower levels of government make parcel-specific decisions while higher levels of government design and develop broader spatial policies. I have identified four types of responsibilities: (1) authorizing spatial policies, (2) designing spatial policies (e.g. definition of what qualifies as an urban center), (3) mapping spatial policies (e.g. designating an area within a community as an urban center), and (4) implementing spatial policies by changing local zoning requirements. In home-rule states, these four responsibilities might all be held at the local level. In growth managing states, these four responsibilities might be distributed across multiple levels of government, intentionally creating interdependencies that need to be managed by integrating procedures.

I have observed four distinct types of spatial policies (Table 7.1): As shown in Table 7.1, there are positive-allocative policies that affirm development and protective policies that limit growth. Both types of policies can be location specific and/or have quantitative measures attached. Hence, there are **four types of spatial policies:** (1) Location-based positive-allocative policies to affirm growth in preferred locations. These policies create general categories of locations suitable for new growth including urban centers, transit corridors, communities, and the urbanized area in general. A popular example from the United States is transit-oriented development which supports new development near transit. (2) A quantitative element can be added to the positive-allocative spatial policies. For instance, King County set an objective to keep 97% of new growth within the urbanized area. Another example is growth projections for urban centers in Metro Vancouver. (3) Protective spatial policies to restrict growth in open spaces or limit new development to areas already served by infrastructure. An urban containment boundary would be a protective spatial policy. Another example would be a policy to protect a fresh water producing area from urban development. Germany does this to ensure that underground aquifers are replenished. (4) Large lot zoning

Table 7.1 Types of spatial policies to direct growth

Where should urban development occur?	*Location of growth*	*Quantity of growth*
Positive-allocative policies (growth affirming)	Type 1 affirms growth for specific geographies of various scales as desirable for new development (housing, employment, retail). Geographies include: urbanized area, cities/communities, neighborhoods, sites (e.g. urban center/ urban core/ large brownfields).	Type 2 includes spatial policies assigning quantitative growth allocation to a specific geography. This can include population, household, housing, job growth, and other specific targets or projections for an area. For instance, population growth projections for communities are a positive-allocative quantitative spatial policy.
Protective policies (growth limiting)	Type 3 creates categories of areas not suitable for development. These uses include ecosystem services, open spaces, forests, farmlands etc.	Type 4 includes quantitative measures that prevent areas from being developed at urban intensities. This can include large-lot zoning, or limits on the extent of new housing units for specific cities, growth caps.

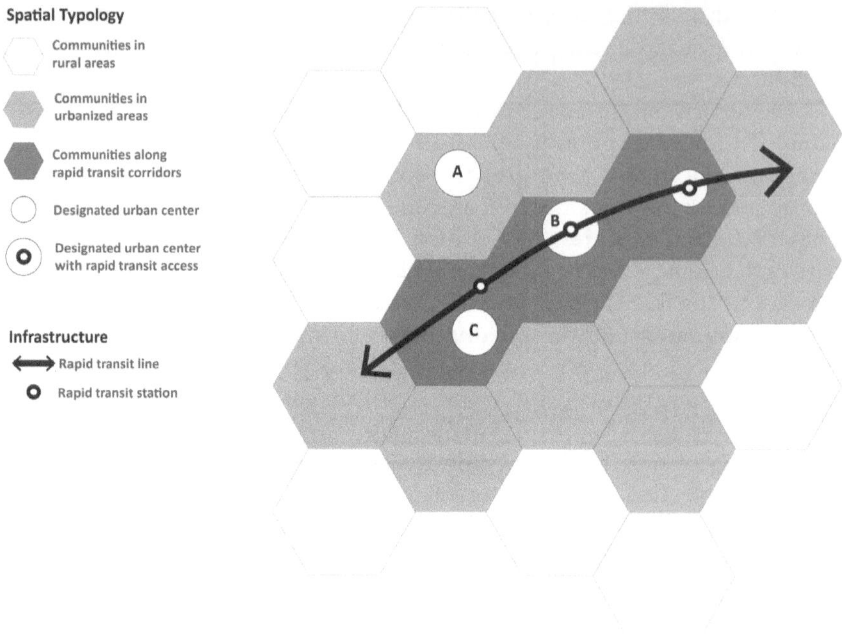

Figure 7.1 Conceptualizing spatial policies targeting various geographies.
Source: Own illustration; modified from Heinen (2021).

or housing quotas as quantitative measures to restrict new development in certain areas. Particularly for quantitative policies, it depends on the phrasing of the policy if they are positive-allocative or protective in nature. The population targets in the Puget Sound region were contested if they are actually caps or minimum requirements. Hence, growth projections and assumptions for certain types of communities can be applied as growth caps (Type 4) or as minimum growth targets (Type 2). Better understanding of spatial policies and how to combine and apply them can further advance research in growth management and spatial planning.

There is much nuance to these four types of spatial policies. Starting with type 1, each employed a different mix of spatial policies to affirm growth in locations of various sizes (Figure 7.1). Underpinning the spatial policies is a spatial typology. Developing spatial typologies is as much a data-drive as a political exercise. Spatial typologies can refer to general areas (e.g. rural, suburban, urban) or to specific communities (e.g. metropolitan core, large cities, rural towns etc.) or to specific locations (urban centers, rural centers, Entwicklungsschwerpunkte). A key task of

Table 7.2 Connecting spatial policies in RGS to low-carbon development patterns

Objective of spatial policy	*Region*	*Name of spatial policy in case study*	*Characteristics of low-carbon development patterns*		
			Density	*Mixed-Uses*	*Transit Access*
Type 1 (positive-allocative spatial policies to direct growth to specific locations)	Puget Sound region	Regional geographies and regional growth centers	Min. density and mix of uses to qualify as regional growth center		Yes
	Stuttgart region	Community classification and preferred location for high-density housing	Density requirement	No	Yes
	Metropolitan Vancouver	Urban centers and FTDAs	Growth targets	Yes	Yes
Type 2 (Quantitative measures for new growth in specific locations)	Puget Sound region	Growth assumptions for regional geographies *(contentious within region if Type 2 or 4)*	No	No	No
	Stuttgart region	Growth percentages for community types	Somewhat	No	No
	Metropolitan Vancouver	Employment and housing growth targets for urban centers	Yes	Yes	No
Type 3 (Growth limiting policies for specific areas)	Puget Sound region	Urban growth area designation	Yes	No	No
	Stuttgart region	Protection of open spaces	No	No	No
	Metropolitan Vancouver	Urban containment boundary; sewer extension permits	Yes	No	No
Type 4 (Quantitative growth limiting policies)	Puget Sound region	Growth assumptions for regional geographies *(contentious within region if Type 2 or 4)*	Somewhat	No	No
	Stuttgart region	Fourth tier communities are permitted to grow 1% of current housing units every five years	Somewhat	No	No
	Metropolitan Vancouver	Zoning in the agricultural areas	No	No	No
Use of maps at the regional level	Puget Sound region	No	No	No	No
	Stuttgart region	Yes	Yes	Somewhat	Yes
	Metropolitan Vancouver	Yes	Yes	Yes	Yes

spatial planning is to develop appropriate typologies that are meaningful to a region: Metro Vancouver directs growth to neighborhood sites (called urban centers) in proximity to rapid transit stations. Verband Region Stuttgart (VRS) directs growth to communities along transit corridors. PSRC, in collaboration with the counties, directs growth to the urbanized area in general and attempts to direct growth to urban centers in particular communities.

The three regions use a variety of approaches to affirm growth for specific locations (Type 1 and 2). Subsequently, I compare several spatial policies in how they are applied in the three regions. First, I start with community classifications. In the Stuttgart region, the state creates a **community typology**. Based on the state typology, VRS assigns growth percentages and density requirements to each community type: Hence, the VRS regional plan permits first and second tier communities along the rapid transit corridors to grow more and at higher densities, while communities further away are permitted to grow less. Similarly, the Puget Sound region works with a community classification called regional geographies. The county level assigns growth targets (called growth projections) for each community. The regional spatial policies encourage some communities to grow while discouraging others. Lastly, Metro Vancouver also works with growth targets which are not assigned only to the communities but also to the locally-designated urban centers along the rapid transit corridors. Therefore, particular locations within each community are encouraged to grow more. The intergovernmental coordination in affirming growth for certain areas is supported by the integrating procedures under state laws.

In the three regions, spatial policies were also used to discourage growth outside of the urbanized area (Type 3 and 4). In the Puget Sound region, counties are authorized under state law to define the urbanized area already served by **sufficient infrastructure**. Outside of the urbanized area, land is protected from development. In the Stuttgart region, VRS is responsible for defining and mapping the open spaces and protected areas including agricultural land, aquifers, forests, environmentally sensitive lands, areas for recreation and fresh air corridors. VRS negotiates the parcel specific boundary with the communities to develop the local land use designations map. Lastly, in metropolitan Vancouver, Metro Vancouver creates and administers a parcel-based boundary between the urbanized area and the **open spaces**. Communities cannot permit development outside of the urban containment boundary.

Deciding which entity gets to draw a parcel-based boundary is a political question and potentially contentious issue. The three regions approach parcel-based mapping differently. In metropolitan Vancouver, the regional level draws the parcel-based urban containment boundary. In the Stuttgart region, communities draw the parcel-based boundary based on the local land use designation map in accordance with regional policies. In the Puget Sound region, the counties draw an **urban containment boundary**.

In North America, urban containment boundaries are frequently critiqued because they tend to increase housing prices within the urbanized area (limiting land supply raises price). Therefore a crucial task for the regional level is to combine growth limiting policies with growth affirming policies. By affirming growth for certain locations within the urbanized area, higher density redevelopment can be encouraged and the pressure on the housing market alleviated. Furthermore, the housing market can be diversified to create a more resilient region. Growth can be intentionally directed with spatial policies such as designating urban centers or community types. These location categories can be combined with quantitative policies such as growth targets, growth percentages, or density requirements. Broadly speaking, combining locations and quantitative growth directing policies pre-structure the regional development patterns without specifying the land uses.

Regional level spatial policies can be controversial at the local level. Therefore having **state-regulated "ground rules of the game"** seemed helpful in Baden-Württemberg and British Columbia. The "ground-rules of the game" seemed to reduce power struggles between the levels of government and tended to allow a focus on the issue at hand. The German federal government and the state of Baden-Württemberg explicitly authorize certain types of spatial policies at the regional level. Legally authorized spatial policies create a nested planning system in which each level provides more details to shape development patterns. For instance, the state legislation in Baden-Württemberg permits the regional level to assign minimum density requirements and growth percentages by community types. The community types are jointly designated at the regional and state levels. Each community type has an assigned minimum average density and allowed growth percentages derived from regional spatial policies. Based on the state and regional spatial policies, the communities determine the locations for new growth when preparing the local land use designations map. Of the approaches, this one intervenes the most in land markets and local government actions. Nevertheless, cultural preference and federal legislation support this type of spatial policy (G-ROG §1(1)).

In contrast, British Columbia legislation does not specifically authorize certain spatial policies but rather focuses on the integrating procedures, ensuring that the local level and regional levels have a clearly defined recourse for conflicts. Since each municipality must adopt the RGS, the local level rather than the state level authorizes the spatial policies in the RGS. Therefore, the local level authorizes Metro Vancouver to assign employment and housing growth targets to communities and to urban centers. To some extent, all 21 local levels of government in Metro Vancouver agree to devolve powers upwards. The growth targets are used during the RCS process to negotiate the appropriate densities of the urban centers. Since the RGS adoption process and RCS alignment process are defined in Provincial law, a level of trust is created between local decision-makers and the regional level. This trust is fundamental to engage the communities in the process of designating centers and assigning growth targets.

Washington State takes another approach by leaving the spatial policies and integrating procedures to self-regulation. The state legislation primarily formulates an integration requirement for joint planning and plan consistency. Based on the integration requirements, PSRC and the counties self-regulate the assignment of growth targets to community types. Overall, PSRC has a more ambiguous role in defining the spatial policies. The ambiguity seems to derive from the extent of self-regulation of integrating mechanisms and spatial policies needed in absence of state regulation. A conversation about any spatial policy immediately sparks a conversation about integrating mechanisms and power relationships.

This means that state legislation on integrating mechanisms combined with spatial policies affect the ability of the regional level to influence the densities and locations of new growth at the local level. The spatial policies presented above do have the potential to foster low-carbon development patterns if combined with integrating mechanisms that balance the powers across levels of government. While all three regional planning organizations have identified spatial policies as helpful to foster low-carbon development patterns, their actual influence seems to depend on the integrating mechanisms. Having a legislatively- or contractually-binding RGS ensures that local decisions are more closely tied to the regional spatial policies. In contrast, a guiding RGS needs to use other integrating mechanisms to achieve similar results. Through an intentional combination of spatial policies supported by integrating mechanisms, regional planning organizations can foster low-carbon development patterns across a region.

Underpinning any use of these spatial policies are the cultural comfort level with and constitutional legality of government interventions in land markets. Of the three case studies, the German planning system intervenes the most by restricting development on open spaces and directing growth to certain communities. The community classification creates clear winners and losers among the municipalities in an effort to ensure that tax dollars are spent prudently and new development is prioritized in locations that have already seen the most public investment. The public good is generally prioritized over individual property rights; however, there are still ample protections for property owners to ensure just compensation and to prohibit takings. In Vancouver, agricultural land, ecologically sensitive areas and resource lands are highly valued. Therefore, interventions in the land markets by senior-level governments seemed warranted. In contrast, tolerance for intervening in land markets is much lower in the United States. This is evident in King County's efforts to purchase land already protected by the urban containment boundary rather than to rely on regulation. Clearly, the level of tolerance for land market interventions shapes the political palatability of spatial policies.

To conclude, all three regions have a longstanding commitment to transit-connected communities as their preferable development pattern (PSRC-Vision 2009, p. 15; VRS-Regionalplan 2009; MV-RGS 2011). Increasingly concerned about climate change, the three regional planning agencies stress the importance of reducing vehicle miles traveled by clustering new development near rapid transit stops. To achieve these development patterns, each RGS contains different types of spatial policies as indicated in Table 7.2. In all three regions, the spatial policies are intended to foster low-carbon development patterns. While the three regional planning organization pursue similar development patterns, the implementation pathways look very different. In each region, implementation depends to some extent on decisions by transit providers and local jurisdictions: Local governments are the ones preparing zoning, issuing development permits, and working with developers. Transit providers plan, invest and build the rapid transit network. Yet, as Chapters 4-6 have illustrated, these implementing entities are held accountable differently to the RGS. A fundamental difference between the three regions is: the divergent legislation on integrating mechanisms.

Note

1 The direction of growth refers to permissible new housing, retail, and job development in certain locations within a region. While permits for property owners in all three regions are administered by the local level, the permitting decisions are pre-structured by regional spatial policies to varying extents. Culturally, directing growth requires some level of comfort in intervening in land markets to ensure the protection of public goods.

8 Integrating mechanisms support implementation

Implementing low-carbon development patterns hinges on integrating local land use and transit decisions. The previous chapters have demonstrated the importance of ensuring that investments in new rapid transit align with local priorities on land uses to actually reduce transportation emissions. In other words, a transit station without sufficient density will not attract enough transit riders. At the same time, density without transit access will create more vehicular traffic. Thus, aligning transit investment and local land use decision is a metropolitan governance challenge that requires coordination among many local governments and transit providers. The three regions have demonstrated how a Regional Growth Strategy (RGS) and affiliated integrating mechanisms can support integrated decision-making.

Integrating mechanisms are rules-in-use that create interdependencies among decision-making centers (integration requirements) and structure interactions in a governance arrangement (integration procedures). This chapter reflects on how legislatively defined integrating mechanisms shape the implementation of low-carbon development patterns. In all three regions, integrating mechanisms support the application of spatial policies to local decisions. Surprisingly, approval mechanisms are not the most significant. Rather alignment mechanisms executed by the local level seem to have a much stronger influence. The chapter introduces the concept of integrating mechanisms that are affiliated with planning documents such as RGS and presents a typology of integrating mechanisms with examples from the three regions.

Types of integrating mechanisms based on empirical findings

The extent to which implementing entities such as transit providers and local governments adhere to an RGS is shaped by the integrating mechanisms. In all three regions, state laws support integrating land use and transit decisions to varying degrees. The three regions use a variety of self-regulated and legislatively defined integrating mechanisms. This section organizes the types of empirically observable integrating mechanisms from the regions in a theoretical typology. Practical examples will follow.

DOI: 10.4324/9781003268505-9

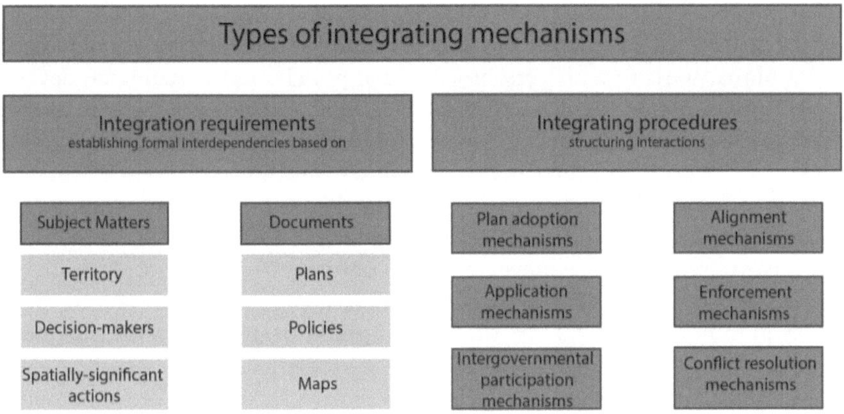

Figure 8.1 Types of integrating mechanisms.
Source: Own illustration.

In state laws, the integrating mechanisms may be abstract requirements or very specific procedural requirements. Based on my empirical analysis, the integrating mechanisms fall into two groups as shown in Figure 8.1: Integration requirements and integrating procedures. Integration requirements establish formal interdependencies while integrating procedures structure interactions. The degree of detail in state legislation can vary widely. For instance, British Columbia is very specific about the procedures used to ensure plan consistency between local OCPs and the RGS. In contrast, Washington State simply requires plan consistency and leaves the procedures up to self-regulation. Subsequently, I explain integration requirements and procedures in more depth comparing examples from the three regions. The three regions clearly diverge in terms of the leveraged types of integrating mechanisms and the extent of legislated and self-regulated integrating mechanisms.

Integration requirements observed in the regions

Frequently, the integration requirement are established in the section of the planning enabling legislation that defines the purpose of planning. In growth managing states, the integration requirements directly establish the formal degree of dependency and define the extent of integrated decision-making. As shown in Figure 8.1, the requirements can refer to various matters such as, the development of the territory, consistency of planning documents, desirable interactions between decision-making centers, and/or responsibilities of implementing entities. Thereby, a planning legislation can encompasses several subject matters simultaneously. The following examples from the three regions will provide more clarity on this concept. Generally speaking, integration requirements define the purpose of cooperating, coordinating and collaborating with other agencies: Is the purpose to ensure the sustainable development of the territory, is the purpose to ensure plan consistency, is the purpose to implement a RGS?

Germany's planning legislation is the most extensive in creating integration requirements. In Germany, **territory** must be developed consistently (whole and parts; principle of reciprocity). This is achieved through a variety of nested spatial **plans**, starting with very broad spatial policies in the statewide development plan and moving through more specific regional spatial policies in the RGS which are then applied by local governments to the land use designations maps. Furthermore, **implementing decision-making** centers (e.g. transportation providers) responsible for **spatially-significant decisions** are required to coordinate those decisions as per the spatial plans. This means integrated decisions are required to achieve consistent outcomes – namely the consistent development of the whole and parts of the German territory. At the center of the integration requirements are the **spatial plans** around which the integrating procedures evolve. The spatial plans get incrementally more specific.

While the German legislation sets requirements for almost all the matters named in Figure 8.1, the British Columbia legislation focuses its integration requirements and procedures around the RGS. For instance, the transit provider TransLink in metropolitan Vancouver is mandated to implement the RGS as part of its statutory responsibilities. Furthermore, legislatively-defined integrating procedures hold local governments accountable to the RGS. Overall, the British Columbia legislation is less specific on integration requirements but more specific on integrating procedures. The interactive planning system is designed to foster coordination among local governments at the regional level and to integrate decisions with the transit provider. In that sense, the British Columbia legislation establishes integrated decision-making by requiring an RGS be prepared.

Table 8.1 Definition of types of integration requirements

Name	*Description*
Integration requirements	Integration requirements establish formal interdependencies among decision-making centers. Integration requirements define to what extent integrated decision-making is a desirable component of planning across multiple levels and/or sectors of government. The mandates define the purpose of planning and can refer to various matters of interdependencies such as the integrated development of the territory, coordination on spatially impactful actions, or coordination among various actors. The purpose of planning can also evolve around jointly preparing planning documents, policies, or maps.
Territory:	Requirement to ensure consistent and coordinated development of the territory where conflicting uses are balanced to enable sustainable development patterns (e.g. principle of reciprocity in Germany).
Plan:	Requirements for plans of multiple decision-making centers to align with one another and be consistent (e.g. plan consistency requirement in Washington State).
Interactions:	Requirements for planning to serve conflict resolution or ensure coordination across levels and sectors of government (e.g. transportation for Metropolitan Planning Organizations in the United States).
Responsibility for implementation	Requirement for implementing decision-making centers to align spatially-significant actions with policies, maps, or planning documents by another entity (e.g. TransLink having to implement the RGS under British Columbia law).

While the integration requirements in Baden-Württemberg and British Columbia place the RGS, including policies and maps, at the center of integrated decision-making, the Washington State legislation does not establish one single planning document as the nexus of integrated decision-making. The Washington State legislation focuses **on plan and policy consistency** in general by requiring the county and local levels to prepare comprehensive planning documents that are consistent with each other. The state legislation authorizes (but does not require) the regional level to create multi-county planning policies. Through a self-regulated effort, these multi-county policies are part of the RGS in the Puget Sound region. The plan consistency requirement and the policy requirements form the basis for the self-regulated efforts to align policies at the local, county, and regional levels. Table 8.1 provides an overview and definitions for the integration requirements. I am describing each requirement in depth in the regions chapters.

Integrating procedures observed in the regions

The integration requirements can be further specified by integrating procedures. The regions vary particularly in legislatively-defined procedures that foster integrated decision-making. In Baden-Württemberg and British Columbia, state laws help resolve conflicts between levels of governments and balance different interests through a set of predefined integrating procedures. These integrating mechanisms evolve around the RGS. In contrast, in the spirit of home-rule, Washington State delegates such procedural aspects to self-regulation at the county and regional levels. The subsequent sections compare the differences and similarities in integration requirements and integrating procedures in more detail.

The integrating procedures structure the interactions of decision-making centers. In Vancouver and Stuttgart, these integrating procedures are directly linked to the RGS. In the Puget Sound region, there are other, primarily self-regulated, integrating procedures. I have identified six subcategories of integrating procedures: the plan adoption mechanisms, the alignment mechanisms, the enforcement mechanisms, the application mechanisms, the participation mechanisms, and the conflict resolution mechanisms.

The **plan adoption mechanisms** are the rules-in-use on how a planning document is formally adopted, which ultimately influences the document's legal status. The RGS has a different legal status in each region: it is legislatively--binding in the Stuttgart region, contractually–binding in metropolitan Vancouver, and primarily guiding in the Puget Sound region. How and to what extent an RGS is adopted determines its legal status. German federal law mandates that states approve an RGS (and that the local level is able to participate in its drafting), which gives it the force of law for local decision-making. Provincial law in Metro Vancouver requires that all municipalities adopt an RGS, which creates a contractual obligation. Lastly, in absence of more specific state legislation in Washington State, an RGS is primarily a guiding document voluntarily adopted. PSRC's RGS is guiding in the sense that the policies do not just apply to local decision-making. The local level creates its own policies (which might be identical to regional policies or might not specify them). For instance, in the Puget Sound region a local policy would be consistent with a regional policy if both read "new development should occur in proximity to transit." In contrast, in the Vancouver region, the local level needs to create more specific policies and map the urban centers. To achieve similar outcomes, PSRC had to develop a self-regulated **application mechanism** as a procedure for local governments to designate urban centers. While PSRC uses a self-regulated application mechanism, the Vancouver and Stuttgart regions rely on state requirement alignment mechanisms.

Alignment mechanisms are procedures that create accountability among decision-making centers by requiring the implementing entity to demonstrate how its plans or actions align with the RGS. The alignment is based on the implementing entity's self-assessment. Frequently, the implementing entity is required to prepare a report or plan that indicates how actions fit within regional spatial policies and, if they do not fit, how they will be aligned in the future. Alignment mechanisms basically charge the implementing entity with identifying needed adjustments to their own planning efforts and engaging in a conversation with the regional level. Examples include the provincially-defined process around the Regional Context Statement (RCS) in metropolitan Vancouver and the federally-defined procedures around the local land use designations map (*Flächennutzungsplan*) and the spatial compatibility assessment (*Raumordnungsverfahren*) in Germany.

The alignment mechanism can be connected to an **approval mechanism**. Approval mechanisms allow a decision-making center such as the state level to ensure compliance. The three regions use a variety of enforcement mechanisms. In metropolitan Vancouver, the entity preparing the RGS also approves the RCSs of the local municipalities. In the Stuttgart region, the approval process is delegated to the counties and state government depending on the size of a community. In the Puget Sound region, the enforcement mechanisms are not accompanied by an alignment mechanism – PSRC directly certifies the transportation element of the local comprehensive plan. Without an alignment mechanism, the approving entity points out the gaps between the local plan and the RGS. In other words, in the Puget Sound region, any gaps between the RGS and local comprehensive plan are "uncovered" during the approval process: it seems that more conflicts arise as the local plan must be adjusted if it is to be certified. Having an intermediating alignment mechanism like in the Stuttgart and Vancouver regions seemed to help foster dialogue between the regional entity and the municipalities prior to the approval process.

There are three other types of integrating procedures. **Application procedures** are frequently used in the Puget Sound region – local governments apply to be a designated regional growth center which creates competition among local governments and spatial policies are implemented voluntarily. Another type is **participation mechanisms** which ensure the participation of multiple decision-making centers along the way to implementation. Intergovernmental review procedures and participation in plan development fall under this category. Lastly, all regions have **conflict resolution**

mechanisms, rules-in-use to resolve conflicts and disagreements, both of which are a central feature of the British Columbia planning system. British Columbia defines these procedures for the adoption of the RGS as well as for the RCS. The German law also includes such procedures with the "permission to deviate from requirements" (*Zielabweichungsverfahren*) for sectoral agencies. In all regions, litigation is another type of conflict resolution mechanism.

The integrating procedures to structure interactions are closely intertwined. For instance, the German planning system uses an alignment mechanism, an approval mechanism, and a participation mechanism to ensure that local land use decisions follow RGS policies. All three procedures depend on the local land use designations map. All three mechanisms are legislatively defined and required by federal and state laws.

In British Columbia, state legislation creates integrating procedures around the RCS. The local governments must prepare the RCS (alignment mechanisms) and Metro Vancouver approves it (enforcement procedure). In case of disagreement, the provincial law defines conflict resolution procedures. The provincial law also creates the context for local governments adopting the RGS (adoption procedures) and has requirements for the participation of local governments in preparing the RGS (participation procedures). TransLink is also required to participate in plan development and to comment on the RCSs (participation procedures). This demonstrates that in Baden-Württemberg and British Columbia the integration requirements and procedures are intentionally organized around specific planning documents such as the RGS, RCS, and local land use designations maps.

In contrast, Washington State does not have extensive legislation on integrating procedures to structure interactions. The integrating procedures are self-regulated in multi-county and countywide planning policies. While there is a state-defined enforcement process for the transportation component of local comprehensive plans to align with the RTP, there is a somewhat self-regulated process for the land use component of local comprehensive plans to align with the RGS. Disagreement about content seemed to be harder to resolve with self-regulated procedures. Conflict resolution primarily occurs in the courts. Overall, Washington State law leaves integrating procedures ambiguous in an effort to respect home-rule.

Concluding, a central difference between the regions is that the planning systems in Baden-Württemberg and British Columbia establish a planning document, namely the RGS, as the focal point of integrated decision-making on development patterns, whereas Washington State does not. Nevertheless, through the plan consistency requirement and multicounty/countywide planning policies, Washington State does enable voluntary coordination on development patterns. The extent of self-regulation and state legislation is clearly different between the regions. Therefore, regional implementation varies greatly despite the fact that regional policies in all three regions promote compact and complete communities along transit corridors (PSRC-Vision 2009; VRS-Regionalplan 2009; MV-RGS 2011; Heinen 2018b). The subsequent section reflects on the integrative nature of a RGS based on the affiliated integrating mechanisms.

Table 8.2 Overview of integrating procedures

Name	*Description*
Integrating procedures	Integrating procedures structure interactions. Integrating procedures are designed to manage frictions and create accountability between decision-making centers.
Plan adoption mechanisms:	Rules-in-use on how a planning document is formally adopted which influence the legal status of the planning document (extent to which the document is binding on other decision-making centers; e.g. legally binding RGS in Stuttgart region, contractually-binding RGS in metropolitan Vancouver, and guiding RGS in Puget Sound region).
Alignment mechanisms:	Rules-in-use defining procedures that create accountability among decision-making centers wherein the implementing entity demonstrates how their plans or actions align with another planning document or policies (e.g. local land use designation map in Germany, Regional Context Statements in British Columbia).
Application mechanisms:	Rules-in-use that require an implementing entity to apply to be included in a planning document at a different level of government (e.g. PSRC process to designate regional growth centers).
Enforcement mechanisms:	Rules-in-use creating procedures to verify if decisions by decision-making centers comply with a planning document or policies (e.g. approval of local land use designations map).
(Intergovernmental) participation mechanisms:	Rules-in-use creating participation procedures for multiple decision-making centers to coordinate on decisions along the way to implementation.
Conflict resolution mechanisms:	Rules-in-use on procedures to address a situation in which the decision-making center that is implementing the planning document needs to deviate from policies within the document for valid reasons.

The integrative nature of a Regional Growth Strategy between self-regulation and state-regulation

Based on the integrating mechanisms, the RGS for each of the regions varied in the degree it affected implementation decisions by local governments and transit providers. Figure 8.2 conceptualizes the potential of a RGS to foster integrated decision-making based on the number of integrating mechanisms and the extent of self-regulation. The subsequent section reviews the implications of having state-legislated integrating mechanisms for the designation of urban centers by local governments followed by a discussion about the transit provider.

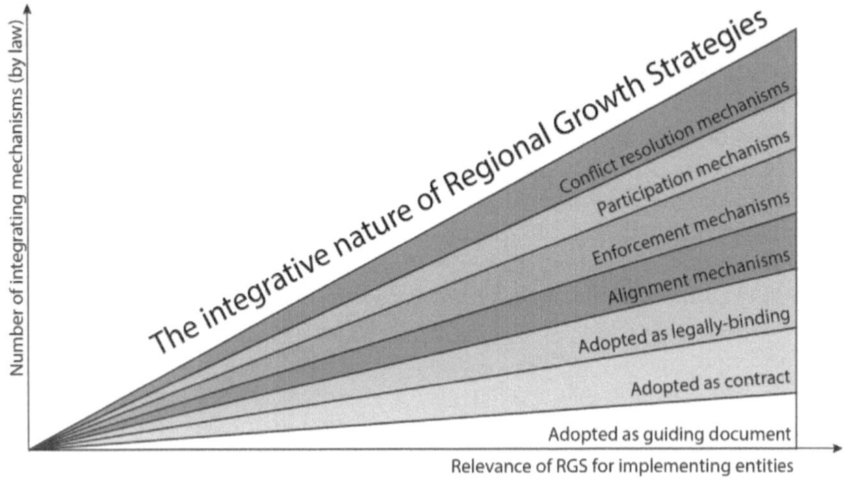

Figure 8.2 The integrative nature of a planning document based on the integrating mechanisms.
Source: Own illustration.

Holding local governments accountable to an RGS

At this point, it needs to be stressed that the extent of self-regulation and state regulation is a political and value-driven decision that derives from the cultural values in each planning system. This means that an RGS can take on very different roles for facilitating implementation of low-carbon development patterns based on how the planning enabling legislation establishes the governance arrangements. One integrating mechanism is the plan adoption process. The RGS in the Stuttgart region is legally binding for local and sectoral decisions. Hence, the same spatial policies contained in the RGS apply to all 179 communities in the Stuttgart region. The spatial policies in the RGS in metropolitan Vancouver are not quite as far reaching. Policies in the Metro Vancouver RGS are limited to issues of regional significance. The local level still creates policies on issues of local significance. However, the policies in the RGS do apply to the 21 communities in metropolitan Vancouver because each community must approve the policies by adopting the RGS, making the RGS contractually-binding.

In contrast, none of the PSRC policies in the RGS apply by default to the 82 communities and four counties in the Puget Sound region. While policies at the county and community levels have to be consistent with the multi-county planning policies; each entity still has to adopt its own set of similar policies in order to be consistent. This means that local land use decisions are based on local policies in the local comprehensive plan, which must be consistent with the county comprehensive plan.

Baden-Württemberg and British Columbia use **alignment mechanisms** to apply regional spatial policies to the local context. The benefit of working with alignment mechanisms is that the local level maintains its authority in designating land while also following regional spatial policies. Accordingly, in Stuttgart and Vancouver, an "in-between" document (alignment document) serves as a buffer between local decisions affecting property owners (zoning) and the regional spatial policies. The legislatively defined alignment documents are named the "Local Land Use Designation Map" in the Stuttgart region and "Regional Context Statements" in metropolitan Vancouver. The alignment mechanisms in both foster the application of regional policies onto a local land use map, which is more general than a zoning map.

For example, in metropolitan Vancouver the RGS asks the local level to designate urban centers whose characteristics are broadly defined in regional policies. While all urban centers share the same characteristics across the region, each municipality decides on the location of its urban center(s). The municipality reports the location of the urban center to Metro Vancouver using the RCS. The RCS is provincially mandated as an alignment mechanism; the use of a map is self-regulated in the Metro Vancouver RGS. During the approval process of the RCS, Metro Vancouver is only involved to the extent of verifying that the local level has designated an urban center, allocated sufficient growth to the urban centers, and adopted policies for the development of the urban center. Metro Vancouver is not as much involved in the specific location choice. Furthermore, the municipality is in charge of preparing more detailed neighborhood plans for the urban centers, including permissible densities and uses.

In contrast, in the Puget Sound region if a regional spatial policy reads "support rapid transit development by intensifying and diversifying uses around the transit stations," PSRC can review if there is also a similar local policy statement. This policy statement does not need to be any more specific than the regional statement and does not need to indicate a specific location. Hence, to identify locations PSRC and King County created a self-regulated **application procedure**. PSRC and King County define criteria that communities have to meet if they want their urban center to qualify. The urban center is ultimately designated by PSRC and King County. A characteristic of the Puget Sound region is that most spatial policies have their own specific integrating mechanisms. Frequently, spatial policies are used as criteria during an application process. The Washington State Growth Management Act does not create a nested or aligned planning system that prompts incrementally more specific decisions, but instead creates a framework to coordinate on overlapping policy interests across levels of government.

Experts in the Stuttgart and Vancouver regions explained the benefit of coordinating maps as part of an alignment mechanism: applying policies to a map made enforcement easier and allowed a differentiated view of various uses within a municipality and the region. It allowed for conversations as to which areas are clearly protected and which areas are expressly desirable for more development. Location decisions remained at the local level. In Stuttgart, experts stressed that the variety of sometimes conflicting regional spatial policy objectives required the application of policies to a map in order to ensure balanced development of the territory.

To summarize, in the Stuttgart region, the RGS is legislatively binding because it is approved by the state government (adoption procedure). The RGS is applied to local decisions through the Local Land Use Designation Map (alignment procedure) and enforced during the approval process of the local map by the counties (enforcement procedure). In metropolitan Vancouver, the RGS is contractually binding as each local government has to adopt the RGS for it to take effect (adoption procedure). If a community disagrees with the content of the RGS, the province provides recourse for conflict among the local governments and regional districts **(conflict resolution mechanisms)**. Local governments then demonstrate how their local plans align with the RGS by preparing the RCS (alignment mechanism). The RCS is approved by Metro Vancouver **(enforcement mechanism)**. In both regions, the state planning enabling legislation intentionally creates the RGS and affiliated integrating mechanisms to ensure integrated decision-making on spatial development patterns. For practitioners in planning systems that do not have state legislation that place a RGS in a significant role, the self-regulated mechanisms in the Puget Sound region are inspiring to foster self-organized efforts.

Holding transit providers accountable to the RGS

We see a few different approaches to connecting transit decisions to the spatial policies in the RGS. The state legislation in the three regions all primarily work with integration requirements and only with a few integration procedures. For instance, while the British Columbia legislation makes the transit provider directly responsible for implementing the RGS, the Baden-Württemberg legislation requires alignment for spatially-significant actions with the spatial policies in the RGS. Lastly, Washington State legislation requires coordination among actors. These details on how decision-making is integrated by law matters for the actors at the regional and local levels. In the three regions, conversations between local governments and transit providers about the transit corridor alignment took development patterns into consideration differently based on the integration requirement.

To be more specific, in the Stuttgart region, state and federal laws create integrating mechanisms to connect the transportation and land use decisions. Based on federal law, "spatially-significant projects" have to align with the spatial policies in the RGS. This creates a clear integration requirement evolving around actions such as transit investments and the RGS as a planning document. To ensure that the requirement is met, federal law specifies an alignment mechanism. The alignment mechanism is called a spatial compatibility assessment (*Raumordnungsverfahren*) which is applied during an early planning stage of a transportation project in order to determine how various possible corridor alignments perform based on spatial policies in the RGS. Both federally-defined integrating mechanisms apply to planning in metropolitan regions across Germany. The state of Baden-Württemberg decided to integrate decision-making further by working with the statutory responsibilities of VRS. VRS is responsible for preparing the regional transportation strategy (RTS) in-house; hence, VRS alters bi-annually between preparing the RGS and the next RTS. To some extent, this serves as an adoption mechanism because the organization adopting the RGS is the same organization that is adopting the RTS. This means that in the Stuttgart region, state and federal legislations deliberately create integrating mechanisms to foster integrated land use and transportation decision-making.

British Columbia attempted a similar approach of combining TransLink with Metro Vancouver into one organization in the early 2000s but was ultimately thwarted due to conflicts with the province (Krawchenko 2012). Nevertheless, British Colombia ensured that transportation and land use decisions were integrated by creating an integration requirement for TransLink. Therefore, TransLink has a statutory responsibility to implement the RGS. Since connecting the urban centers is a spatial policy in the RGS, TransLink has to take this spatial policy into account when considering various alignments of a new transit corridor. Furthermore, provincial legislation created an adoption procedure for the RTS that connects the RTS with the RGS. The RTS is adopted by the Mayors' Council at TransLink which is almost identical to Metro Vancouver's board. The Mayors' Council used the Regional Transportation Strategy to communicate to the province the need for more transit funding to build the envisioned rapid transit network. Involving the Mayors' Council in these decisions is an adoption mechanism that loosely links decisions to the RGS by creating similar board compositions.

While British Columbia and Baden-Württemberg create formally interdependent transit decision-makers, Washington State creates a rapid transit provider that is fairly independent from land use decision-makers. In the Puget Sound region, state legislation empowers Sound Transit to act fiscally independent since Sound Transit is primarily accountable to voters. Voters essentially adopt the Regional Transportation Strategy and authorize the taxes for funding the construction and operation of the rapid transit system. Sound Transit, thus, can unilaterally select a transit corridor alignment. The local level has veto-power since it could block the construction of the rapid transit line as a land use. So, Sound Transit negotiates the corridor alignment with the communities. However, this is only loosely connected to the spatial policies in the Puget Sound RGS. While PSRC can certify (enforcement procedure) Sound Transit's System Plan as consistent with PSRC's long-range transportation plan, the transit alignment in the system plan is so vague that missing an urban center by two miles would not show on the generalized map. Subsequently, connecting the urban centers has primarily been a guiding principle rather than a binding policy – leading to mixed results.

This means that spatial policies in an RGS can vary in their influence on transit corridor alignments depending on the state-legislated integrating mechanisms. In metropolitan Vancouver and in the Stuttgart region, the spatial policies in the RGS must be considered when selecting a corridor alignment. Thus, the RGS is binding on the transit provider. In contrast, the spatial policies in the Puget Sound RGS can only be guiding in the absence of any state legislated integrating mechanisms. Because they are self-regulated, decision-making centers can take unilateral action which leads to frustration on both sides; the transit provider is frustrated with communities not leveraging the transit investments and the local level is frustrated with the transit provider for not serving the community's chosen location. Certainly, there were also cases in the Puget Sound region where bilateral negotiations resulted in a win-win situation but these were less frequent than in the other two regions. To some extent, the RGS in metropolitan Vancouver and Stuttgart creates accountability between communities and transit providers regarding the desirable development patterns for the region.

Implementing transit-connected urban centers with and without a binding Regional Growth Strategy

The Vancouver and Stuttgart regions both hold the local level and the transit provider accountable to the spatial visions in the RGS, their spatial visions slightly differ. The Stuttgart region directs growth to communities while the Vancouver region directs growth to urban centers – particularly locations with rapid transit access. However, the Vancouver region does share its spatial vision with the Puget Sound region. Therefore, after briefly discussing the Stuttgart case, this section compares the experiences in metropolitan Vancouver with the Puget Sound region.

The spatial vision for the Stuttgart region can best be summarized as transit-connected communities rather than transit-connected urban centers. The spatial policies in the Stuttgart RGS direct population growth to communities serviced by the rapid transit system built along the designated priority development corridors. I learned from the interviews that increasing densities in the transit stop locations was not a primary concern. Historically, many transit stops serve the downtown of communities. Many spatial policies in the Stuttgart RGS have been in place for decades. Furthermore, it should be highlighted that the Stuttgart transit system is mostly considered to be built out while the transit systems in the other two regions are continuing to grow and evolve. Therefore, the subsequent discussion only focuses on metropolitan Vancouver and the Puget Sound region.

The RGS in both metropolitan Vancouver and the Puget Sound region contains a spatial vision of connecting the locally-designated urban centers with rapid transit. Provincial law mandates that TransLink's investments be used to implement the RGS. In contrast, Sound Transit is not bound to the RGS prepared by PSRC. Under Washington State law, Sound Transit's decisions are clearly framed by its responsibilities to the taxpayers who want evidence that spending is not wasteful. While Sound Transit generally makes an effort to connect as many designated urban centers as possible, some may be deemed cost prohibitive because Sound Transit faces severe pressure to make short-term cost-effective decisions in order to not lose voter support.

For the Puget Sound region, the Tukwila case demonstrates the downside of a non-binding RGS. To be fair, Sound Transit has since learned from the case and made self-organized improvements to its procedures for working with the communities, but the Tukwila case does demonstrate the challenges any region may face. The City of Tukwila in the Puget Sound region is committed to developing its designated urban center but the city is hesitant to put the same energy into development around the transit station at Tukwila International Boulevard. While Sound Transit had multiple reasons to not connect the urban center to the transit system, it created a situation in which neither transit investment nor redevelopment in the city are completely leveraged to ensure low-carbon development patterns. The densities in the designated urban center are increasing and the transit system is running, but unfortunately not in the same place. Both parties (Sound Transit and the City of Tukwila) discussed several possible alignments, but, ultimately, Sound Transit's cost constraints and local resistance to a third alignment sunk the deal. During negotiations, regional development patterns were not the deciding factor. As predicted by theory, unilateral actions were taken instead, ultimately resulting in an underleveraged transit investment.

In contrast, the alignment decision was fundamentally different in the Vancouver region. To connect the City of Coquitlam to the rapid transit network, TransLink prioritized alignments that connected more urban centers rather than those along the less costly interstate corridor. The integrating mechanisms held TransLink accountable to the regional vision laid out in the RGS.[1] It appears that TransLink is able to create more value when its investment is based on the RGS. Since the RGS and RCS process ensure that the local level is committed to the urban centers, there is much more active redevelopment around the station areas across the Vancouver region. The RGS in Vancouver helps frame municipalities' and transit providers' decisions since it is a binding document for both. This facilitates public investment and efforts in the same locations. Provincial law creates a fairly high degree of interdependency among the implementing entities by holding all entities accountable to the RGS which is adopted like a contract by all entities.

Based on the rules-in-use in the planning system, the corridor alignment decision was fiscally-driven in the Puget Sound region but spatially-driven in the Vancouver region (Figure 8.3). Ultimately, the integrating mechanisms around the RGS seem to have facilitated a spatial match in efforts in metropolitan Vancouver, unlike in the Puget Sound region.

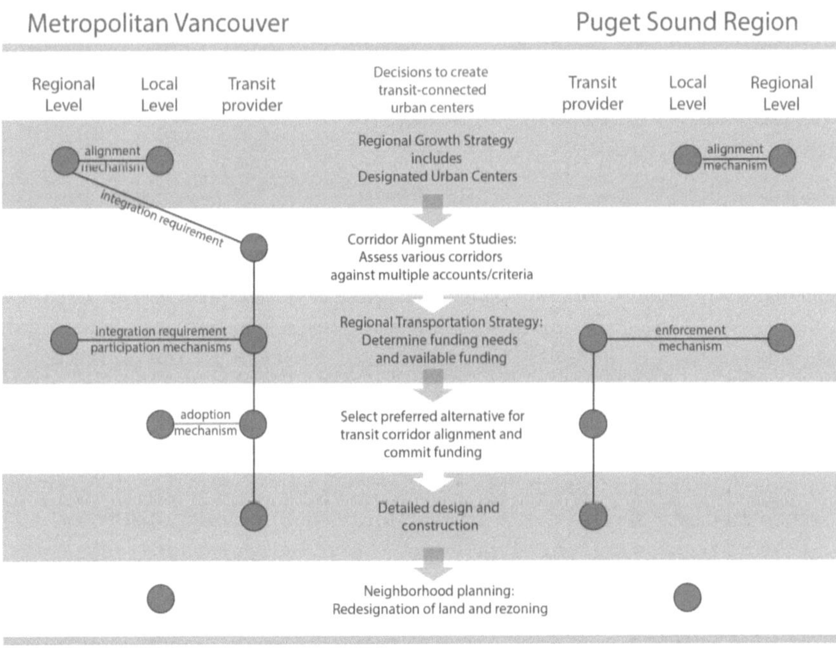

Figure 8.3 Determining corridor alignment in metropolitan Vancouver and in the Puget Sound region.

Source: Own illustration.

The timing of the funding decision may have also played a role. TransLink first determined the specific corridor alignments prior to securing funding. RGS spatial policies guided the route alignments which were determined through multiple accounts assessments.[2] In contrast, Sound Transit secured funding for a general alignment first by appealing to voters. The particular corridor alignments were then negotiated with the communities. Having a fixed amount of funding may have also intensified the cost pressure on Sound Transit.

The absence of a binding RGS creates a situation in which more unilateral actions by implementing entities are possible. To some extent, this may have hurt the communities' ability to recapture some of the value of the transit investment in the Puget Sound region. Certainly, it is hard to justify a more expensive corridor alignment to taxpayers, but connecting urban centers may have helped to pay for the transit system in the long run (as new people move near the transit stops). It seems that the primary contribution of a legislatively binding RGS is that it requires the transit agency to negotiate the corridor alignment with multiple communities at once instead of negotiating with them individually. This is particularly the case for Vancouver as the RGS is adopted as a contract by 21 communities. Yet, each one of the three planning systems has evolved in response to particular cultural values with regard to interdependencies among public sector actors.

The trouble with rezoning around any rapid transit station

To successfully implement low-carbon development patterns, each actor has to uphold their part of the bargain: the transit provider has to advance transit projects that connect urban centers and the local level needs to update land use designations, rezone and work with developers on permits. In all three regions, local governments decide whether to change land uses around a transit station. The extent to which the local level can act is closely tied to the cultural norms for government involvement in land markets. As discussed in Chapter 1, development can be market-led, government-led or a combination of both. Development is more market-led in the Puget Sound region and more government-led in the Stuttgart region. Vancouver presents an in-between case. I discuss the role of the local level in more detail below.

In the market-led context of the Puget Sound region, rezoning oftentimes happens at the request of a developer. Broadly speaking, a developer already needs to own the property to apply for rezoning and to argue his case in front of the planning commission. During the rezoning process, there may be neighborhood opposition to increased densities or particular uses. Accordingly, developers are hesitant to take on the risk of purchasing land and applying for a zoning amendment which may, in turn, be rejected. Some of that risk to private developers is absorbed by the local governments in the Vancouver and Stuttgart regions. In the Stuttgart region, the local government assembles the land and creates new land use designations. Then it seeks development proposals for the site. The Vancouver region does not go as far, but it does create a neighborhood vision (public engagement) during which densities and mix-of-uses for the whole urban center are revised. Based on the new land use designations map, individual property owners can then apply for rezoning. This benefits the developer and current property owners. Some of the risk to the developer is absorbed by the local government and current property owners can negotiate a higher price for their property based on the designated land use category.

When we compare the regions, we see that the tasks at the local level are very different. In metropolitan Vancouver, the local governments proactively re-designate land through a community-wide planning process. Afterwards, developers can apply for rezoning based on the newly created land use designations map. In Stuttgart, the local government takes on more responsibilities and actively assembles parcels, develops a neighborhood plan, and selects developers to build the new neighborhood or individual buildings in a competitive process. Lastly, in the Puget Sound region, the local level acts primarily in a regulatory role where the city responds to developers' requests to rezone land in accordance with a local comprehensive or neighborhood plan.

In the Puget Sound region, the City of Shoreline actively engaged in a neighborhood planning process around the transit stops to create new planning policies and land use designations along the newly build rapid transit line. The narrative in the chapter demonstrates the political challenge of re-designating land in a predominantly single-family neighborhood – it literally involved talking to every single person in the neighborhood individually. The city council ultimately approved the rezoning but even today new council members are still trying to change the adopted plan. It will take vigilant leadership to protect it.

To some extent, the rezoning around the transit stops in the Puget Sound region was harder because they were in single-family neighborhoods. In contrast, the transit network in the Vancouver region connects the locally designated urban centers. In The urban centers in Metro Vancouver are mostly indoor malls with large empty parking lots and already existing multi-family housing. It is generally easier to rezone a primarily rental area or a previous surface parking lot than a home-owner area. So, in a way the cities and centers in metropolitan Vancouver were set up for a different rezoning conversation.[3] Local planners highlighted the need to ensure that older rental housing stock is replaced with newer affordable and market priced housing. The approach to redevelop the areas around indoor malls as urban centers is a regional strategy outlined in Metro Vancouver's RGS. The RGS has been shaping implementation decisions at the local level through the integrating procedures around the Regional Context Statements. Furthermore, TransLink is obligated to implement the RGS (integration requirement). Hence, implementation of low-carbon development patterns has been very successful.

To reflect, it appears that successful implementation of low-carbon development patterns depends on the RGS and its affiliated integrating mechanisms to integrate decisions on the preferred corridor alignment. A primary difference between the Puget Sound and Vancouver is who gets to determine which neighborhood receives rapid transit access. In the Puget Sound region, the transit provider, after negotiating with the city, decides which neighborhood will receive rapid transit access. In metropolitan Vancouver, the local level decides which neighborhood ought to be served by transit by designating the urban centers in the RGS. Having locally-designated urban centers assures that communities support the location that receives rapid transit access. Furthermore, a community is probably in the best position to judge which neighborhoods are ripe for redevelopment and suitable for rapid transit access.[4] At the same time, the local preferences need to fit within a regional strategy. As demonstrated in Vancouver, having all communities designate their urban centers in the RGS gives the communities a collective bargaining position with the transit provider. As transit providers have many other considerations, the requirement to implement the RGS ensures that connecting the urban centers is prioritized. Rather than settling for a less costly alignment with lower prospects of redevelopment opportunities, the mayors in the Vancouver region lobbied the Province for more funding.

Of all three regions, new construction is most consistently placed along the rapid transit network in Vancouver. While all three regions experienced a building boom in the past decade, much of this new growth has occurred along the rapid transit corridors in metropolitan Vancouver. In contrast, in the Puget Sound region, this growth occurred throughout the urbanized area. In the Stuttgart region, new development is oriented toward communities that lie along the rapid transit network but are not closely connected to the rapid transit system. One might argue that the planning system in metropolitan Vancouver has implemented low-carbon development patterns the most successfully and widely. Legislatively defined integrating mechanisms hold local leadership and transit leadership accountable to spatial policies that promote low-carbon development patterns. It appears to make the system a little less dependent on leadership. While TransLink and Metro Vancouver have had a rocky relationship, TransLink's investments do support the vision of transit-connected urban centers as outlined in the RGS.

Each level of government has its own view of and knowledge about implementing low-carbon development patterns. Successful implementation seems to rely on rules-in-use that support each decision-making center's own expertise. The local level knows best which locations should be served by rapid transit within the municipality. The planning systems in British Columbia affirm this role and give the local level collective bargaining leverage with the transit provider by creating a binding RGS that has a bearing on the transit provider's decisions. The regional planning organization Metro Vancouver facilitates this collective bargaining by preparing an RGS.

Concluding, the integrating mechanisms influence the extent to which the spatial policies in the RGS are binding on decision makers. This has implications for the implementation of low-carbon development patterns. This book shows that the spatial outcomes were more desirable if decisions were integrated by law. This is achieved through thoughtfully designed rules-in-use that create formal interdependencies among decision-makers. These rules-in-use still maintain responsibilities for zoning (mix-of-use and density) at the local level and transit prioritization and alignment with the transit provider; however, the rules-in-use create clear guidance on power-relationships in decision-making, ensuring that both sides can equally participate in the decision-making processes.

Notes

1 Furthermore, several experts mentioned the following phrase: "The best transportation plan is a good land use plan" which seems to have informed the multiple accounts assessment approach. The connection to land use is very clearly articulated throughout the transportation plans, including the expectation for land uses to change.
2 During the multiple accounts assessment, several alternatives were discussed and the performance on those accounts analyzed. One account included the redevelopment potentials along the corridors.
3 It needs to be pointed out that one downside in the local decision-making throughout metropolitan Vancouver is the displacement of renters because the new high-rise residential buildings are all condominiums. Currently, Metro Vancouver is trying to create affordability policies to ensure more social redevelopment. This demonstrates the complexity of these decisions – experts agreed that it is important to include social policies earlier, prior to new development.
4 When connecting urban centers, TransLink created additional transit stops which were eventually designated as Frequent Transit Development Areas on the RGS.

9 Implementing low-carbon development patterns

My objective was to develop an understanding of how rules-in-use can facilitate integrated decision-making across levels and sectors of government using the example of implementing low-carbon development patterns. The examples in the three regions point to particularly relevant leverages in planning legislation: the integrating mechanisms. Besides shifting responsibilities across levels of government, planning and climate researchers may wish to study integrating mechanisms in depth to learn what types are particularly suited to foster solutions to interdependent policy problems. Prior to offering more specific recommendations, I will briefly discuss the limitations of the findings.

Certainly, studying only a few regions limits my ability to draw general conclusions about an issue. Integrating mechanisms need to be studied further as a particularly relevant factor for plan implementation. The regions I present in this book are all examples of state planning laws that deliberately create integrating mechanisms to ensure plan implementation and consistency. When I compare the regions, it appears that the integrating mechanisms facilitated the implementation of low-carbon development patterns. However, none of the regions have a planning system characterized by command-and-control or a completely market-led planning system (see Chapter 1). As a result, my recommendations primarily apply to planning systems that are accustomed to working on land use and transportation questions across multiple levels of government and to planning systems in which government regulation of land markets is acceptable to at least a small extent. In fact, the three regions show that there is a wide variety of nuance between command-and-control and market-led planning systems. Neither of the three regions represents an extreme.

Furthermore, my findings cannot be generalized for climate governance without further study of other climate actions. By studying the implementation of low-carbon development patterns, I have examined a particular policy problem with a heightened need for deeply integrated decisions in the land use and transportation sector. Particularly for creating low-carbon development patterns, a spatial match of transit investment with land use changes is crucial to achieve emission savings as discussed in Chapter 1. Other climate

DOI: 10.4324/9781003268505-10

issues may not have the same need for a deep integration of decision-making. Nevertheless, there are still a few lessons for future climate research.

By examining the relevance of the rules-in-use for a particular policy problem, this book contributes to the larger climate and metropolitan governance discourses. Both discourses are characterized by a debate over what the most appropriate levels of government are to regulate, coordinate, or take collective actions. A central challenge is matching a problem's natural scale with the regulatory scale (Newig & Fritsch 2009). The three regions showed different approaches to this question for creating low-carbon development patterns.

This book provides a more nuanced approach to conceptualizing the extent of state regulatory involvement in climate governance and metropolitan governance arrangements that implement low-carbon development patterns. I have documented the variety of regulatory involvement of state governments in fostering integrated decision-making among public sector decision-makers at the metropolitan regional level. The qualitative findings of my research suggest that state-regulation can hold actors accountable to the regionally agreed-upon spatial policies in the Regional Growth Strategy (RGS) through integrating mechanisms.

Findings for urban planning

State planning enabling legislation significantly shapes how low-carbon development patterns are implemented. The legislation shapes the realm of influence of organizations, the integrating mechanisms, and the spatial policies. None of the governments I studied reformed its planning system in efforts to foster more low-carbon development patterns. However, by looking at the existing systems, I learned relevant lessons about which factors in the planning system help integrate decisions of multiple actors towards achieving transit-connected urban centers. This section discusses those lessons and the need for further research in spatial planning, growth management, and climate governance.

I observed several types of integrating mechanisms in the three regions. The identified types of integrating mechanisms are likely not an exhaustive list. However, the typology I presented in Chapter 8 provides more nuance than assuming senior-level governmental regulation is top-down or deterrence-based. By layering multiple integrating mechanisms together, senior-level governments can structure accountability among decision-making centers within a governance arrangement. Thereby, multiple combinations are possible and senior-level governments can decide on the extent of self-regulation. Appreciating this variety of possible senior-level governmental actions can help inform policy-making approaches to fit the cultural preferences within a given location.

Governments and other planning actors in the three regions use various combinations of integrating mechanisms to create accountability among decision-making centers for creating low-carbon development patterns.

Planning researchers in North America typically examine enforcement mechanisms as the only type of integrating mechanisms to ensure that decision-making centers are held accountable to a planning document, such as an RGS. From my research in the metropolitan Vancouver and Stuttgart regions, I have discerned that alignment mechanisms are particularly suited to ensure implementation of spatial policies. Alignment mechanisms place the burden of proof on the implementing entity, which must document how it is implementing the spatial policies in an RGS. Underpinning the use of alignment mechanisms is a clear understanding of the level of detail that is best regulated at the local, regional, or state-level (which is different in each region). While alignment mechanisms encourage coordination about disagreements, enforcement mechanisms put the two entities in conflict from the beginning. Therefore, by legislatively-defining alignment mechanisms, state legislators can strengthen the regional level's coordinating position.

The qualitative evidence I gathered shows that the **Vancouver** region implements low-carbon development patterns the most widely. In comparison to the other two regions, the integrating mechanisms in Vancouver ensured that RGS spatial policies were followed by the transit provider and local governments. In contrast, in the absence of similar integrating mechanisms, other considerations assumed priority in the Puget Sound region. There, when the preferred alignment was negotiated, other urgent challenges such as cost assumed priority over the RGS spatial policies. It seemed that the integrating mechanisms in the Vancouver regions helped to keep the spatial policies front and center throughout the process, which can take decades. This book identifies the Vancouver framework as a way to legislatively strengthen the collective bargaining powers of local governments in their negotiations with a transit provider. Nevertheless, some metropolitan regions may have hundreds of local governments, so the practicality of applying such a framework is certainly worth questioning.

My research shows that the extent to which state legislation defines integrating mechanisms may explain discrepancies in outcomes in governance arrangements that pursue similar goals. The integrating mechanisms can explain how and when decision-makers continue to pursue a common goal and find mutually agreeable solutions even in the face of conflict, rather than taking unilateral actions or disengaging from the effort. Nevertheless, my research also illustrates the unique cultural preferences for acceptable senior-level government involvement. Experts at all levels of government in Washington State did not see the need for more state legislative involvement in growth management or transit investment. Therefore, the Puget Sound region exemplifies a state government deliberately choosing to permit and require self-regulation but remaining mostly uninvolved in the details. Remember that the integrating mechanisms can also be created through self-regulation and manifested in contractual agreements. In fact, contractual agreements were widely used within the climate governance arrangements across the regions. Rather than arguing for state-legislated integrating mechanisms, the book presents the typology of integrating mechanisms which can be employed in creative ways to strengthen accountability among decision-makers.

Regional level as a facilitator to align local and transit visions

There are a few lessons to take from my research about the distribution of responsibilities across levels of government that facilitate integrated decision-making on low-carbon development patterns. There are three functions that may be executed by the various levels of government: regulatory, coordinating, and implementing. For instance, in British Columbia, the Province has a regulatory function, Metro Vancouver has a coordinating function in setting spatial policies, and the municipalities and TransLink have an implementation function in applying the spatial policies to particular properties. The underpinning philosophy is a functional separation of powers which also underpins the distribution of responsibilities in Baden-Württemberg.

In its regulatory function, the state level can create clear integrating mechanisms and statutory responsibilities. Creating "ground rules of the game," as this was called in the Stuttgart region, seems to help build trust among decision-making centers and reduce power struggles. Having clear rules-of-the-game appeared to facilitate the development of win-win-solutions in conflicts between the local level and transit provider. Where mandated by state law, the regional level can ensure that transit investment decisions match local land use decisions on densities and uses. The regional level then serves as an outside third party to guide negotiations towards a shared regional vision. This does not mean the regional level is at the table during transit corridor alignment negotiations, but rather that the RGS as a document provides a framework for individual interaction. The integrating mechanisms ultimately hold the transit provider, as well as the local level, accountable to the RGS. While the transit provider has a responsibility to make fiscally responsible decisions, having a previously agreed-upon spatial vision can help reframe and give context to fiscal decisions. Rather than arguing over alignments to save short-term costs like in the Puget Sound region, other factors such as redevelopment potentials may shift into focus to ensure long-term viability of the transit system. If the local level is committed to its center, it may be more likely to pursue the needed land use changes. The regional level can facilitate this regional conversation by asking the local level to designate centers while also asking the transit provider to commit to connecting such centers. This could perceivable be done through contracts in absence of state legislation.

The respect for sectoral and local expertise is a fundamental principle underlying integrating mechanisms. An RGS should not determine the details of connecting two urban centers. Determining the exact locations to which a spatial policy applies is a task most suited to the local level. Therefore, state legislation needs to protect the rights of the implementing entities to make decisions concerning the implementation details. Hence, conflict resolution mechanisms in state planning laws are crucial as well – there are going to be different priorities between entities at the local and regional levels. Achieving a balance in powers between the local level, regional level, and transit provider can be one contribution of state legislation towards achieving spatially aligned efforts.

This is reflected in the Stuttgart and Vancouver regions with their state-legislated alignment mechanisms. In metropolitan Vancouver, the local level reports its urban center to Metro Vancouver during the RCS process. Metro Vancouver defines the characteristics of urban centers and the local level designates them. The example from the Stuttgart region is the designation of the actual growth boundary. The RGS defines policies on what areas are protected from development, but the actual boundary is designated by the local level. Again, the basic principle is that a higher level of government determines the spatial policies, but the local level applies them to particular parcels during the alignment process. Similarly, a transit builder has certain technical considerations that the RGS should not address.

There is a certain value proposition to orchestrating local and transit decisions within an RGS. Namely, that enabling a regional entity to coordinate the various spatial needs within the region will hopefully create a more livable region for residents. Again, incremental decisions by local and sectoral agencies do result in built transit stations and denser places, but in worst case scenarios, efforts do not occur at the same location – leaving a dense place without transit access which, in turn, creates more road congestion; and a transit location without riders to ultimately pay for the transit operation. While one might think this mutual interest would be reflected in a direct negotiation between the local level and a transit provider, the Seattle case shows that is not always the case. As Scharpf (2000) points out, a negotiation is framed by the rules-in-use. Sound Transit's decision to prioritize cost considerations is shaped by the state legislation. In contrast, TransLink's ability to take on more up-front investment costs to connect the locally-desirable urban centers is shaped by the Provincial legislation that promotes a spatial decision based on the RGS. In the long term, TransLink's investment might spark more redevelopment and thus a bigger increase in ridership. When visiting both regions in 2018, I saw more redevelopment around station areas in Vancouver than in Seattle – especially in locations outside of the core cities.

Recommendations on spatial policies

I also gained some insight on promising spatial policies for fostering low-carbon development patterns. An underpinning philosophy is a differentiated approach to the territorial development of the region; rather than applying the same set of spatial policies to all land, there are locations that serve particular purposes. The purposes include areas to be protected from urban development, areas that are prioritized for new development, and areas that likely will not change much (which might resonate with NIMBYs). In the three regions, several spatial policies work in conjunction to structure the development patterns to reduce VMT and GHG emissions, including policies for urban centers, density requirements, community classifications, growth targets, urban growth areas, and growth boundaries.

Particularly in how they prioritized areas for new development, the three regions deviated. The Puget Sound region prioritized the urbanized area in general, the Stuttgart region prioritized certain communities, and metropolitan Vancouver prioritized specific locations within a walkable radius of new and existing rapid transit stops, namely the urban centers and Frequent Transit Development Areas (FTDAs). In all likelihood, metropolitan Vancouver's approach is most suited for fostering low-carbon development patterns, particularly since the transit provider is actually connecting the urban centers with transit access.

To be more specific, it seems that local governments designating urban centers is a crucial component of pursuing low-carbon development patterns if the transit provider is required to connect these urban centers. The regional spatial policies can define characteristics of urban centers, including growth targets or density requirements, to ensure consistency across the region. As urban centers are clusters of employment and higher density housing, the urban centers then serve as the primary destinations within the rapid transit network. A debatable point is whether the urban centers may be designated based on existing or future land uses (zoned capacity). However, from the three case studies, it seems crucial that the local level identifies the most appropriate location for these urban centers. Again, the regional level defines development patterns (a network of transit-connected urban centers) while the local level identifies the specific locations (land use designation as urban center) and appropriate zoning within the urban center. There is a clear separation of powers in federally organized states. The designation of urban centers is self-regulated in the Puget Sound region and part of the RGS/RCS process in the Vancouver region.

To encourage redevelopment in urban centers, cities rely on private investment and interest in infill locations. I found evidence that having an urban containment boundary drives market interest into the urbanized area. As I pointed out in Chapter 1, a common critique with urban containment boundaries is the increase in housing prices – as the available land within the boundary saturates, prices increase. I observed this effect in the three regions. Yet, to mediate housing prices, it is crucial to simultaneously diversify the housing stock, increase densities, and adopt housing affordability policies. Further research is needed in places critiqued for their growth boundaries to discern if efforts were actually accompanied by regional spatial policies and subsequent local actions to increase zoned densities. The evidence I gathered suggests that spatial policies on urban containment need to happen in conjunction with policies on urban centers or other approaches to increase densities throughout the urbanized area to avoid negative externalities.[1]

Considerations for growth management; impact on spatial development patterns

Growth management researchers have frequently observed a lack of implementation of spatial policies or regional plans in North America. My hypothesis is that a lack of state-legislated integrating mechanisms fails to hold implementing entities accountable to the spatial policies. Furthermore, some studies document negative externalities of urban containment boundaries which may be explained by the lack of other spatial policies proactively directing growth to certain locations. One could analyze the findings of previous studies for instances in which spatial policies are described as failures by deliberately examining if there are any integrating mechanisms in place. Obviously, politicians would like to know if a spatial policy can achieve results when connected with integrating mechanisms and other spatial policies.

Lastly, there may be other factors in the planning system influencing an entity's ability to implement low-carbon development patterns besides integrating mechanisms. This includes the constitutional rights of each level of government, the decision-making for sewer and water permits, the expertise of real estate developers in a region, the fiscal system and the relevance of property rights pertaining to the highest and best use of land. In the United States, most local government revenue stems from property taxes which thus incentivizes zoning for single-family homes at the local level. In Germany, local revenue partly comes from the redistribution of taxes by the federal government (*Finanzausgleich*). Property rights and environmental protection are both constitutional rights in Germany. While there is due compensation for property owners, there is also constitutional protection of environmental uses of land. Hence, the constitutions in both countries create different higher level rules-in-use that influence the planning system.

This means other rules-in-use as observable features in planning systems may be relevant and should be added to future research. With this book, I hope to draw attention to how a state's planning legislation can foster integrated decision-making on growth management through integrating mechanisms that make an RGS a point of coordination on development patterns. However, there needs to be a political will to coordinate on development patterns. Policy transfer always relies on unique values. This book shows that just within federally organized countries there is a wide diversity of approaches with many nuanced details. This should discourage placing countries into particular typologies and encourage better understanding of the particularities along the five governance dimensions outlined in Chapter 2. Hypothetically, there is a wide diversity in empirically observable combinations along the five governance dimensions in planning systems and climate governance arrangements.

Findings for climate governance

Policy-makers and researchers involved in climate governance may be able to learn from my findings about integrated decision-making in urban planning. Both climate action plans and RGSs are planning documents that rely on the actions of implementing entities. I have examined in depth how implementing entities are held accountable to the spatial policies in the RGS based on the integrating mechanisms. However, integrated decision-making is not just a challenge for creating low-carbon development patterns but also for implementing other climate action plans. The typology of integrating mechanisms may be applicable to climate governance. In the three regions, climate actions were integrated primarily through working groups and contracts among multiple entities. A primary outcome of my research is that alignment mechanisms, as a type of integrating mechanism, may be particularly suited to translating climate objectives into climate actions. An interesting example for an alignment mechanism, I encountered in Baden-Württemberg, is the "European Energy Award." Communities sign-up to participate in a self-evaluation of their climate efforts. By creating a cross-departmental energy team, communities assess their efforts for over 100 action items and create a local work program.

As described in Chapter 2, some urban climate governance researchers have argued that systems with more local control and more self-regulation should perform better than systems with more senior-level involvement. However, my evidence suggests that there is a role for senior-level involvement, which at the very least can create "ground rules of the game" and ultimately frame the choices of other decision-making centers. Furthermore, state-level government can provide funding. Within Germany, the state of Baden-Württemberg funds communities to participate in the European Energy Award – they are seeing very high participation rates. My findings also suggest that thoughtfully designed state legislation can spark additional climate actions at lower levels of government. In the absence of such state legislation, self-regulated efforts can be successful but are limited to the jurisdictional boundaries of the climate active communities or counties.

Agenda setting and financial powers of the state level

I have demonstrated how the state level can leverage its agenda setting, as well as its financial and regulatory powers. All three states passed legislation to reduce GHG emissions. While Washington State only applied the legislation to state agencies, British Columbia and Baden-Württemberg regulations applied to all lower levels of government. To support this regulation, British Columbia and Baden-Württemberg also authorized funds to incentivize actions at the local level. Furthermore, British Columbia and Baden-Württemberg both created compacts (contracts) with communities to foster voluntary actions. British Columbia engages its local governments through the BC Climate Action Charter (BCCAC) and Baden-Württemberg created the Klimaschutzpakt (Climate mitigation compact). Having these compacts in place has deeply engaged communities and fostered political support (Dale et al. 2018, p. 347). While both states utilized the full set of governing resources to foster climate actions at the lower level, Washington State decided to limit its intervention to providing information. A state-level expert explained that climate action is controversial in Washington, so a compromise was reached to commit state agencies legislatively to actions, but also to provide information to local governments (a less intrusive approach).

Without a state framework, climate activity in the Puget Sound region is diverse, with the City of Seattle and King County as leading examples. In the absence of state leadership, local decision-making centers with the capacity and political will to pursue climate actions decided to create and implement climate action plans. My empirical findings echo the concerns raised by climate researchers about the "cities as saviors" narrative and the geographic limitations of large cities able to take action (Hughes 2016, p. 13; Setzer & Nachmany 2018; van der Heijden 2019.

Besides the extent of encouragement for local climate actions, another difference between the state climate action strategies is the relevance of land use actions. The recommended climate actions in all three regions do include those conducive to low-carbon development. Germany and the Province of British Columbia updated their planning enabling legislation to add climate mitigation as a concern in spatial planning. However, British Columbia is the only state-level government that has set a clear local agenda around development pattern changes for climate mitigation. Washington State opted to provide information on low-carbon development patterns to interested communities. Baden-Württemberg's climate efforts pertaining to land use primarily emphasize the determination of sites for renewable energy. Furthermore, none of the three planning systems was significantly changed to enhance implementation of low-carbon development patterns. This means that the state-level governments all included low-carbon development patterns in their climate action plans without making significant changes to their planning and growth management. Figure 9.1 provides an overview of the different approaches to climate actions by the three state-level governments.

Having provincial legislation like in British Columbia can ensure that climate mitigation is consistently addressed across the province. Of the three regions, British Columbia has the most extensive legislative requirement as it requires all local governments to include climate targets and actions in the OCP. To some extent, one might argue that this provincial requirement serves as an integration requirement – namely to integrate climate targets and actions in local comprehensive plans. This is further incentivized by the BCCAC. Several local planners indicated that having a state legislative requirement helped them engage with locally elected officials on how to best work on climate issues. The provincial level did not require specific targets or

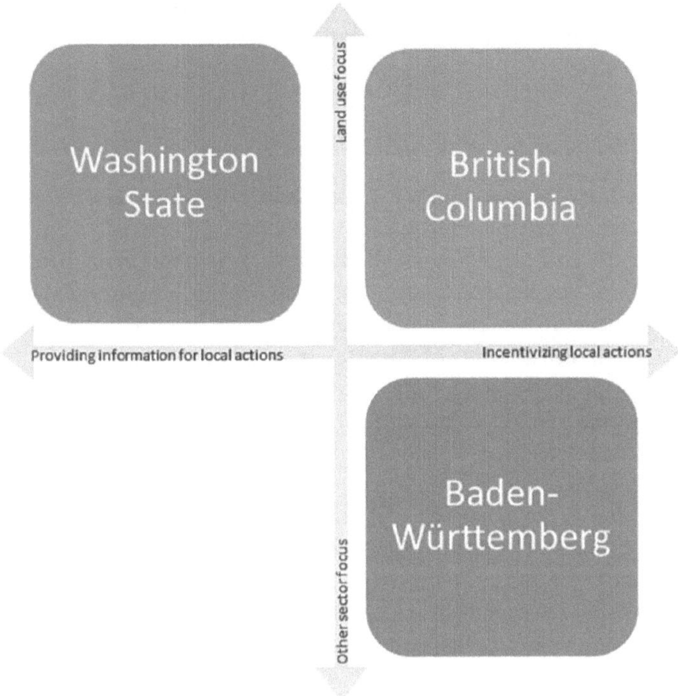

Figure 9.1 State agenda setting for local land use actions to foster GHG reductions.
Source: Own illustration.

specific actions, but it was able to influence the local agendas, ensuring that climate actions would be discussed during the OCP development process. I observed a similar effect in Baden-Württemberg where federal legislation placed renewable energy facilities on the local and regional planning agendas. In the absence of state legislation, this has not been the case in Washington State. Individual jurisdictions are extremely active and passionate about climate actions but not all communities share their enthusiasm.

Overall, communities in the Vancouver and Stuttgart regions receive strong support from state (and partly federal) government through regulations, funding, organization, and information for climate action. While there is an intention at the state level in Washington State to reduce GHG emissions, the leveraged governance resources are less diverse. Washington State supports communities interested in climate action by providing information and assistance to those who request it, but there is no significant regulation or funding specifically for the communities. When it comes to implementing low-carbon development, the responsibility lies at the local level. In contrast, communities in British Columbia and Baden-Württemberg have financial and institutional support to implement climate actions in general.

British Columbia in particular has made low-carbon development patterns a central feature of its climate action strategy. Therefore, low-carbon development patterns are supported to varying extents by the state level across all three regions.

Rethinking climate action plans and creating integrating mechanisms

This book has explored the integrating mechanisms around the RGS and their implications for implementing low-carbon development patterns. To some extent, there are similarities between climate action plans and an RGS – both depend on actions of many different decision-makers and agencies for implementation. One difference between them is the binding status of the RGS in contrast to the guiding status of climate action plans. As discussed above, the integrating mechanisms around the RGS have facilitated a deeper integration and more consistent implementation of its spatial policies. Therefore, future research may want to consider how and if legislated integrating mechanisms could realistically be applied to climate action plans.

Within climate governance, self-organized integrating mechanisms are currently predominant. This includes working groups, monitoring reports and designated staffers to work on climate issues (expert interviews). For instance, in the Puget Sound region, working groups were the primary mechanism to coordinate actions on climate issues. King County and the City of Seattle were able to propel many climate actions within their jurisdictions based on strategically designed working groups. Some climate governance studies suggest that frequent group meetings build trust and encourage learning exchanges. However, if the actions span multiple levels and sectors of government, more formalized interdependencies in decision-making may be needed to reduce the reliance on trust and leadership. Neither working groups, nor monitoring reports or staffers, establish formal interdependencies in the same way that integrating mechanisms do. It might be worthwhile to examine if there is an inverse relationship between rules-in-use and the reliance on trust and leadership, meaning that in the absence of rules-in-use, trust and leadership become determining factors for climate actions.

For spatial planning, integrating mechanisms that bridge the leadership gap are crucial for successful implementation. Integrating mechanisms ensure that planning documents influence the decisions by implementing entities. Some integrating mechanisms to consider for future research are changes to adoption, participation and alignment procedures. Currently, climate action plans are guiding planning documents which point multiple decision-making centers towards a set of desirable actions. Experts I interviewed appreciated the guiding character of the climate action plan as it allowed for faster adoption and creation of the document. However, the core of the implementation problem is the need to create accountability of implementing entities to the agreed upon climate action plan. One might even argue that there is an inverse relationship between the agreement to a plan from implementing entities and the speed by which it was prepared. Usually in spatial planning, for a legislatively binding RGS, there are extensive participation requirements for the development of the plan since the plan is binding on implementing entities. One could therefore consider adjusting the preparation and adoption procedures of climate action plans. A state-level government could decide to create climate action plans as legislatively-binding documents. Alternatively, a group of decision-making centers may jointly develop a climate action strategy that could be adopted as a contract.

Besides planning documents, contracts seemed to work particularly well in the regions to structure self-organized efforts. Vancouver used contracts quite frequently with the BCCAC, the partnership agreements, and the contractually-binding RGS. The use of contracts as self-regulated integrating mechanisms may be a viable option in the absence of state-level legislation that clarifies the "ground rules" of climate actions. While my research has found that state-regulated integrating mechanisms facilitate integrated decision-making on low-carbon development patterns, the relevance of state-regulation in contrast to self-regulation would still have to be determined for other areas of climate actions. Again, creating low-carbon development patterns requires a deeper integration of decisions than other sets of climate actions.

While one could consider creating more binding climate action plans through revising the adoption procedure and creating more stringent participation requirements, another approach may be to develop alignment mechanisms. Certainly, implementing entities do have the expertise within their sectoral field, and this expertise is best acknowledged through alignment mechanisms. The alignment mechanisms prompt the implementing entity to demonstrate how they are including climate action items within their efforts. The challenge would be to identify the documents relevant for implementation actions of the implementing entities (e.g. budgets or funding programs). One could argue that British Columbia's requirement to include climate targets and actions into the OCP serves as an alignment mechanism. Furthermore, the European Energy Award and the Baden-Württemberg state funding for local participation is another example for an alignment mechanism. Nevertheless, the alignment mechanisms could even be self-regulated and fit within the context of already established working groups and monitoring reports. It may be interesting for future researchers to examine this in more depth as appropriate for the various action fields in climate action plans.

Concluding, integrating decisions across multiple levels and sectors of government is not just a challenge for creating low-carbon development patterns but also for other subsets of climate mitigation and adaptation actions. While this book provides insights into mechanisms that can integrate decisions on land use and transportation matters, researchers may wish to explore existing integrating mechanisms in other sectors in cross-country comparative analysis. For practitioners and researchers, it may be worthwhile to determine what integrating mechanisms in the climate context are already utilized, which ones are particularly effective and which new mechanisms may be envisioned based on the typology presented in Chapter 8. Thinking about climate actions within this context leads to a few questions decision-makers may want to ask: to what extent would it be helpful for a state-level government to create integrating mechanisms to improve coordination on outcomes among multiple actors on climate actions? Would it be feasible to self-regulate integrating mechanisms by entering into a contract with the other decision-making centers?

Conclusion

The book adds to the theoretical discussion on climate and metropolitan governance by providing a view on how to integrate decisions in governance arrangements. Frequently, metropolitan and urban climate governance researchers advocate delegating authority to just one level of government to facilitate integrated decision-making. This is often impractical given cultural preferences, existing governance arrangements in metropolitan areas, and existing power relationships. Therefore, an alternative approach is to focus on integrating mechanisms that can facilitate integrated decision-making among multiple actors by creating formal interdependencies in decision-making and by pre-structuring interactions. Integrating mechanisms are the glue in polycentric and multi-level governance arrangements that ensure coordinated actions.

Ultimately, legislators, political parties, and other stakeholders will have different views on the acceptability of state and regional-level involvement. Nevertheless, if state governments in federal systems are interested in fostering low-carbon development patterns, it may be worthwhile carefully reviewing planning or climate legislation for opportunities to create integrating mechanisms. Policy transfer from one country to another is always a value-driven political decision (Dolowitz & Medearis 2009). For land use and even for climate questions, the values include acceptable levels of senior-level government involvement in local affairs, tolerance for creating interdependent levels of government, and a willingness to intervene in markets with regulation that does not over- or under-regulate. Certainly, climate action plans touch many policy sectors, and therefore, for each policy sector state regulation may be crucial.

Based on the findings presented here, polycentric, multi-level, and urban climate governance researchers may need to re-examine the emphasis on factors such as local control, leadership, and trust and critically ask if these factors serve to patch a gap within the rules-in-use (self-regulated or state-regulated). I was able to identify rules-in-use, regardless as to whether they were self-regulated or state-regulated, as a relevant factor in climate governance arrangements. It appeared from the expert interviews that leadership came up more frequently as an explanation for successful climate actions in less regulated settings. In the more regulated settings, experts frequently cited clear "ground rules of the game" as a factor of successful actions. It appeared that clear rules also contributed to trust among decision-making centers and encouraged collaborative behavior. Nevertheless, I did not examine this in depth and there needs to be more detailed research on the relationship between leadership, trust, and state legislation of climate governance arrangements.

Overall, this book identifies legislatively-designed integrating mechanisms as an alternative to rescaling of powers to foster the implementation of low-carbon development patterns. However, there is need for more research to broaden the focus to other planning systems and other subsets of climate actions. For the particular policy problem of creating low-carbon development patterns, my research qualitatively confirms the hypothesis that state regulation can facilitate integrated decision-making more consistently than self-regulated efforts. This hypothesis needs to be verified quantitatively for other metropolitan regions and examined in more depth for other fields of climate actions that may not require integrated decision-making to the same extent.

My research objective was not to assess the performance of the regions based on the integrating mechanisms utilized, but rather to develop a theory to understand the role of rules-in-use for integrated decision-making. By uncovering the typology of integrating mechanisms (Chapter 8), I have introduced an analytical concept to the governance and planning literature that can structure further quantitative research to assess the performance of governance arrangements based on the unique combinations of integrating mechanisms.

To conclude, when working on solving an interdependent policy problem such as creating low-carbon development patterns, integrating mechanisms have clear implications for advancing plans towards implementation. Integrating mechanisms can ensure that implementing entities are held accountable to policies or action items, ideally jointly agreed upon, in a planning document. There is evidence from the three regions that state-regulated integrating mechanisms foster more consistent implementation of low-carbon development patterns. The state-regulated integrating mechanisms create a clear degree of dependency among decision-making centers and structure interactions. The integrating mechanisms ensure that locally desirable land use patterns are translated into regional development patterns to which the transit provider is held accountable. Rather than having one locus of power, the integrating mechanisms create a context for power sharing and joint implementation. Given the urgency of climate actions, it is a worthwhile academic and political effort to further explore integrating mechanisms as an approach to fostering joint implementation among governmental decision-making centers.

Note

1 Using urban centers in conjunction with urban growth boundaries also addresses another challenge in planning, namely the protection of historic single family neighborhoods. Having spatial policies for a variety of lands in the region acknowledges that some neighborhoods will be preserved in their current character, while others may undergo rapid change. Implementing this differentiated view on land uses within the region requires a regional coordinating body that has a responsibility in dealing with these types of questions about development patterns.

Bibliography

A–C

Abbott, C. (2006). Urban Growth and Environmental Concerns. In American Planning Association (Ed.), *Planning and Urban Design Standards* (p. 86). Hoboken, NJ: John Wiley & Sons.

Abromeit, H., & Stoiber, M. (2006). *Demokratien im Vergleich–Einführung in die vergleichende Analyse politischer Systeme.* Wiesbaden: VS Verlag für Sozialwissenschaften.

Addie, J.-P. (2017). Governing the Networked Metropolis–The Regionalization of Urban Transportation in Southern Ontario. In R. Keil, P. Hamel, J.-A. Boudreau, & S. Kipfer (Eds.), *Governing Cities through Regions. Canadian and European Perspectives* (pp. 121–142). Waterloo: Wilfrid Laurier University Press.

Alterman, R. (2001). National-Level Planning in Democratic Countries: A Comparative Perspective. In R. Alterman (Ed.), *National-Level Planning in Democratic Countries: An International Comparison of City and Regional-Policy Making* (pp. 1–42). Liverpool: Liverpool University Press.

Altshuler, A., Morrill, W., Wolman, H., & Mitchell, F. (1999). *Governance and Opportunity in Metropolitan America.* Washington, D.C.: National Academy Press.

Amundsen, H., Berglund, F., & Westskog, H. (2010). Overcoming Barriers to Climate Change Adaptation–a Question of Multilevel Governance? *Environmental and Planning C: Government and Policy, 28*, 276–289. https://doi.org/10.1068/c0941

Andrew, C., & Goldsmith, M. (1998). From Local Government to Local Governance: And Beyond? *International Political Science Review, 19*(2), 101–117. https://doi.org/10.1177/019251298019002002

ARL-Akademie für Raumforschung und Landesplanung [German Academy for Spatial Research and Planning] (2005). *Handwörterbuch der Raumplanung [Dictionary of Spatial Planning in Germany].* Hannover: VSB Verlagsservice Braunschweig.

ARL-Akademie für Raumforschung und Landesplanung [German Academy for Spatial Research and Planning] (2009). *Klimawandel als Aufgabe der Regionalplanung [Climate Change as a Responsibility of Regional Planning].* Positionspapier aus der ARL. Nr. 81. Hannover.

Artibise, A., Cameron, K., & Seeling, J. (2004). Metropolitan Organization in Greater Vancouver: "Do It Yourself" Regional Government. In D. Phares (Ed.), *Metropolitan Governance without Metropolitan Government?* (pp. 195–211). Wiltshire: Ashgate.

Banister, D., & Anable, J. (2009). Transport Policies and Climate Change. In S. Davoudi, J. Crawford, & A. Mehmood (Eds.), *Planning for Climate Change–Strategies for Mitigation and Adaptation for Spatial Planners* (pp. 55–69). London & Sterling, VA: Earthscan.

Barnes, W.R., & Foster, K.A. (2012). *Toward a More Useful Way of Understanding Regional Governance. A* Paper for Presentation at the September 2012 Conference of the European Research Association. Retrieved June 30, 2015 from Building Resilient Regions–A Macarthur Foundation Research Network http://brr.berkeley.edu/wp-content/uploads/2012/10/Barnes-Foster-Toward-a-more-useful-way-of-understanding-regional-governance.pdf

Bassett, E., & Shandas, V. (2010). Innovation and Climate Action Planning. *Journal of the American Planning Association, 76*(4), 435–450.

Bauer, A.H., Thess, M., Kleinschmit, B., & Creutzig, F. (2013). Urban Climate Change Mitigation in Europe: Looking at and Beyond the Role of Population and Density. *Journal of Urban Planning and Development, 140*(1), 1–12.

BC-Province of British Columbia

BC-ALCA (2002). *British Columbia Agricultural Land Commission Act 2002.* Retrieved July 11, 2019, from http://www.bclaws.ca/civix/document/id/complete/statreg/02036_01

BC-Bill 27 (2008). *Local Government (Green Communities) Statutes Amendment Act 2008.* Retrieved October 29, 2019, from http://www.bclaws.ca/civix/document/id/lc/billsprevious/4th38th:gov27-1

BC-Bill 44 (2007). *Bill 44- Greenhouse Gas Reduction Targets 2007, 38th Parliament, 3rd Session, First Reading.* Retrieved May 22, 2018, from https://www.leg.bc.ca/pages/bclass-legacy.aspx#/content/legacy/web/38th3rd/1st_read/gov44-1.htmBC-Budget (2017). *Budget and Fiscal Plan 2017/19-2019/2020.* Prepared by the Ministry of Finance. Retrieved November 12, 2019, from https://www.bcbudget.gov.bc.ca/2017/bfp/2017_Budget_and_Fiscal_Plan.pdf

BC-CAC (2011). *The British Columbia Climate Action Charter between the Province of British Columbia and the Union of British Columbia Municipalities and signatory local governments.* Retrieved October 26, 2020, from https://www2.gov.bc.ca/assets/gov/british-columbians-our-governments/local-governments/planning-land-use/bc_climate_action_charter.pdf

BC-CAP (2016). *Climate Leadership Plan.* Retrieved May 23, 2018, from https://climate.gov.bc.ca/app/uploads/sites/13/2016/10/4030_CLP_Booklet_web.pdf

BC-CSCD (2018a). *About the BC Climate Action Charter.* Retrieved May 22, 2018, from https://www.toolkit.bc.ca/BC-Climate-Action-Charter

BC-CSCD (2018b). *Climate Action Revenue Incentive Program.* Retrieved May 22, 2018, from https://www2.gov.bc.ca/gov/content/governments/local-governments/grants-transfers/climate-action-revenue-incentive-program-carip

BC-LGA (2018). *British Columbia Local Government Act 2018.* Retrieved July 6, 2018, from http://www.bclaws.ca/civix/document/id/lc/statreg/r15001_00

BC-RGS Guide (2005). *Regional Growth Strategy–An Explanatory Guide.* Prepared by the Ministry of Community Services. Retrieved May 23, 2018, from https://www2.gov.bc.ca/assets/gov/british-columbians-our-governments/local-governments/planning-land-use/rgs_explanatory_guide_2005.pdf

BC-SCBCTAA (1998). *South Coast British Columbia Transportation Authority Act 1998.* Retrieved December 06, 2019, from https://www.bclaws.ca/civix/document/id/complete/statreg/98030_01

BC-Toolkit (2018a). *BC Climate Action Toolkit.* Retrieved March 09, 2020, from https://www.toolkit.bc.ca/

BC-Toolkit (2018b). *Regional Growth Strategy–How can a Regional Growth Strategy Be Used to Take Action on Climate Change*? Retrieved March 09, 2020, from https://www.toolkit.bc.ca/tool/regional-growth-strategy

BC-Vancouver Charter (1953). Retrieved July 6, 2018, from http://www.bclaws.ca/civix/document/id/lc/statreg/vanch_00

Bengston, David N., Fletcher, Jennifer O., Nelson, Kristen C. (2004). Public Policies for Managing Urban Growth and Protecting Open Space: Policy Instruments and Lessons Learned in the United States. *Landscape and Urban Planning,* 69, 271–286.

Ben-Zadok, E. (2005). Consistency, Concurrency and Compact Development: Three Faces of Growth Management Implementation in Florida. *Urban Studies, 42*(12), 2167–2190.

Benz, A. (2007). Multilevel Governance. In A. Benz, S. Lütz, U. Schimank, & G. Simonis (Eds.), *Handbuch Governance. Theoretische Grundlagen und empirische Anwendungsfelder [Governance. Theoretical Foundations and Empirical Applications]* (pp. 297–310). Wiesbaden: VS Verlag für Sozialwissenschaften | GWV Fachverlage GmbH.

Benz, A. (2009). *Politik in Mehrebenensystemen.* Wiesbaden: VS Verlag für Sozialwissenschaft.

Benz, A., Lütz, S., Schimank, U., & Simonis, G. (2007). Einleitung [Introduction]. In A. Benz, S. Lütz, U. Schimank & G. Simonis (Eds.), *Handbuch Governance. Theoretische Grundlagen und empirische Anwendungsfelder [Governance. Theoretical Foundations and Empirical Applications]* (pp. 9–25). Wiesbaden: VS Verlag für Sozialwissenschaften | GWV Fachverlage GmbH.

Bestor, C. (2010). Networks, Neighborhoods, and Markets: Fieldwork in Tokyo. In G. Gmelch, R. Kemper, & W. Zenner (Eds.), *Urban Life. Readings in the Anthropology of City* (5th ed., pp. 20–35). Long Grove, IL: Waveland Press.

Betsill, M. (2001). Mitigating Climate Change in US Cities: Opportunities and Obstacles. *Local Environment, 6*(4), 393–406.

Betsill, M., & Bulkeley, H. (2006). Cities and the Multilevel Governance of Global Climate Change. *Global Governance, 12,* 141–159.

Birch, E.L. (2005). U.S. Planning Culture Under Pressure: Major Elements Endure and Flourish in the Face of Crisis. In B. Sanyal (Ed.), *Comparative Planning Cultures* (pp. 331–357). New York and London: Routledge-Taylor and Francis Group.

Blair, J.P., & Caroll, M.C. (2009). *Local Economic Development. Analysis, Practices and Globalization* (2nd ed.). Los Angeles, London, New Delhi, Singapore: Sage.

BMVBS (2012). *Regionalplanerische Instrumente zur Reduzierung der Flächeninanspruchnahme [Regional Spatial Policies to Limit Sprawl]. Online-Publikation, Nr. 20/2012.* Prepared by the Federal Ministry for Transportation, Construction and Urban Development. Retrieved May 16, 2020, from https://www.bbsr.bund.de/BBSR/DE/Veroeffentlichungen/ministerien/BMVBS/Online/2012/DL_ON202012.pdf;jsessionid=CBC863D-179804B165040F230DD7ACC96.live11294?__blob=publicationFile&v=2

BMVBW (2001). *Auf dem Weg zu einer nachhaltigen Siedlungsentwicklung. Nationalbericht der Bundesrepublik Deutschland zur 25. Sondersitzung der Generalversammlung der Vereinten Nationen ("Istanbul +5") [Path to Sustainable Urban Development Patterns. National Report of Germany to the 25th Assembly of the United Nations–Istanbul + 5].* Prepared by the Federal Ministry for Economic Cooperation and Development. Retrieved March 20, 2017, from http://www.bbsr.bund.de/BBSR/DE/Veroeffentlichungen/BMVBS/Sonderveroeffentlichungen/2005undaelter/DL_Istanbul5.pdf?__blob=publicationFileandv=6;

Boarnet, M.G., McLaughlin, R.B., & Carruthers, J.I. (2011). Does State Growth Management Change the Pattern of Urban Growth? Evidence from Florida. *Regional Science and Urban Economics, 41*(3), 236–252. https://doi.org/10.1016/j.regsciurbeco.2010.12.004

Bogart, W.T. (2006). *Don't Call It Sprawl. Metropolitan Structure in the Twenty-First Century.* Cambridge, New York, Melbourne, Madrid, Cape Town, Singapore, São Paulo: Cambridge University Press.

Bohnsack, R. (2003*). Rekonstruktive Sozialforschung. Einführung in qualitative Methoden* (5th ed.). Opladen: Leske and Budrich.

Bollens, S.A. (1992). State Growth Management: Intergovernmental Frameworks and Policy Objectives. *Journal of the American Planning Association, 58*(4), 454–466. https://doi.org/10.1080/01944369208975829

Bollens, S.A. (1993). Restructuring Land Use Governance. *Journal of Planning Literature,* 7(3), 211–226.

Bolleyer, N., & Börzel, T.A. (2010). Non-Hierarchical Policy Coordination in Multilevel Systems. *European Political Science Review, 2*(2), 157–158. https://doi.org/10.1017/S175577391000007X

Booth, P. (2005). The Nature of Difference: Traditions of Law and Government and Their Effects on Planning in Britain and France. In B. Sanyal (Ed.), *Comparative Planning Cultures* (pp. 259–283). New York and London: Routledge-Taylor & Francis Group.

Bortz, J., & Döring, N. (2006).*Forschungsmethoden und Evaluation für Human- und Sozialwissenschaftler* (4th ed.). Heidelberg: Springer.

Boswell, M.R., Greve, A.I., & Seale, T.L. (2012) *Local Climate Action Planning.* Washington, D.C.: Island Press.

Boswell, M.R., & Mason, S.G. (2018). Regional Climate Planning and Local Outcomes in California. In S. Hughes et al. (Eds.), *Climate Change in Cities* (pp. 19–38). Cham: Springer International Publishing–The Urban Book Series.

Boudreau, J.-A., Hamel, P., Jouve, B., & Keil, R. (2006). Comparing Metropolitan Governance: The Cases of Montreal and Toronto. *Progress in Planning, 66*, 7–59. https://doi.org/10.1016/j.progress.2006.07.005

Bräutigam D.A., & Knack, S. (2004). Foreign Aid, Institutions, and Governance in Sub-Saharan Africa. *Economic Development and Cultural Change, 52*, 255–285. https://doi.org/10.1086/380592, ISSN: 0013-0079

Breu, C., Priebs, A., & Tönnes, M. (Eds.), (2015). *Regionalverbände–Starke Partner für die Zukunftsgestaltung in den Ballungsräumen [Regional planning organizations–strong partners for designing the future of metropolitan areas].* Hannover: Arbeitsgemeinschaft der Regionalverbände in Ballungsräumen.

Brown, D.M. (2012). Comparative Climate Change Policy and Federalism: An Overview: Comparative Climate Change Policy and Federalism. *Review of Policy Research, 29*(3), 322–333.

Brunet-Jailly, E., & Arcand, È. (2017). Provincial Distrust Weighs on Vancouver's Regional Governance. In R. Keil, P. Hamel, J.-A. Boudreau, & S. Kipfer (Eds.), *Governing Cities through Regions. Canadian and European Perspectives* (pp. 239–258). Waterloo: Wilfrid Laurier University Press.

Brunnengräber, A. (2013) Multi-Level Climate Governance: Strategic Selectivities in International Politics. In J. Knieling, & W. Leal Filho (Eds.), *Climate Change Governance: Series Climate Change Management* (pp. 70–85). Heidelberg: Springer.

Bryson, J. (2004). What to Do When Stakeholders Matter. *Public Management Review, 6*(1), 21–53. https://doi.org/10.1080/14719030410001675722

Bulkeley, H., & Betsill, M. (2005). Rethinking Sustainable Cities: Multilevel Governance and the 'Urban' Politics of Climate Change. *Environmental Politics, 14*(1), 42–63. http://dx.doi.org/10.1080/0964401042000310178

Bundesgesetzblatt (2017, Teil I Nr. 30). *Gesetz zur Änderung raumordnungsrechtlicher Vorschriften vom 23. Mai 2017 [Law on Changing the Spatial Planning Requirements from May 23, 2017]* (pp. 1245–1252). Retrieved March 12, 2018, from http://www.bgbl.de/xaver/bgbl/start.xav?startbk=Bundesanzeiger_BGBlandjumpTo=bgbl117s1245.pdf

Burch, S., Shaw, A., Dale, A., & Robinson, J. (2014). Triggering Transformative Change: A Development Path Approach to Climate Change Response in Communities. *Climate Policy, 14*(4), 467–487. http://dx.doi.org/10.1080/14693062.2014.876342

Burns, E., & Ondernonk, D. (1993). Urban Growth and Environmental Protection at the Local Level. In J. Stein (Ed.), *Growth Management. The Planning Challenge of the 1990s* (pp. 129–142). Newbury Park, CA: SAGE Publications.

Burrows, L. (1978). *Growth Management, Issues, Techniques and Policy Implications.* New Brunswick, NJ: Center for Urban Policy Research.

BW-Baden-Württemberg

BW-Drucksache 15/3842 (2013). *Gesetz zur Förderung des Klimaschutzes in Baden-Württemberg, Landtag von Baden-Württemberg. 15. Wahlperiode [Law to Foster Climate Mitigation in Baden-Württemberg-Adopted by the 15th State Assembly].* Retrieved June 18, 2018, from https://um.baden-wuerttemberg.de/fileadmin/redaktion/m-um/intern/Dateien/Dokumente/4_Klima/Klimaschutz/Klimaschutzgesetz/Gesetzesbeschluss_Klimaschutzgesetz.pdf

BW-GVRS. *Gesetz über die Errichtung des Verbands Region Stuttgart (GVRS) [Law creating the Verband Region Stuttgart].* Vom 7. Februar 1994 [Adopted February 7, 1994]. Retrieved June 19, 2018, from http://www.landesrecht-bw.de/jportal/?quelle=-jlink&query=RegStuttgG+BW&psml=bsbawueprod.psml&max=true&aiz=true

BW-IEKK (2014). *Integriertes Energie- und Klimaschutzkonzept Baden-Württemberg (IEKK) [Integrated Energy and Climate Mitigation Plan Baden-Württemberg].* Retrieved June 18, 2018, from https://um.baden-wuerttemberg.de/fileadmin/redaktion/m-um/intern/Dateien/Dokumente/2_Presse_und_Service/Publikationen/Klima/140715_IEKK.pdf

BW-KEA (2018). *Regionale Energieagenturen in Baden-Württemberg [Regional Energy Consulting Agencies in Baden-Württemberg].* Retrieved June 18, 2018, from https://www.kea-bw.de/service/energieagenturen/regionale-agenturen/

BW-Klimaschutzpakt (2018). *2. Klimaschutzpakt 2018/2019 des Landes Baden-Württemberg mit den kommunalen Landesverbänden [Second Climate Compact 2018/2019 between the State of Baden-Württemberg and the Unions of Local Governments].* Published by the Ministry of the Environment, Climate Protection and the Energy Sector Baden-Württemberg (2018/2019). Retrieved March 28, 2020, from https://um.baden-wuerttemberg.de/fileadmin/redaktion/m-um/intern/Dateien/Dokumente/4_Klima/Klimaschutz/Zweiter_Klimaschutzpakt_2018-2019.pdf

BW-Klimaschutz Plus (2020). *Program Klimaschutz-Plus [State Funding Program for Local Climate Actions].* Published by the Ministry of the Environment, Climate Protection and the Energy Sector Baden-Württemberg. Retrieved March 27, 2020, from https://um.baden-wuerttemberg.de/de/klima/informieren-beraten-foerdern/klimaschutz-plus/

BW-LEP (2002). *Landesentwicklungsplan [State Development Plan].* Published by the Ministry of Transportation. Retrieved March 20, 2019, from https://vm.baden-wuerttemberg.de/fileadmin/redaktion/m-mvi/intern/Dateien/Brosch%C3%BCren/Landesentwichlungsplan_2002.PDF

BW-LplG - *Landesplanungsgesetz Baden-Württemberg [Planning Law in Baden-Württemberg].* Retrieved July 17, 2019, from http://www.landesrecht-bw.de/jportal/?quelle=jlink&query=LPlG+BW&psml=bsbawueprod.psml&max=true&aiz=trueBW-Mobility (2020). *Land organisiert den Schienenpersonennahverkehr [State Organizes the Rail Transit Network].* Published by the Ministry of Transportation in Baden-Württemberg. Retrieved April 23, 2020, from https://vm.baden-wuerttemberg.de/de/mobilitaet-verkehr/schiene/planung-finanzierung-und-ausschreibungen/planung-und-finanzierung/

BW-ÖPNVG. *Gesetz über die Planung, Organisation und Gestaltung des öffentlichen Personennahverkehrs vom 08. Juni 1995. [Law on Planning, Organising and Composition of Public Transit in Baden-Württemberg].* Retrieved April 25, 2020, from http://www.landesrecht-bw.de/jportal/portal/t/jmb/page/bsbawueprod.psml/action/portlets.jw.MainAction?p1=0&eventSubmit_doNavigate=searchInSubtreeTOC&show-doccase=1&doc.hl=0&doc.id=jlr-%C3%96PNVGBWrahmen&doc.part=R&toc.poskey=#focuspoint

BW-ÖPNV-Pakt (2014). ÖPNV-Pakt für die Region Stuttgart [Public *Transportation Compact for the Stuttgart Region].* Published by the Ministry of Transportation in Baden-Württemberg. Retrieved June 21, 2018, from https://vm.baden-wuerttemberg.de/de/mobilitaet-verkehr/bus-und-bahn/oepnv-pakt-stuttgart/

BW-Procurement (2016). *Verträge für Stuttgarter Netze unterzeichnet [Contracts Signed with Rapid Transit Operator].* Published by the Ministry of Transportation in Baden-Württemberg. Retrieved September 27, 2020, from https://vm.baden-wuerttemberg.de/de/service/presse/pressemitteilung/pid/vertraege-fuer-stuttgarter-netze-unterzeichnet/

BW-Statistics (2019). *Statistischer Bericht Baden-Württemberg: Bevölkerung und Erwerbstätigkeit [Statistical Report for Baden-Württemberg: Population and Employment Figures].* Retrieved May 23, 2019, from https://www.statistik-bw.de/Service/Veroeff/Statistische_Berichte/312218001.pdf

BW-Verkehr (2017). *Verkehrsinfrastruktur 2030 – Ein klimaschutzszenario für Baden-Württemberg [Transportation Infrastructure 2030 - A Climate Scenario for Baden-Württemberg].* Published by the Ministry of Transportation in Baden-Württemberg. Retrieved March 20, 2019, from https://vm.baden-wuerttemberg.de/fileadmin/redaktion/m-mvi/intern/Dateien/Brosch%C3%BCren/Klimaschutzszenario_10-2017_web.pdf

BW-Zielkonzept (2025). *Zielkonzept 2025 für den Schienenpersonennahverkehr (SPNV) in Baden-Württemberg. [Vision 2025 for Rail Transit in Baden-Württemberg].* Published by the Ministry of Transportation in Baden-Württemberg. Retrieved April 23, 2020, https://vm.baden-wuerttemberg.de/de/service/publikation/did/zielkonzept-2025-fuer-den-schienenpersonennahverkehr-spnv-in-baden-wuerttemberg/

Calthorpe, P. (2015, April). *Urbanism in the Age of Climate Change.* Paper presented at the National Conference of American Planning Association, Seattle, WA.

Campbell, H. (2006). Is the Issue of Climate Change too Big for Spatial Planning? *Planning Theory & Practice,* 7(2), 201–230. http://dx.doi.org/10.1080/14649350600681875

Canadian Constitution Act (1982). *Canada–Justice Laws Website.* Retrieved April 4, 2019, from https://laws-lois.justice.gc.ca/eng/const/page-15.html#h-38

Carlisle, K., & Gruby, R. (2017). Polycentric Systems of Governance: A Theoretical Model for the Commons. *The Policy Studies Journal, 47*(2), 1–26.

Carruthers, J.I. (2002). Evaluating the Effectiveness of Regulatory Growth Management Programs an Analytic Framework. *Journal of Planning Education and Research, 21*(4), 391–405.

CEC-Commission of the European Communities (1997). *The EU Compendium of Spatial Planning Systems and Policies.* Luxembourg: Office for Official Publications of the European Communities.

Chan, K. (Dec 13, 2018, 11:40pm). *Mayors' Council Approves TransLink's 15-Month Timeline to Plan New Surrey SkyTrain.* Retrieved October 2, 2019, from https://dailyhive.com/vancouver/mayors-council-translink-planning-skytrain-fraser-highway-december-2018

Chan, K. (Sept 3, 2020, 03:51 pm). *Premier Horgan Says Announcement on Surrey-Langley SkyTrain Expected Soon.* Retrieved September 18, 2020, from https://dailyhive.com/vancouver/surrey-langley-skytrain-update-september-2020

Cole, D.H. (2015). Advantages of a Polycentric Approach to Climate Change Policy. *Nature Climate Change, 5,* 114–118. https://doi.org/10.1038/nclimate2490

COQ-City of Coquitlam

COQ-BLLUD (2020). *Burquitlam-Lougheed Neighbourhood Plan–Land use designations–Schedule A, Adopted: June 27, 2017.* Retrieved October 07, 2020, from https://www.coquitlam.ca/docs/default-source/citywide-ocp/part-3---chapter-9-2---burquitlam-lougheed-neighbourhood-plan-schedule-a.pdf?sfvrsn=2

COQ-BLNP (2017). *Burquitlam–Lougheed Neighborhood Plan. Chapter 9.2 in Citywide Official Community Plan. Adopted June 26, 2017.* Retrieved September 10, 2020, from https://www.coquitlam.ca/DocumentCenter/View/2932/Burquitlam-Lougheed-Neighbourhood-Plan-PDF

COQ-LLUD (2020). *Southwest Coquitlam Area Plan–Schedule A. Last Amended: Feb. 24, 2020.* Retrieved October 07, 2020, from https://www.coquitlam.ca/docs/default-source/citywide-ocp/Part_3_-_9_Schedule_A.pdf?sfvrsn=12

COQ-Market Analysis (2015). *Burquitlam-Lougheed Neighbourhood Plan Market Analysis.* Issued on May 14, 2015. Internal Communication with Interviewed Experts.

COQ-RCS (2013). *Introduction and Regional Context Statement–Part 1 of Citywide Official Community Plan. Amended December 2, 2013.* Retrieved September 11, 2020, from https://www.coquitlam.ca/docs/default-source/citywide-ocp/Part_1_-_Ch_1_-_Introduction_and_Regional_Context_Statement.pdf?sfvrsn=2

COQ-TDS (2012). *Transit-Oriented Development Strategy. Approved by Council Resolution on July 30, 2012.* Retrieved September 10, 2020, from https://www.coquitlam.ca/docs/default-source/community-planning-documents/Coquitlam_Transit-Oriented_Development_Strategy.pdf?sfvrsn=0

Cradock, A.L., Troped, P.J., Fields, B., Melly, S.J., Simms, S.V, Gimmler, F., & Fowler, M. (2009). Factors Associated with Federal Transportation Funding for Local Pedestrian and Bicycle Programming and Facilities. *Journal of Public Health Policy, 30,* 38–72.

Crane, R., & Landis, J. (2010). Introduction to the Special Issue Planning for Climate Change: Assessing Progress and Challenges. *Journal of the American Planning Association, 76*(4), 389–401. http://dx.doi.org/10.1080/01944363.2010.512036

Cullingworth, B., & Caves, R.W. (2009). *Planning in the USA. Policies, Issues, and Processes.* (3rd ed.). New York: Routledge.

D–F

Dabrowski, M. (2018). Boundary Spanning for Governance of Climate Change Adaptation in Cities: Insights from a Dutch Urban Region. *Environment and Planning C: Politics and Space, 36*(5), 837–855. https://doi.org/10.1177/2399654417725077

Dale, A., Burch, S., Robinson, J., & Strashok, C. (2018). Multilevel Governance of Sustainability Transitions in Canada: Policy Alignment, Innovation, and Evaluation. In S. Hughes et al. (Eds.), *Climate Change in Cities* (pp. 343–358). Springer International Publishing:–The Urban Book Series. https://doi.org/10.1007/978-3-319-65003-6_17Daniels, T. L. (2009). A Trail Across Time. American Environmental Planning from City Beautiful to Sustainability. *Journal of the American Planning Association, 75*(2), 178–192.

Davoudi, S. (2017). Spatial Planning: The Promised Land or Rolled Out Neoliberalism? In M. Gunder, A. Madanipour, & V. Watson (Eds.), *The Routledge Handbook of Planning Theory* (pp. 15–27). London: Taylor and Francis.

Davoudi, S. (2013). Climate Change and the Role of Spatial Planning in England. In J. Knieling& W. Leal Filho (Eds.), *Climate Change Governance: Series Climate Change Management* (pp. 151–167). Heidelberg: Springer.

Davoudi, S., Crawford, J., & Mehmood, A. (Eds., 2009). *Planning for Climate Change-Strategies for Mitigation and Adaptation for Spatial Planners* (pp. 55–69). London & Sterling, VA: Earthscan.

Deangelo, B. J., & Harvey, D. (1998). The Jurisdictional Framework for Municipal Action to Reduce Greenhouse Gas Emissions: Case Studies from Canada, the USA and Germany. *Local Environment, 3*(2), 111–136.

DeGrove, J.M., & Metzger, P.M. (1993). Growth Management and the Integrated Roles of State, Regional and Local Governments. In J.M. Stein (Ed.), *Growth Management. The Planning Challenge of the 1990s* (pp. 3–17). Newbury Park, CA: Sage Publications.

Dente, B. (2014). *Understanding policy decisions.* Milano: PoliMI SpringerBriefs.

Destatis (2011). *Zensus 2011, Bevölkerung nach Geschlecht und Nationalität–Stichtag 09.05.2011–regionale Tiefe: Kreise und krfr. Städte [German Census Bureau (2011). Census Data 2011, Population by Gender and Nationality on May 09, 2011–Geographic Detail: Counties and Cities].* Retrieved April 6, 2018, from https://www.regionalstatistik.de/genesis/online/data;jsessionid=18F040B7B23BF840E0DBF928591CE602.reg1?operation=abruftabelleBearbeiten&levelindex=2&levelid=1523001743651&auswahloperation=abruftabelleAuspraegungAuswaehlen&auswahlverzeichnis=ordnungsstruktur&auswahlziel=werteabruf&selectionname=12111-01-01-4&auswahltext=&werteabruf=Werteabruf

DIFU-Deutsches Institute für Urbanistik (2011, Ed.) *Klimaschutz in Kommunen. Praxisleitfaden.* Retrieved April 18, 2016, from http://www.leitfaden.kommunaler-klimaschutz.de/sites/leitfaden.kommunaler-klimaschutz.de/files/pdf/klimaschutzleitfaden.pdf

Di Gregorio, M., Fatorelli, L., Paavola, J., Locatelli, B., Pramova, E., Nurrochmat, & Sari, I.M. (2019). Multi-Level Governance and Power in Climate Change Policy Networks. *Global Environmental Change, 54,* 64–77. https://doi.org/10.1016/j.gloenvcha.2018.10.003

Diller, C. (2015). *Bewertung in der Evaluation regionaler Siedlungsentwicklung: ein Vergleich Deutschland-USA [Ratings in Evaluating Regional Urban Development Patterns: A Comparison between Germany and the USA].* Im Rahmen des DEGEVAL-Kolloquiums: "Zwischen Objektivität und Normativität: Wie kommt die Evaluation zu(m) Werten?" am 27.2.2015 in Gießen [Presented at the Colloquium "Between Objective and Normative Research: How Does Evolutions Get Results? on February 27, 2015 in Gießen]. Retrieved October 12, 2020, from https://docplayer.org/7723428-Bewertung-in-der-evaluation-regionaler-siedlungsentwicklung-ein-vergleich-deutschland-usa.html

Diller, C. (2018). Instrumente der Raumplanung [Mechanisms in German Spatial Planning]. In Akademie für Raumforschung und Landesplanung (Ed.), *Handwörterbuch der Stadt- und Raumentwicklung [Dictionary of Urban and Regional Development]* (pp. 1023–1035). Hannover: ARL. Retrieved October 06, 2018, from https://shop.arl-net.de/media/direct/pdf/HWB%202018/Instrumente%20der%20Raumplanung.pdf

Dolowitz, D.P., & Medearis, D. (2009). Considerations of the Obstacles and Opportunities to Formalizing Cross-National Policy Transfer to the United States: A Case Study of the Transfer of Urban Environmental and Planning Policies from Germany. *Environment and Planning C: Government and Policy, 27*, 684–697.

Dooley, L. (2002). Case Study Research and Theory Building. *Advances in Developing Human Resources, 4*(3), 335–354.

Dorsch, M.J., & Flachsland, C. (2017). A Polycentric Approach to Global Climate Governance. *Global Environmental Politics, 17*(2), 45–64.

Downs, A. (1997). The Challenge of Our Declining Big Cities. *Housing Policy Debate, 8*(2), 359–408.

Drucksache 18/10883-*Gesetzentwurf der Bundesregierung Entwurf eines Gesetzes zur Änderung raumordnungsrechtlicher Vorschriften vom 18.01.2017.* Retrieved March 14, 2018, from http://dip21.bundestag.de/dip21/btd/18/108/1810883.pdf

Echenique, M., Hargreaves, A., Mitchell, G., & Namdeo, A. (2012). Growing Cities Sustainably. *Journal of the American Planning Association, 28*(2), 121–137.

EEA 2020. *European Energy Award.* Retrieved March 27, 2020, from https://www.european-energy-award.org/european-energy-award

Eliadis, P., Hill, M.M., & Howlett, M. (2007). Introduction. In P. Eliadis, M.M. Hill, & M. Howlett (Eds.), *Designing Government. From Instruments to Governance* (pp. 3–18). Montreal & Kingston, London, Ithaca, NY: McGill Queen's University Press.

Ewing, R., & Cervero, R. (2017). "Does Compact Development Make People Drive Less?" The Answer Is Yes. *Journal of the American Planning Association, 83*(1), 19–25. http://dx.doi.org/10.1080/01944363.2016.1245112

Falk, M. (2006). *Die kommunalen Aufgaben unter dem Grundgesetz. Eine Untersuchung der rechtlichen Stellung der Aufgaben der kommunalen Körperschaften in der Staatsorganisation der Bundesrepublik Deutschland [Statutory Responsibilities at the Local Level Based on the German Constitution. A Study of the Legal Status of Local Jurisdictions in the Organizational Structure of the German Republic].* Baden-Baden: Nomos Verlagsgesellschaft.

Farinos Dasi, J. (2006). *ESPON Project 2.3.2, Governance of Territorial and Urban Policies from EU to local level, Final Report.* Esh-sur-Alzette: ESPON Coordination Unit.

FHWA-Federal Highway Administration (2008). *Summary Report-MPO Peer Workshop on Planning for Climate Change.* Retrieved October 4, 2015, from www.fhwa.dot.gov/planning/processes/metropolitan/mpo/seattle_mpo/index.cfm

Fischer, F., Miller, G., &Sidney, M. (2007). *Handbook of Public Policy Analysis. Theory, Politics, and Methods.* Boca Raton, London, New York: CRC Press.

Fischler, R. (1995). Strategy and History in Professional Planning. In H. Liggett, & D. Perry (Eds.), *Spatial Practice* (pp. 13–58). Thousand Oaks, CA: SAGE Publications Inc.

Fitzgerald, J. (2020). *Greenovation: Urban Leadership on Climate Change.* New York: Oxford University Press.

Friedmann, J. (2005). Planning Cultures in Transition. In B. Sanyal (Ed.), *Comparative Planning Cultures* (pp. 26–44). New York and London: Routledge-Taylor & Francis Group.

Friedrichs, J. (1990). *Methoden der empirischen Sozialforschung.* Wiesbaden: VS Verlag für Sozialwissenschaften.

Fröhlich, J., & Knieling, J. (2013) Conceptualizing Climate Change Governance. In J. Knieling, & W. Leal Filho (Eds.), *Climate Change Governance: Series Climate Change Management* (pp. 14–31). Heidelberg: Springer.

Fürst, D. (2009). Planning Cultures en Route to a Better Comprehension of 'Planning Process'? In J. Knieling & F. Othengrafen (Eds.), *Planning Cultures in Europe. Decoding Cultural Phenomena in Urban and Regional Planning* (pp. 23–38). Burlington, VT: Ashgate Publishing.

Fürst, D. (2010). *Raumplanung–Herausforderungen des deutschen Institutionensystems [Spatial Planning–Challenges of the German Institutions].* Detmold: Verlag Dorothea Rohn.

Fürst, D. (2014). Koordination und Führung in der Regionalplanung [Coordination and Leadership in Regional Planning]. *Raumforschung Raumordnung, 72*, 451–462. http://dx.doi.org/10.1007/s13147-014-0311-x

Fürst, D., Klinger, W., Knieling, J., Mönnecke, M, & Zeck, H. (1990). Regionalverbände im Vergleich: Entwicklungssteuerung in Verdichtungsräumen [Comparing Regional Planning Organizations: Steering Development Patterns in Urban Areas]. In J.J.Hesse, & A. Benz (Eds.), *Schriften zur kommunalen Wissenschaft und Praxis.* Baden-Baden: Nomos Verlagsgesellschaft.

G–I

Gale, D.E. (1992). Eight State-Sponsored Growth Management Programs: A Comparative Analysis. *Journal of the American Planning Association, 58*(4), 425–439. https://doi.org/10.1080/01944369208975827

G-Germany

G-BauGB-*Bau Gesetzbuch [Federal Zoning Code].* Published by the Federal Ministry of Justice and Consumer Protection. Retrieved May 31, 2019, from https://www.gesetze-im-internet.de/bbaug/

G-BVWP 2030 (2017), *Bundesverkehrswegeplan 2030 [Federal Transportation Plan 2030].* Published by the Federal Ministry of Transport and Digital Infrastructure. Retrieved June 18, 2018, from http://www.bmvi.de/DE/Themen/Mobilitaet/

Infrastrukturplanung-Investitionen/Bundesverkehrswegeplan-2030/bundesverkehrswegeplan-2030.html

G-FStrG-*Bundesfernstraßengesetz [Law on Federal Highways]*. Published by the Federal Ministry of Justice and Consumer Protection. Retrieved November 1, 2020, from https://www.gesetze-im-internet.de/fstrg/index.html#BJNR009030953BJNE002310305

G-Gesetz zur Förderung (22. July 2011). *Gesetz zur Förderung des Klimaschutzes bei der Entwicklung von Städten und Gemeinden [Law to Foster Climate Actions During the Development of Cities and Local Municipalities]*. Published in Bundesgesetzblatt Teil I–2011-Nr. 39 on July 29, 2011. Retrieved October 29, 2019, from http://www.bgbl.de/xaver/bgbl/start.xav?startbk=Bundesanzeiger_BGBl&jumpTo=bgbl111s1509.pdf

GG-*Grundgesetz für die Bundesrepublik Deutschland* [*Constitution of the German Federal Republic 1949/2019]*. Published by the Federal Ministry of Justice and Consumer Protection. Retrieved May 31, 2019, form https://www.gesetze-im-internet.de/gg/BJNR000010949.html

G-GVFG-*Gesetz über Finanzhilfen des Bundes zur Verbesserung der Verkehrsverhältnisse der Gemeinden (Gemeindeverkehrsfinanzierungsgesetz-GVFG) [Law on Federal Program to Support Local Transportation Networks]*. Published by the Federal Ministry of Justice and Consumer Protection. Retrieved April 23, 2020, from https://www.gesetze-im-internet.de/gvfg/index.html#BJNR002390971BJNE000210126

G-Klimaschutz (2018a). *Nationale Klimaschutzinitiative [National Climate Mitigation Program]*. Published by the Federal Ministry of the Environment, Nature Conservation and Nuclear Safety. Retrieved March 27, 2020, from https://www.klimaschutz.de/die-nationale-klimaschutzinitiative

G-Klimaschutz (2018b). *Allgemeine Informationen. Zahlen und Fakten, [General Information–Data about the Program]*. Published by the Federal Ministry of the Environment, Nature Conservation and Nuclear Safety. Retrieved March 27, 2020, from https://www.klimaschutz.de/zahlen-und-fakten

G-Klimaschutzplan 2050 (2016). *Klimaschutzplan 2050- Klimaschutzpolitische Grundsätze und Ziele der Bundesregierung [Climate Mitigation Policy Principles and Requirements of the Federal Government]*. Published by the Federal Ministry of the Environment, Nature Conservation and Nuclear Safety. Retrieved June 13, 2018, from https://www.bmu.de/fileadmin/Daten_BMU/Download_PDF/Klimaschutz/klimaschutzplan_2050_bf.pdf

G-Klimaschutz in Zahlen (2017). *Klimaschutz in Zahlen Fakten, Trends und Impulse deutscher Klimapolitik*. Published by the Federal Ministry of the Environment, Nature Conservation and Nuclear Safety. Retrieved June 13, 2018, from https://www.bmu.de/fileadmin/Daten_BMU/Pools/Broschueren/klimaschutz_in_zahlen_2017_bf.pdf

G-ÖPNV (2020). *Heute fahr' ich Öffis. Bundesmittel für öffentlichen Nahverkehr werden massiv aufgestockt [I Take Public Transit Campaign–Planned Increases of Federal Funding for Public Transit]*. Published by the Federal Ministry of Transport and Digital Infrastructure. Retrieved April 23, 2020, from https://www.bmvi.de/SharedDocs/DE/Artikel/K/bundesmittel-oepnv.html

G-PBefG-*Personenbeförderungsgesetz [Law on Transportation Services]*. Published by the Federal Ministry of Justice and Consumer Protection. Retrieved April 25, 2020, from https://www.gesetze-im-internet.de/pbefg/index.html#BJNR002410961BJNE002308305

G-RegG-*Gesetz zur Regionalisierung des öffentlichen Personennahverkehrs [Law on Regional Organization of Public Transit].* § 5 Finanzierung und Verteilung [§5 Financing and *Apportionments].* Published by the Federal Ministry of Justice and Consumer Protection. Retrieved April 23, 2020, from http://www.gesetze-im-internet.de/regg/__5.html

G-ROB (2011). *Raumordnungsbericht [Federal Spatial Monitoring Report].* Published by BBSR [Federal Office for Building and Regional Planning]. Retrieved March 15, 2018, from https://www.bbsr.bund.de/BBSR/DE/veroeffentlichungen/sonder-veroeffentlichungen/2012/DL_ROB2011.pdf;jsessionid=B0E918D4E9E0968D-2A497C489A39497F.live21304?__blob=publicationFile&v=1

G-ROG (2017). *Raumordnungsgesetz [Federal Spatial Planning Law].* Published by the Federal Ministry of Justice and Consumer Protection. Retrieved July 6, 2018, from https://dejure.org/gesetze/ROG

G-ROV-*Raumordnungsverordnung [Regulations for Spatial Planning].* Published by the Federal Ministry of Justice and Consumer Protection. Retrieved May 8, 2020, from, http://www.gesetze-im-internet.de/rov/

G-VwVfG-*Verwaltungsverfahrensgesetz [Federal Administrative and Procedural Law of Germany].* Published by the Federal Ministry of Justice and Consumer Protection. Retrieved July 15, 2019, from https://www.gesetze-im-internet.de/vwvfg/BJNR012530976.html

Geertz, C. (1992). Kulturbegriff und Menschenbild. In R. Habermas, R., & M. Minkmar (Eds.), *Das Schwein des Häuptlings–Sechs Aufsätze zur historischen Anthropologie* (pp. 56–82). Berlin: Wagenbach.

Geertz, C. (1994). Thick Descriptions–Towards an Interpretive Theory of Culture. In M. Martin, & L.C. McIntyre (Eds.), *Readings in the Philosophy of Social Science* (pp. 213–232). Cambridge, MA: MIT Press.

Gerring, J. (2004). What Is a Case Study and What Is It Good for? *American Political Science Review, 98*(2), 341–454.

Gillard, R., Gouldosn, A., Paavola, J., & Van Alstine, J. (2017). Can National Policy Blockages Accelerate the Development of Polycentric Governance? Evidence from Climate Change Policy in the United Kingdom. *Global Environmental Change, 45*, 174–182. https://doi.org/10.1016/j.gloenvcha.2017.06.003

Glaeser, B., & Strauss, A. (1967). *The Discovery of Grounded Theory-Strategies for Qualitative Research.* New York: Aldine De Gruyter.

Gläser, J., & Laudel, G. (2010). *Experteninterviews und qualitative Inhaltsanalyse [Expert Interviews and Qualitative Interview Analysis]* (4th ed.). Wiesbaden: VS Verlag.

GoC-Government of Canada

GoC (2016a). *Pan-Canadian Framework on Clean Growth and Climate Change: [Canada's plan to address climate change and grow the economy].* Published by the Ministry for Environment and Climate Change. Retrieved May 17, 2018, from http://publications.gc.ca/collections/collection_2017/eccc/En4-294-2016-eng.pdf

GoC (2016b). *Federal Actions for a Clean Growth Economy. [Delivering on the Pan-Canadian Framework on Clean Growth and Climate Change].* Retrieved May 17, 2018, from https://www.canada.ca/content/ dam/themes/environment/documents/weather1/20170119-en.pdf

Gonzales, Richard (March 15, 2018). *FEMA Drops 'Climate Change' From Its Strategic Plan. National Public Radio.* Retrieved on May 14, 2018 from https://www.npr.org/sections/thetwo-way/2018/03/15/594140026/fema-drops-climate-change-from-its-strategic-plan

Goppel, K. (2005) Landesplanung [State Planning]. In ARL-Akademie für Raumforschung und Landesplanung (Ed.), *Handwörterbuch der Raumplanung [Dictionary of Spatial Planning]* (pp. 561–573). Hannover: VSB Verlagsservice Braunschweig.

Gordon, D.J. (2013). Between Local Innovation and Global Impact: Cities, Networks, and the Governance of Climate Change. *Canadian Foreign Policy Journal, 19*(3), 288–307. http://dx.doi.org/10.1080/11926422.2013.844186

Gregoire, C. (2009). *Executive Order 09-05–Washington's Leadership on Climate Change.* Retrieved May 15, 2018, from http://governor.wa.gov/sites/default/files/exe_order/eo_09-05.pdf

Gualini, E. & Gross, S. (2019). Introduction–Actors, Policies and Processes in the Construction of Metropolitan Space: Conceptual and Analytical Differences. In S. Gross, E. Gualini, & L. Ye (Eds.), *Constructing Metropolitan Space–Actors, Policies and Processes in World Metropolises* (pp. 3–28). New York: Routledge.

Gullestrup, H. (2006). *Cultural Analysis, Towards Cross-Cultural Understanding.* Aalborg: University Press.

Gullestrup, H. (2009). Theoretical Reflections on Common European (Planning-) Cultures. In J. Knieling, & F. Othengrafen (Eds.), *Planning Cultures in Europe. Decoding Cultural Phenomena in Urban and Regional Planning* (pp. 3–22). Burlington: Ashgate Publishing.

Guth, D., Holz-Rau, C., Maciolek, M., & Scheiner, J. (2010). Beschäftigungssuburbanisierung, Siedlungsstruktur und Berufspendelverkehr: Ergebnisse für deutsche Agglomerationsräume 1999–2007 [Suburban Employment Centers, Spatial Structure and Commuting Patterns in German Metropolitan Regions, 1999–2007]. *Raumforschung Raumordnung, 68*, 283–295.

Hamel, P. (2017). Shortcomings and Promises of Governing City-Regions in the Canadian Federal Context. The Example of Montreal. In R. Keil, P. Hamel, J.-A. Boudreau, & S. Kipfer (Eds.), *Governing Cities through Regions. Canadian and European Perspectives* (pp. 173–196). Waterloo: Wilfrid Laurier University Press.

Hamilton, M., & Lubell, M. (2017). Collaborative Governance of Climate Change Adaptation Across Spatial and Institutional Scales. *Policy Studies Journal, 46*(2), 222–247. https://doi.org/10.1111/psj.12224

Handy, S. (1996). Methodologies of Exploring the Link between Urban form and Travel Behavior. *Transportation Research Part D: Transport and Environment, 1*(2), 151–165. https://doi.org/10.1016/S1361-9209(96)00010-7

Handy, S. (2017). Thoughts on the Meaning of Mark Stevens's Meta-Analysis. *Journal of the American Planning Association, 83*(1), 26–28.

Hardinghaus, M. (2004). *Zur amerikanischen Entwicklung der Stadt. Ein Beitrag zur Kulturgenese des City-Suburb Phänomens unter besonderer Berücksichtigung protestantisch-calvinistischer Leitbilder. [About the American Development of the City. A Contribution to the Cultural Evolution of the City-Suburb Phenomenon with a Particular Focus on Protestant-Calvinistic Values].* Europäischer Verlag der Wissenschaft: Peter Lang.

Harris, M. (1998). *The Theory of Culture in Postmodern Times.* Walnut Creek, Lanham, New York, Oxford: AltaMira Press.

Harrison, K. (2007). The Road Not Taken: Climate Change Policy in Canada and the United States. *Global Environmental Politics,* 7(4), 92–117.

Haughton, G., Allmendinger, P., Counsell, D., & Vigar, G. (2010). *The New Spatial Planning. Territorial Management with Soft Spaces and Fuzzy Boundaries.* Oxon: Routledge.Heinelt, H., & Lamping, W. (2015a). *Wissen und Entscheiden.*

Lokale Strategien gegen den Klimawandel in Frankfurt am Main, München und Stuttgart [Knowledge and Decisions. Local Strategies Against Climate Change in Frankfurt Main, Munich and Suttgart]. Frankfurt am Main: Campus Verlag GmbH.

Heinelt, H. & Lamping, W. (2015b). The Development of Local Knowledge Orders: A Conceptual Framework to Explain Differences in Climate Policy at the Local Level. *Urban Research & Practice, 8*(3), 283–302. http://dx.doi.org/10.1080/17535069.2015.1051378

Heinen, D. (2018a). Comparing Planning Systems–A Framework to Analyze How Land-Use and Spatial Activities Are Governed. In J. Knieling (Ed.), *Wege zur großen Transformation. Herausforderungen für eine nachhaltige Stadt- und Regionalentwicklung [Pathways to Transitions–Challenges for Sustainable Urban and Regional Development]* (pp. 155–169). Ahrensburg: Oekam.

Heinen, D. (2018b). *The Role of Regional Planning for Spatial Climate Mitigation Actions. Regional Governance of Land Use and Transportation in the US, Canada, and Germany. 54th ISOCARP Congress 2018- Cool planning: Changing climate and our urban future–Proceedings* (pp. 161–173). Retrieved April 3, 2019, from https://isocarp.org/app/uploads/2018/10/ISOCARP_54th-Congress_Proceedings.pdf

Heinen, D. (2020). Growth Management for Low-Carbon Development Patterns–Leverages in State Planning Enabling Legislation. *Urban Research & Practice, 15*(1), 71–93. http://dx.doi.org/10.1080/17535069.2020.1722736

Heinen, D., Arlati, A., & Knieling, J. (2021). Five Dimensions of Climate Governance Arrangements–Comparing Perspectives on Polycentric and Multi-Level Climate Governance to Inform Empirical Research, Resubmitted to *Environmental Policy and Governance* in October 2020.

Heinen & Knieling (forthcoming). A Comparative Perspective on Metropolitan Planning in Germany, the US, and Canada, submitted in *Journal of Planning Education and Research*.

Heinz, W. (2000). Interkommunale Kooperation in Stadtregionen–ein internationaler Vergleich [Cooperation between Communities in City Regions–An International Comparison]. In W. Heinz (Ed.), *Stadt & Region–Kooperation oder Koordination? Ein internationaler Vergleich [City & Region–Cooperation or Coordination? – An International Comparison]* (pp. 31–60). Stuttgart, Berlin, Köln: Kolhammer–Dt. Gemeindeverlag.

Helmholz, A. (2013). *Raumplanung und Planungskultur in Deutschland und Österreich Vergleichsanalyse der Großprojekte „Stuttgart 21" und „Hauptbahnhof Wien"*. Institute of Geography at University of Tübingen–Global Studies Working Paper. Retrieved November 10, 2015, from https://publikationen.uni-tuebingen.de/xmlui/bitstream/handle/10900/49905/pdf/GSWP_11_2013_Anouk_Helmholz.pdf?sequence=1&isAllowed=y; June 19, 2016].

Hendler, R. (2005). Raumordnungsrecht [Spatial Planning Law]. In ARL–Akademie für Raumforschung und Landesplanung (Ed.), *Handwörterbuch der Raumplanung [Dictionary of Spatial Planning]* (pp. 877–884). Hannover: VSB Verlagsservice Braunschweig.

Hess, D.B., & Lombardi, P.A. (2005). Governmental Subsidies for Public Transit: History, Current Issues, and Recent Evidence. *Public Works Management & Policy, 10*(2), 138–156. https://doi.org/10.1177/1087724X05284965

Hirt, S. (2007). The Devil Is in the Definition. Contrasting American and German Approaches to Zoning. *Journal of the American Planning Association, 73*(4), 436–450.

Hirt, S. (2012). Mixed Use by Default: How the Europeans (Don't) Zone. *Journal of Planning Literature, 27*(4), 375–393.

Hirt, S. (2013). Home, Sweet Home: American Residential Zoning in Comparative Perspective. *Journal of Planning Education and Research, 33*(3), 292–309.

Hodge, G., Hall, H.M., & Robinson, I.M. (2017). *Planning Canadian Regions* (2nd ed.). Vancouver: UBC Press.

Höhnberg, U. (1998). Raumordnungsverfahren [Spatial Compatibility Assessment]. In E.-H. Ritter & K. Wolf (Eds.), *Methoden und Instrumente räumlicher Planung. Handbuch [Methods and Instruments in Spatial Planning - A Toolkit]* (pp. 222–237). Hannover: Verlag der Akademie für Raumforschung und Landesplanung.

Höhnberg, U. (2005). Instrumente zur Verwirklichung von Raumordnung und Landesplanung. In ARL-Akademie für Raumforschung und Landesplanung (Ed.), *Handwörterbuch der Raumplanung [Dictionary of Spatial Planning]* (pp. 483–488). Hannover: VSB Verlagsservice Braunschweig.

Homsy, G.C. (2018). Size, Sustainability, and Urban Climate Planning in a Multilevel Governance Framework. In S. Hughes et al. (Eds.), *Climate Change in Cities* (pp. 19–38). Springer International Publishing: The Urban Book Series.

Homsy, G.C., & Warner M.E. (2015). Cities and Sustainability: Polycentric Action and Multilevel Governance. *Urban Affairs Review, 51*(1), 46–73.

Hood, C. (1986). *The Tools of Government.* Chatham, GA: Chatham House Publishers.

Hooghe, L., & Marks, G. (2001). *Types of Multi-Level Governance.* Retrieved from http://eiop.or.at/eiop/texte/2001-011.htm

Hooghe, L., & Marks, G. (2003). Unraveling the Central State, But How? Types of Multilevel Governance. *The American Political Science Review, 97*(2), 233–243.

Hörning, K.H. (2004). Soziale Praxis zwischen Beharrung und Neuschöpfung. Ein Erkenntnis- und Theorieproblem. In K.H. Hörning, & J. Reuter (Eds.), *Doing Culture. Neue Positionen zum Verhältnis von Kultur und sozialer Praxis* (pp. 19–39). Bielefeld: Transcript Verlag.

Howlett, M. (2007). What is a Policy Instrument? Tools, Mixes and Implementation Styles. In P. Eliadis, M.M. Hill and M. Howlett (Eds.), *Designing Government. From Instruments to Governance* (pp. 31–50). Montreal & Kingston, London, Ithaca, NY: McGill Queen's University Press.

Howlett, M. (2009). Governance Modes, Policy Regimes and Operational Plans. A Multi Level Nested Model. *Policy Science 42*, 73–89. http://dx.doi.org/10.1007/s11077-009-9079-1.

Hughes, S. (2017). The Politics of Urban Climate Change Policy: Toward a Research Agenda. *Urban Affairs Review, 53(2), 362–380.* https://doi.org/10.1177/1078087416649756

ILS (2018). *International vergleichende Stadtforschung. Eine Handreichung für die wissenschaftliche Praxis im ILS [International Comparative Urban Research-A Report for the Academic Praxis at the Research Institute for Regional and Urban Development].* Dortmund: ILS–Institut für Landes- und Stadtentwicklungsforschung. Retrieved Mai 8, 2018, from https://www.ils-forschung.de/files_publikationen/pdfs/handreichung_intern_vergleichende_stadtforschung.pdf

Inslee, J. (2014) *Executive Order 14-04–Washington Carbon Pollution Reduction and Clean Energy Action.* Retrieved May 15, 2018, from https://www.governor.wa.gov/sites/default/files/exe_order/eo_14-04.pdf

IPCC (2014). *The Intergovernmental Panel on Climate Change. Fifth Assessment Report. Climate Change 2014: Mitigation of Climate Change.* Retrieved March 15, 2015, from http://www.ipcc.ch/report/ar5/wg3/

J–L

Jänicke, M. (2017). The Multi-Level System of Global Climate Governance-the Model and Its Current State. *Environmental Policy and Governance, 27*(2), 108–121. https://doi.org/10.1002/eet.1747

Jänicke, M., & Quitzow, R. (2017). Multi-Level Reinforcement in European Climate and Energy Governance: Mobilizing Economic Interests at the Sub-National Levels. *Environmental Policy and Governance, 27*(2), 122–136. https://doi.org/10.1002/eet.1748

Jessen, J., & Roost, F. (2015). Editorial: Refitting Suburbia–Umbau der Siedlungstrukturen des 20. Jahrhunderts [Editorial–Refitting Suburbia–Modification of Development Patterns of the 20th Century]. In J. Jessen & F. Roost (Eds.), *Refitting Suburbia. Erneuerung der Stadt des 20. Jahrhunderts in Deutschland und den USA [Refitting suburbia–Revitalization of the City of the 20th Century in Germany and the United States]* (pp. 07–21). Berlin: JOVIS Verlag.

Jordan, A., Huitema, D., Hildén, M., van Asselt, H., Rayner, T.J., Schoenefeld, J.J., Boasson, E.L. (2015). Emergence of Polycentric Climate Governance and Its Future Prospects. *Nature Climate Change, 5*, 977–982. https://doi.org/10.1038/nclimate2725

Jordan, A., Huitema, D., Schoenefeld, J., Van Asselt, H., & Forster, J. (2018a). Governing Climate Change Polycentrically–Setting the Scene. In A. Jordan, D. Huitema, H.van Hasselt & J. Forster (Eds.*), Governing Climate Change. Polycentricity in Action?* (pp. 3–26). New York: Cambridge University Press. http://dx.doi.org/10.1017/9781108284646

Jordan, A., Huitema, D., Van Asselt, H., & Forster, J. (2018b). Governing Climate Change. The Promise and Limits of Polycentric Governance. In A. Jordan, D. Huitema, H. van Hasselt & J. Forster (Eds.), *Governing Climate Change. Polycentricity in Action*? (pp. 359–383). New York: Cambridge University Press. https://doi.org/10.1017/9781108284646

Jordan, A., van Asselt, H., Berkhout, F., Huitema, D., & Rayner, T. (2012). Understanding the Paradoxes of Multilevel Governing: Climate Change Policy in the European Union. *Global Environmental Politics, 12*(2), 43–66. https://doi.org/10.1162/GLEP_a_00108

Kaiser, J.K., & Godschalk, D.R. (1995). Twentieth Century Land Use Planning. Reprinted In M. Stein (Ed.), *Classic Readings in Urban Planning* (2nd ed., pp. 124–146). New York: Planners Press.

Kantor, P. (2013). The Two Faces of American Urban Policy. *Urban Affairs Review, 49*(6), 821–850.

Kayden, J. (2001). National Land-Use Planning and Regulation in the United States: Understanding Its Fundamental Importance. In R. Alterman (Ed.), *National-Level Planning in Democratic Countries. An International Comparison of City and Regional-Policy Making* (pp. 43–64). Liverpool: Liverpool University Press.

KC-King County

KC-BLR (2014). *Buildable Land Report.* Retrieved July 17, 2019, from https://www.kingcounty.gov/~/media/depts/executive/performance-strategy-budget/regional-planning/buildable-lands-report/king-county-buildable-lands-report-2014.ashx?la=en

KC-Comp Plan (2012, Amended 2013). *Comprehensive Plan.* Retrieved May 31, 2019, from https://www.kingcounty.gov/depts/executive/performance-strategy-budget/regional-planning/king-county-comprehensive-plan/2012Adopted.aspx

KC-CPP (2012). *King County Countywide Planning Policies.* With amendments ratified by June 25, 2016. Retrieved May 30, 2020, from https://www.kingcounty.gov/~/media/depts/executive/performance-strategy-budget/regional-planning/CPPs/2012-CPPsAmended062516withMaps.ashx?la=en

KC-K4C (2020). *King County-Cities Climate Collaboration.* Retrieved June 6, 2020, from https://www.kingcounty.gov/services/environment/climate/actions-strategies/climate-strategies/partnerships-collaborations/k4c.aspx

KC-K4C-Commitment Letters (2016). *Joint Letter of Commitment: Climate Change Actions in King County.* Retrieved June 6, 2020, from https://your.kingcounty.gov/dnrp/library/dnrp-directors-office/climate/2016-K4C-LetterOfCommitments.pdf

KC-Metro Connects (2017). *Metro Connects–Long Range Plan 2016.* Adopted January 2017. Prepared by the Department of Transportation, Metro Transit Division. Retrieved June 15, 2018, from https://drive.google.com/file/d/0B44RYEx3kgpoZUJqbXVScnR4cjg/view

KC-Metro Sustainability Strategy (2014). *Metro Transit Sustainability Plan.* Prepared by the Department of Transportation, Metro Transit Division. Retrieved June 15, 2018, from https://metro.kingcounty.gov/am/reports/2014/metro-sustainability-plan-2014.pdf

KC-SCAP (2015). *Strategic Climate Action Plan.* Retrieved May 8, 2019, from https://your.kingcounty.gov/dnrp/climate/documents/2015_King_County_SCAP-Full_Plan.pdf

KC-Strategic Plan (2015). *Metro Strategic Plan for Public Transportation 2011–2012.* Update 2015. Adopted April 2016. Prepared by the Department of Transportation, Metro Transit Division. Retrieved June 15, 2018, fromhttp://metro.kingcounty.gov/planning/pdf/2011-21/2015/metro-strategic-plan-042816.pdf

Keil, R., & Addie, J.-P. (2017). Internalized Globalization and Regional Governance in the Toronto Region. In R. Keil, P. Hamel, J.-A. Boudreau, S. Kipfer (Eds.), *Governing Cities through Regions. Canadian and European Perspectives* (pp. 101–120). Waterloo: Wilfrid Laurier University Press.

Keil, R., Hamel, P., Boudreau, J.-A., & Kipfer, S. (Eds.) (2017). *Governing Cities through Regions. Canadian and European Perspectives.* Waterloo: Wilfrid Laurier University Press.

Kilper, H. (2010). Governance und die soziale Konstruktion von Räumen. Eine Einführung. In H. Kilper (Ed.), *Governance und Raum* (pp. 9–24). Baden-Baden: Nomos.

Kivimaa, P., Hilden, M., Huitema, D., Jordan, A., & Newig, J. (2015). *Experiments in Climate Governance e Lessons from a Systematic Review of Case Studies in Transition Research.* SPRU Working Paper Series, ISSN 2057e6668. Retrieved October 18, 2019, from http://sro.sussex.ac.uk/id/eprint/59245/1/2015_36_SWPS_Kivimaa_et_al.pdf

Knaap, G.-J., Avin, U., & Fang, L. (2017). Driving and Compact Growth: A Careful Look in the Rearview Mirror. *Journal of the American Planning Association, 83*(1), 32–35. http://dx.doi.org/10.1080/01944363.2017.1251276

Knieling, J., & Klindworth, K. (2016). Climate Adaptation Governance in Cities and Regions between Hierarchical Steering and Network Cooperation: Fndings from Theoretical Considerations and International Practice. In J. Knieling (Ed.), *Climate Adaptation Governance in Cities and Regions. Theoretical Fundamentals and Empirical Evidence* (pp. 405–419). London: Wiley-Blackwell.

Knieling, J., & Leal Filho, W. (Eds., 2009). *Climate Change Governance: Series Climate Change Management.* Heidelberg: Springer.

Knieling, J., & Othengrafen, F. (2009). En Route to a Theoretical Model for Comparative Research on Planning Cultures. In J. Knieling, & F. Othengrafen (Eds.), *Planning Cultures in Europe. Decoding Cultural Phenomena in Urban and Regional Planning* (pp. 39–62). Burlington: Ashgate Publishing.

Krawchenko, T. (2012). *Institutional Solutions to Jurisdictional Fragmentation: The Implications of Regional Special Purpose Bodies for How City-Regions are Governed in Canada.* Ontario: Dissertation, Carleton University Ottawa.

Kreis Böblingen (2013). *Integriertes Klimaschutzkonzept für den Kreis Böblingen–Energie und Verkehr Endbericht. Band I–Kreiskonzept. [Integrated climate action plan for Böblingen county–energy and transportation final report–Book 1–county plan.]* Retrieved February 5, 2019, from https://www.ifeu.de/wp-content/uploads/KSK_LK_BB_Band_2_Endbericht_Steckbriefe_Hauptteil_final.pdf

Kuzel, A. (1999). Sampling in Qualitative Inquiry. In B. Craftree, & W. Miller (1999), *Doing Qualitative Research* (2nd ed., pp. 33–45). Thousand Oaks, CA: SAGE Publications Inc.

Landauer, M., Juhola, S., & Klein, J. (2018). The Role of Scale in Integrating Climate Change Adaptation and Mitigation in Cities. *Journal of Environmental Planning and Management, 62*(5), 741–765. https://doi.org/10.1080/09640568.2018.1430022

Lloyd, S. (2019). *Seattle's Long History of Transit Funding. Paying for Transit Has Always Been Complicated.* Published on Curbed Seattle Website. Retrieved on November 05, 2020, from https://seattle.curbed.com/2019/10/29/20938796/seattle-king-county-transit-funding

Lodge, M. (2007). Comparative Public Policy. In F. Fischer, & G. Miller (Eds.), *Handbook of Public Policy Analysis. Theory, Politics and Methods* (pp. 273–288). Boca Raton, FL: Taylor & Francis Group–CRC Press.

Lynch, K. (1981). *A Theory of Good City form.* Cambridge, MA and London: MIT Press.

M–O

Manville, M. (2017). Travel and the Built Environment: Time for Change. *Journal of the American Planning Association, 83*(1), 29–32. http://dx.doi.org/10.1080/01944363.2016.1249508

Marquardt, J. (2017). Conceptualizing Power in Multi-Level Climate Governance. *Journal of Cleaner Production, 154*, 167–175. https://doi.org/10.1016/j.jclepro.2017.03.176

Marshall, G.R. (2015). *Polycentricity and Adaptive Governance.* Working Paper presented at the 15th Biannual International Conference of the International Association for the Study of the Commons, Edmonton, Canada.

Marzoughi, R., & Vanderburg, W.H. (2010). A Precautionary Approach to City Building: Interpreting the Relationship between Urban Form and Mobility. *Bulletin of Science, Technology & Society, 30*(2), 86–95. https://doi.org/10.1177/0270467610361233

Masterplan 100% Stuttgart (2017). *IBP-Bericht WB 198/2017- Masterplan 100% Klimaschutz der Landeshauptstadt Stuttgart [Climate Action Plan for the City of Stuttgart].* Retrieved May 7, 2019, from https://www.stuttgart.de/img/mdb/item/620298/129654.pdf

Mayntz, R. (2008). Von der Steuerungstheorie zu Global Governance [From Steering Theories to Global Governance]. In G.F. Schuppert, & M. Zürn (Eds.),

Governance in einer sich wandelnden Welt [Governance in a Changing World] (pp. 43–60). Wiesbaden: VS Verlag für Sozialwissenschaften.

Mayntz, R., & Scharpf, F. (1995). Steuerung und Selbstorganisation in staatsnahen Sektoren. In R. Mayntz, & F. Scharpf (Eds). *Gesellschaftliche Selbstregelung und politische Steuerung* (pp. 9–38). Frankfurt am Main: Campus Verlag.

Mayntz, R., & Schneider, V. (1995). Die Entwicklung technischer Infrastruktursysteme zwischen Steuerung und Selbstorganisation. In R. Mayntz, & F. Scharpf (Eds.), *Gesellschaftliche Selbstregelung und politische Steuerung* (pp. 9–38). Frankfurt am Main: Campus Verlag.

McCarney, P. (2013). Cities and Governance: Coming to Terms with Climate Challenges. In J. Knieling, & W. Leal Filho (Eds.), *Climate Change Governance: Series Climate Change Management* (pp. 86–105). Heidelberg: Springer.

McDowell, B. (1999). *Improving Regional Transportation Decisions. MPOs and Certification*. Washington, D.C.: Brookings Institute.

Meadowcroft, J. (2009). *Climate Change Governance. Policy Research Working Paper 4941*. Washington, D.C.: World Bank. http://www-wds.worldbank.org/external/default/WDSContentServer/WDSP/IB/2009/05/19/000158349_20090519144015/Rendered/PDF/WPS4941.pdf

Meck, S. (2006). State Enabling Legislation. In APA-American Planning Association (Ed.), *Planning and Urban Design Standards* (p. 589). Hoboken, NJ: John Wiley & Sons.

Meuser, M., & Nagel, U. (1991). Experteninterviews–vielfach erprobt, wenig bedacht [Expert Interviews–Often Used, Rarely Examined]. In D. Garz, & K. Kraimer (Eds.), *Qualitativ-empirische Sozialforschung Konzepte, Methoden, Analysen [qualitative empirical research–concepts, methods and analysis]* (pp. 441–471). Opladen: Westdeutscher Verlage.

Miller, B. (2017). Sustainability Fix Meets Growth Machine. Attempting to Govern the Calgary Metropolitan Region. In R. Keil, P. Hamel, J.-A. Boudreau, & S. Kipfer (Eds.), *Governing Cities through Regions. Canadian and European Perspectives* (pp. 213–238). Waterloo: Wilfrid Laurier University Press.Mills, G. (2007). Cities as Agents of Global Change. *International Journal of Climatology 27*, 1859–1857.

Mills, G. (2006). Progress Toward Sustainable Settlements: A Role for Urban Climatology. *Theoretical and Applied Climatology, 84*, 69–76. http://dx.doi.org/10.1997/s00704-005-0145-0

MPO database (N.Y.). *Resource Hub-Metropolitan Planning Organizations (MPO) Database*. Prepared by the Federal Highway Administration of the United States–Transportation Planning Capacity Building Division. Retrieved October 4, 2015, from https://www.planning.dot.gov/MPO/

Mullin, J.R. (1976). American Perception of German City Planning at the Turn of the Century. *Landscape Architecture and Regional Planning Faculty Publication Series*, Paper 35.

MV-Metro Vancouver

MV-Board Strategy (2015–2018). *Board Strategic Plan 2015 to 2018*. Retrieved May 25, 2018, from http://www.metrovancouver.org/about/aboutuspublications/BoardStrategicPlan2015-2018.pdf

MV-CCAP (2010). *Corporate Climate Action Plan*. Retrieved May 25, 2018 from http://www.metrovancouver.org/services/air-quality/AirQualityPublications/CorporateClimateActionPlan.pdf

MV-Climate 2050-DP (2018). *Climate 2050 Discussion Paper*. Presented in April 2018. Retrieved May 25, 2018, from http://www.metrovancouver.org/

services/air-quality/AirQualityPublications/AQ_C2050-DiscussionPaper.pdf#search=%22Integrated%20climate%22

MV-COQ RCS. (September 20, 2013). *Consideration of the City of Coquitlam's Regional Context Statement. Memo to the Metro Vancouver Regional Planning and Agricultural Committee.* Retrieved February 02, 2020, from http://www.metrovancouver.org/services/regional-planning/RegionalContextStatements/Coquitlam_acceptance_report_to_GVRD_Board_October_11_2013.pdf

MV-FGT (2016). *Greater Vancouver Regional District–Intergovernment and Finance Committee–Federal Gas Tax Task Force–Regular Meeting on Friday, April 29, 2016 1:30 p.m.* Retrieved May 28, 2018, from http://www.metrovancouver.org/boards/FederalGasTax/FGT_Apr_29_2016_Agenda.pdf#search=%22Greater%20Vancouver%20Regional%20FUnd%22

MV-LRSP (1996). *Livable Region Strategic Plan.* Adopted by the Greater Vancouver Regional District Board of Directors January 26, 1996. Retrieved March 11, 2020, from http://www.metrovancouver.org/services/regional-planning/PlanningPublications/LRSP.pdf

MV-RGS (2011). *Regional Growth Strategy–Bylaw No. 1136, 2010. Metro Vancouver 2040. Shaping Our Future. Adopted by the Greater Vancouver Regional District Board on July 29, 2011. Updated to July 28, 2017.* Retrieved May 28, 2018, from http://www.metrovancouver.org/services/regional-planning/PlanningPublications/RGSAdoptedbyGVRDBoard.pdf

MV-RLUD (2020). *Regional Land Use Designation Map.* Retrieved October 07, 2020, from http://www.metrovancouver.org/services/regional-planning/PlanningPublications/Map2.pdf

Nadin, V., & Stead, D. (2008). European Spatial Planning Systems, Social Models and Learning. *disP, 44*(1), 35–47.

Nationale Klimaschutzinitiative (2015). *Richtlinie zur Förderung von Klimaschutzprojekten in sozialen, kulturellen und öffentlichen Einrichtungen im Rahmen der Nationalen Klimaschutzinitiative vom 22.09.2015. [Guidelines for Funding of Climate Mitigation Projects in Social, Cultural and Public Organizations within the Context of the Federal Program to Fund Climate Mitigation Actions].* Retrieved April 18, 2016, from http://www.klimaschutz.de/sites/default/files/page/downloads/mb_klimaschutzkonzepte_0.pdf

NCA (2014). *National Climate Assessment for the United States conducted under the Obama Administration.* Hosted by globalchange.gov under the Trump Administration. Retrieved on November 1, 2020, from https://nca2014.globalchange.gov/highlights/overview/overview

Nelson, A.C. (2017). Compact Development Reduces VMT: Evidence and Application for Planners—Comment on 'Does Compact Development Make People Drive Less?' *Journal of the American Planning Association, 83*(1), 36–41. http://dx.doi.org/10.1080/01944363.2016.1246378

Nelson, A.C., Burby, R.J., Feser, E., Dawkins, C.J. Malizia, E.E., & Quercia, R. (2004). Urban Containment and Central-City Revitalization. *Journal of the American Planning Association, 70*(4), 411–425. http://dx.doi.org/10.1080/01944360408976391

Newig, J., & Fritsch, O. (2009). Environmental Governance: Participatory, Multi-Level–and Effective? *Environmental Policy and Governance, 19*, 197–214. https://doi.org/10.1002/eet.509

Newman, P. (1999). Sustainability and Cities: Extending the Metabolism Model. *Landscape and Urban Planning, 44*, 219–226. As quoted in Mills, 2006.

Newman, P., & Thornley, A. (1996). *Urban Planning in Europe–International Competition, National Systems and Planning Projects*. London: Routledge.

Oberlander, P., & Smith, P. (1993). Governing Metropolitan Vancouver: Regional Intergovernmental Relations in British Columbia. In D. N. Rothblatt, & A. Sancton (Eds.), *Metropolitan Governance revisited. American/ Canadian Intergovernmental Perspectives* (pp. 329–373). Berkeley, CA: Institute of Governmental Studies Press.

OECD (2017). *The Governance of Land Use in OECD Countries: Policies Analysis and Recommendations*. Paris: OECD Publishing. Retrieved March 26, 2018, from https://www.keepeek.com//Digital-Asset-Management/oecd/urban-rural-and-regional-development/the-governance-of-land-use-in-oecd-countries_9789264268609-en#page4

Orfield, M., & Luce, F.T. (2009). Governing American Metropolitan Areas–Spatial Policy and Regional Governance. In C.L. Ross (Ed.), *Megaregions–Planning for Global Competitiveness* (pp. 250–279). Washington, D.C., Coveland, and London: Island Press.

Orum, M., Feagin, J., & Sjoberg, G. (1991). The Nature of the Case Study. In M. Orum, J. Feagin, & G. Sjoberg (Eds.), *A Case for the Case Study* (pp. 1–23). Chapel Hill and London: The University of North Carolina Press.

Ostrom, E. (1990). *Governing the Commons: The Evolution of Institutions for Collective Action*. Cambridge: Cambridge University Press.

Ostrom, E. (2010a). Polycentric Systems for Coping with Collective Action and Global Environmental Change. *Global Environmental Change, 20*, 550–557.

Ostrom, E. (2010b). Beyond Markets and States: Polycentric Governance of Complex Economic systems. *American Economic Review, 100*(3), 641–672. Retrieved from www.jstor.org/stable/27871226

Ostrom, E. (2011). Background on the Institutional Analysis and Development Framework. *Policy Studies Journal, 38*(1), 7–27.

Ostrom, V., Tiebout, C.M., & Warren, R. (1961). The Organization of Government in Metropolitan Areas: A Theoretical Inquiry. *American Political Science Review, 55*, 831–842.

P–R

Paavola, J. (2016). Multi-Level Environmental Governance: Exploring the Economic Explanations. *Environmental Policy and Governance, 26*(3), 143–154. https://doi.org/10.1002/eet.1698

Patton, M. (1987) *How to Use Qualitative Methods in Evaluation*. Newbury Park, CA: Sage.

PCLD-Mandelker, D., Brown, C.N., Meck, S., Merriam, D., Salsich, P., Stroud, N., & Tappendorf, J. (2011). *Planning and Control of Land Development: Cases and Materials* (8th ed.). Durham: Carolina Academic Press - Lexis Nexis.

Peine, F.-J. (1998). Interessenermittlung und Interessenberücksichtigung im Planungsprozess [Determining and Considering Interests During the Planning Process]. In E.-H. Ritter, & K. Wolf (Eds.), *Methoden und Instrumente räumlicher Planung. Handbuch [Methods and Instruments of Spatial Planning. A Handbook]* (pp. 169–185). Hannover: Verlag der Akademie für Raumforschung und Landesplanung.

Peters, G. (2007). Conclusion: The Future of Instrument Research. In P. Eliadis, M.M. Hill & M. Howlett (Eds.), *Designing Government. From Instruments to*

Governance (pp. 353–364). Montreal & Kingston, London, Ithaca, NY: McGill Queen's University Press.

Peters, G., & Hoornbeek, J.A. (2007). The Problem of Policy Problems. In P. Eliadis, M.M. Hill & M. Howlett (Eds.), *Designing Government. From Instruments to Governance* (pp. 77–105). Montreal & Kingston, London, Ithaca, NY: McGill Queen's University Press.

Peters, G., & Pierre, J. (2016). *Comparative Governance.* Cambridge, New York, Port Melbourne, Delhi, Singapore: Cambridge University Press.

Phares, D. (2004). Governance or Government in Metro Areas?–Introduction. In Phares, D. (Ed.), *Metropolitan Governance without Metropolitan Government?* (pp. 1–6). Wiltshire: Ashgate.

Pizarro, R. (2009). Urban Form and Climate Change: Towards Appropriate Development Patterns to Mitigate and Adapt to Global Warming. In S. Davoudi, J. Crawford, & A. Mehmood (Eds.), *Planning for Climate Change–Strategies for Mitigation and Adaptation for Spatial Planners* (pp. 33–45). London & Sterling, VA: Earthscan.

Popper, F.J. (1988). Understanding American Land Use Regulation Since 1970. Reprinted In M. Stein (Ed.), *Classic Readings in Urban Planning* (2nd ed., pp. 98–111). New York: Planners Press.

PSCAA Strategic Plan (2014). *Strategic Plan 2014–2020 Clean Healthy Air for Everyone, Everywhere, All the Time.* Prepared by Puget Sound Clean Air Agency. Retrieved May 30, 2018, from https://pscleanair.gov/DocumentCenter/View/445/2014-to-2020-Strategic-Plan-PDF?bidId=

PSRC-Puget Sound Regional Council

PSRC-GHG Strategy (2018). *Appendix L Greenhouse Gas 4-Part Strategy.* Retrieved May 30, 2018, from https://www.psrc.org/sites/default/files/appendix_l_-_greenhouse_gas_4-part_strategy.pdf

PSRC-GTC (2013). *Growing Transit Communities.* https://www.psrc.org/sites/default/files/gtcstrategy.pdf

PSRC-Interlocal Agreement (1993). *Interlocal Agreement for Regional Planning in the Central Puget Sound Area.* Retrieved May 30, 2018, from https://www.psrc.org/sites/default/files/interlocal.pdf

PSRC-Plan Review (2014). *Plan Review Manual–A Resource to Assist with Plan Development and Review–Including Certification.* Retrieved May 30, 2018, from https://www.psrc.org/plan-review-manual

PSRC-Policy (2003). *Appendix A: Puget Sound Regional Council Adopted Policy and Plan Review Process.* Retrieved May 30, 2018, from https://www.psrc.org/sites/default/files/appendix_a.pdf

PSRC-RC Frame (2018). *Regional Centers Framework Update-Adopted March 22, 2018.* Retrieved July 7, 2020, from https://www.psrc.org/sites/default/files/final_regional_centers_framework_march_22_version.pdf

PSRC-Reference Map (2018). *Central Puget Sound Region–Showing Urban Centers and Regional Geographies.* Retrieved on November 1, 2020, from https://www.psrc.org/sites/default/files/psrcregion_0.pdf

PSRC-RTP (2018). *The Regional Transportation Plan 2018.* Retrieved May 30, 2018, from https://indd.adobe.com/view/1af394e0-4e37-4982-9155-a2ee1e221b75

PSRC-UCA (2016). *Regional Centers Framework Update Project. Stakeholder Working Group–June 22nd Meeting–Transit Discussion Follow-up Materials.* Provided by PSRC staff after personal communication.

PSRC-Vision (2009) *Vision 2040–People. Prosperity. Planet.* Retrieved May 30, 2018, from https://www.cascadia.edu/discover/about/sustainability/documents/Vision%202040.pdf

PTIF (2020). *Building Strong Cities through Investments in Public Transit.* Prepared by the Government of Canada. Retrieved March 04, 2020, from https://www.infrastructure.gc.ca/plan/ptif-fitc-eng.php

Puentes, R., & Bailey, L. (2003). *Improving Metropolitan Decision Making in Transportation: Greater Funding and Devolution for Greater Accountability.* Washington, D.C.: Brookings Institute, Transportation Reform Series.

Quesnel, L. (2000). Intraregionale Kooperation in Kanada [Cooperation at the Regional Level in Canada]. In W. Heinz (Ed.), *Stadt & Region–Kooperation oder Koordination? Ein internationaler Vergleich [City & Region-Cooperation or Coordination?–An International Comparison]* (pp. 111–168). Stuttgart, Berlin, Köln: Verlag W. Kohlhammer.

RCW-Revised Code of Washington,

RCW 36.70A (Growth Management). Retrieved May 23, 2018, from https://app.leg.wa.gov/RCW/default.aspx?cite=36.70A

RCW 47 (Public Highways and Transportation). Retrieved May 23, 2018, from https://apps.leg.wa.gov/rcw/default.aspx?Cite=47

RCW 47.80 (Regional transportation planning organizations). Retrieved December 06, 2019, from https://app.leg.wa.gov/RCW/default.aspx?cite=47.80

RCW 70 (Public Health and Safety). Retrieved May 24, 2018, from https://app.leg.wa.gov/RCW/default.aspx?Cite=70

RCW 81.104 (High Capacity Transportation System). Retrieved October 30, 2020 from https://app.leg.wa.gov/rcw/default.aspx?cite=81.104

RCW 81.112 (Regional Transit Authorities). Retrieved December 06, 2019, from https://app.leg.wa.gov/RCW/default.aspx?cite=81.112

Reckien, D., Flacke, J., Dawson, R.J., Heidrich, O., Olazabal, M., Foley, A., Hamann, J.J.-P., Orru, H., Salvia, M., De Gregorio Hurtado, S., Geneletti, D., & Pietrapertosa, F. (2014). Climate Change Response in Europe: What's the Reality? Analysis of Adaptation and Mitigation Plans from 200 Urban Areas in 11 Countries. *Climatic Change (2014), 122*, 331–340. http://dx.doi.org/10.1007/s10584-013-0989-8

Reimer, M., Getimis, P., & Blotevogel, H.H. (Eds.), (2014). *Spatial Planning Systems and Practices in Europe–A Comparative Perspective on Continuity and Change.* London and New York: Routledge–Taylor & Francis Group.

Rhodes, R. (2007). Understanding Governance: Ten Years On. *Organization Studies, 28*(8), 1243–1264. https://doi.org/10.1177/0170840607076586

RMK-Rems-Murr-Kreis (County)

RMK-Klima (2019). *Das 3. Klimaschutz-Handlungsprogramm für den Rems-Murr-Kreis 2019 bis 2022- Klimaschutz zum Mitmachen [Third Climate Mitigation Implementation Plan for the Rems-Murr-County for the Years 2019 to 2022-Participate in Climate Mitigation].* Prepared by Rems-Murr-Kreis, Amt für Umweltschutz, Geschäftsstelle Klimaschutz [Rems-Murr county, department of environmental protection, division for climate mitigation]. Retrieved April 10, 2019, from https://www.rems-murr-kreis.de/fileadmin/Dateien/Dateien/%C3%84mter/Umwelt/FB_321/Klimaschutz/HPs_und_UVA_Vorlagen/Klimaschutz_zum_Mitmachen_-_3._Klimaschutz-Handlungsprogramm_f%C3%BCr_den_Rems-Murr-Kreis_2019-2022.pdf

RMK-NVP (2017). *Nahverkehrsplan für den Rems-Murr-Kreis 2. Fortschreibung April 2015, Änderungsstand 24.4.2017 gem. Kreistagsbeschluss [Public Transportation Plan for Rems-Murr-County-Adopted April 2015, Last Change April 24, 2017]*. Retrieved February 11, 2019, from https://www.rems-murr-kreis.de/fileadmin/Dateien/Dateien/%C3%84mter/OEPNV/NVP_RMK_Stand_April_2017.pdf

Rohrbach-Langenhagen, C. (2005). *Raumordnung und Raumplanung*. Darmstadt: Wissenschaftliche Buchgesellschaft.

Romero-Lankao, P. (2012). Governing Carbon and Climate in the Cities: An Overview of Policy and Planning Challenges and Options. *European Planning Studies, 20*(1), 7–26.

Romo, V., & Parkes, M. (September 16, 2017). Confusion Continues: The United States' Position on the Paris Climate Agreement. *National Public Radio*. Retrieved May 14, 2018, from https://www.npr.org/sections/thetwo-way/2017/09/16/551551083/u-s-still-out-of-paris-climate-agreement-after-conflicting-reports

Roodbol-Mekkes, P.H., & van den Brink, A. (2015). Rescaling Spatial Planning-Spatial Planning Reforms in Denmark, England, and the Netherlands. *Environment and Planning C: Government and Policy, 33*, 184–198.

Rothblatt, D.N. (1994). North American Metropolitan Planning: Canadian and U.S. Perspectives. *Journal of the American Planning Association 60*(4), 501–520. http://dx.doi.org/10.1080/01944369408975607

Runkel, P. (2005). Ziele, Grundsätze, Erfordernisse der Raumordnung [Requirements, Principles and Other Issues in Spatial Planning]. In ARL-Akademie für Raumforschung und Landesplanung (Ed.), *Handwörterbuch der Raumplanung [Dictionary of Spatial Planning]* (pp. 1315–1322). Hannover: VSB Verlagsservice Braunschweig.

S–U

Sancton, A. (2009). *A Review of Canadian Metropolitan Regions: Governance and Government for the Symposium on Regional Government in the Vancouver Region*. Delivered on Friday, December 11, 2009 at Richmond Airport Executive Inn Hotel, Richmond BC. [Modified from Article in Don Phares (2008, Ed.) Governing Metropolitan Regions in the 21st Century (pp. 221–236). Armonk, NY].

Sanyal, B. (Ed.). (2005a). *Comparative Planning Cultures*. New York and London: Routledge-Taylor & Francis Group.

Sanyal, B. (2005b). Hybrid Planning Cultures: The Search for the Global Cultural Commons. In B. Sanyal (Ed.), *Comparative Planning Cultures* (pp. 3–25). New York and London: Routledge-Taylor & Francis Group.

Scharpf, F.W. (2000). *Interaktionsformen. Akteurzentrierter Institutionalismus in der Politikforschung [Games Real Actors Play. Actor-Centered Institutionalism in Policy Research]*. Wiesbaden: Springer.

Schimank, U. (2007). Elementare Mechanismen [Basic Mechanisms]. In A. Benz, S. Lütz, U. Schimank, & G. Simonis (Eds.), *Handbuch Governance. Theoretische Grundlagen und empirische Anwendungsfelder [Governance. Theoretical Foundations and Empirical Applications]* (pp. 29–45). Wiesbaden: VS Verlag für Sozialwissenschaften | GWV Fachverlage GmbH.

Schmidt, S., & Buehler, R. (2007). The Planning Process in the US and Germany: A Comparative Analysis. *International Planning Studies, 12*(1), 55–75.

Schmitz, G. (2005). Regionalplanung [Regional Planning]. In ARL-Akademie für Raumforschung und Landesplanung (Ed.), *Handwörterbuch der Raumplanung [Dictionary of Spatial Planning]* (pp. 963–973). Hannover: VSB Verlagsservice Braunschweig.

Schönwandt, W., & Jung, W. (2006). *Ausgewählte Methoden und Instrumente in der räumlichen Planung. Kritische Sondierung als Beitrag zur Diskussion zwischen Planungswissenschaft und -praxis [Selected Methods and Instrument in Spatial Planning. A Critical Exploration as a Contribution to the Discussion between Academic Discourses and Practitioners in Planning]*. Hannover: Verlag der ARL.

Schorndorf (2015). *Erläuterungsbericht zum Gemeinsamen Flächennutzungsplan Schorndorf– Winterbach [Supplementary Report to the Land Use Designation Map of Schorndorf and Winterbach]*. Retrieved May 24, 2020, from https://www.schorndorf.de/ceasy/resource/?id=9544&download=1

Schorndorf-Arcadis (2016). *Neugestaltung des ehemaligen Breuninger-Areals in Schorndorf [Revitalization of the Former Leather Manufacturing Site Breuninger in the City of Schorndorf]*. Retrieved May 25, 2020, from https://www.schorndorf.de/ceasy/resource/?id=15240&download=1

Schorndorfer Nachrichten (2019). *Bebauungsplan fürs Breuninger-Areal: kein Einkaufsmarkt, mehr Wohnungen [Zoning Map for the Breuninger Site: No Retail but More Apartments]*. In Schorndorf News 86 on April 11, 2019. Retrieved May 25, 2020, from https://www.schorndorf.de/ceasy/resource/?id=15316&download=1

Schreurs, M.A. (2010). Multi-Level Governance and Global Climate Change in East Asia. *Asian Economic Policy Review, 5*(1), 88–105. https://doi.org/10.1111/j.1748-3131.2010.01150.x

Schreus, M.A., & Tiberghien, Y. (2007). Multi-Level Reinforcement: Explaining European Union Leadership in Climate Change Mitigation. *Global Environmental Politics,* 7(4), 19–46.

SEA-City of Seattle

SEA-CAP (2013). *Climate Action Plan*. Retrieved November 15, 2015, from http://www.seattle.gov/Documents/Departments/OSE/2013_CAP_20130612.pdf

SEA-CAP (2018). *Seattle Climate Action-Released by Mayor Jenny A. Durkan*. Retrieved November 20, 2019, from http://greenspace.seattle.gov/wp-content/uploads/2018/04/SeaClimateAction_April2018.pdf

Setzer, J., & Nachmany, M. (2018). National Governance–The State's Role in Steering Polycentric Action. In A. Jordan, D. Huitema, H. van Hasselt, & J. Forster (Eds.), *Governing Climate Change. Polycentricity in Action?* (pp. 47–62). New York: Cambridge University Press. http://dx.doi.org/10.1017/9781108284646

SHO-Shoreline, City of

SHO-185th Street Plan (2015). *185th Street Station Subarea Plan*. Retrieved on November 1, 2020, from https://www.shorelinewa.gov/home/showdocument?id=42338

SHO-145th Street Plan (2016). *145th Street Station Subarea Plan*. Retrieved on November 1, 2020, from https://www.shorelinewa.gov/home/showdocument?id=26591

SHO-CAP (2013). *Shoreline Climate Action Plan*. Retrieved on November 1, 2020, from https://www.shorelinewa.gov/home/showdocument?id=38435#:~:text=-This%20Climate%20Action%20Plan%20(the, (GHG)%20emissions%20in%20Shoreline.&text=Inform%20the%20community%20about%20what, do%20to%20address%20climate%20change

SHO-Center Plan (2011). *City of Shoreline Town Center Subarea Plan. Adopted by City Council July 25, 2011*. Retrieved on November 1, 2020, from https://www.shorelinewa.gov/home/showdocument?id=9997

SHO-Comp Plan (2012). *Comprehensive Plan. Adopted by Ordinance 649 on December 10, 2012*. Retrieved on November 1, 2020, from https://www.shorelinewa.gov/home/showdocument?id=12641

SHO-FLUM 145th (2016). *145th Street Station Subarea Plan. Comprehensive Plan Future Land Use Map.* Retrieved on November 1, 2020, from https://www.shorelinewa.gov/home/showdocument?id=29090

SHO-Framework Policy (2012). *Light Rail Station Area Planning Framework Policy for Shoreline.* Adopted on 5/14/2012. Retrieved on November 1, 2020, from https://www.shorelinewa.gov/Home/ShowDocument?id=11296

SHO-Zoning 145th (2016). *145th Street Station Subarea Plan. Official Zoning Map Adopted September 26, 2016.* Retrieved on November 1, 2020, from https://www.shorelinewa.gov/home/showdocument?id=29094

Siedentop, S. (2015). Suburbane Räume unter Anpassungsdruck. Ein deutsch-amerikanischer Vergleich [Suburbia Under Pressure to Adopt. A German-American Comparison]. In J. Jessen, & F. Rooster (Eds.), *Refitting Suburbia–Erneuerung der Stadt des 20. Jahrhunderts in Deutschland und den USA [Refitting Suburbia– Revitalization of the city of the 20th century in Germany and the USA]* (pp. 23–42). Berlin: Jovis Verlags GmbH.

Siedentop, S., Roos, S., & Fina, S. (2013). Ist die 'Autoabhängigkeit' von Bewohnern städtischer und ländlicher Siedlungsgebiete messbar? [Is the Car Dependency of Urban and Rural Residents a Measurable Phenomenon?]. *Raumforschung und Raumordnung 71 [German Spatial Planning Journal], 71*, 329–341.

Siener, M. (2004). *Organizing Growth? Zum Zusammenhang zwischen regionalen Organisationsstrukturen und Ansätzen zur Steuerung der Siedlungsflächenentwicklung in Großstadtregionen [Organizing Growth? About the Connection between Regional Organizational Structures and Approaches to Govern Development Patterns in Metropolitan Areas].* Berlin: Universitätsverlag TU.

Sindelfingen Planungsworkshop (2016). *Planungsworkshop II in Maichingen am 21.04.2016 [Public Participation for the Allmendäcker Development in Maichingen on April 21, 2016].* Prepared by KE Baldauf Architekten und Stadtplaner. Retrieved May 24, 2020, from https://www.maichingen.de/site/Sindelfingen-Maichingen-Internet/get/params_E1848868018/12177576/160421_Allmend%C3%A4cker%20B%C3%BCrgerworkshop.pdf

Sindelfingen Zoning Map (2017). *Allmendäcker II Planbereich 105/5- Bebauungsplan und örtliche Bauvorschriften [Zoning Map for the New Development Allmendäcker II in area 105/5].* Prepared by Stadt Sindelfingen–Bürgeramt Stadtentwicklung und Bauen [City of Sindelfingen–Department of development and construction]. Retrieved November 1, 2020, from https://www.sindelfingen.de/site/Sindelfingen-Internet/get/params_E218727783/14908216/170802_Allmend%C3%A4ckerII_S_1_500.pdf

Sinz, M. (2005). Raumordnung/Raumordnungspolitik [Spatial Politics]. In ARL-Akademie für Raumforschung und Landesplanung (Ed.), *Handwörterbuch der Raumplanung [Dictionary of Spatial Planning]* (pp. 863–872). Hannover: VSB Verlagsservice Braunschweig.

SKKK (2014). *Klimaschutz mit Konzept [Climate Mitigation with a Plan].* Prepared by Service- und Kompetenzzentrum Kommunaler Klimaschutz [Center for Local Climate Mitigation]. Retrieved April 19, 2016, from http://www.klimaschutz.de/sites/default/files/page/downloads/skkk_einleger_klimaschutzkonzepte_sep14_barrierefrei.pdf

Smith, J., Flower, P., & Larkin, M. (2009). *Interpretative Phenomenological Analysis.* Los Angeles, CA: Sage.

Smith, P., & Oberlander, P. (1998). Restructuring Metropolitan Governance: Greater Vancouver-British Columbia Reforms. In D.N. Rothblatt, & A. Sancton (Eds.), *Metropolitan Governance revisited. American/Canadian Intergovernmental Perspectives Revisited.* Berkeley, CA: Institute of Governmental Studies Press.

Sovacool, B. (2011). An International Comparison of Four Polycentric Approaches to Climate and Energy Governance. *Energy Policy, 39*(6), 3832–3844. https://doi.org/10.1016/j.enpol.2011.04.014

Sovacool, B., & Van de Graaf, T. (2018). Building or Stumbling Blocks? Assessing the Performance of Polycentric Energy and Climate Governance Networks. *Energy Policy, 118*, 317–324. https://doi.org/10.1016/j.enpol.2018.03.047

SoW-State of Washington

SoW-CAP (2008). *Growing Washington's Economy in a Carbon Constrained World–A Comprehensive Plan to Address the Challenges and Opportunities of Climate Change.* Prepared by Departments of Ecology and Community, Trade and Economic Development. Retrieved May 29, 2018, from https://fortress.wa.gov/ecy/publications/documents/0801025.pdf

SoW-CTED (2008). *Planning for Climate Change. Addressing Climate Change Through Comprehensive Planning under the Growth Management Act. Report to the Legislature.* Prepared by Community, Trade and Economic Development. Retrieved May 15, 2018, from https://deptofcommerce.app.box.com/s/za1cy5wbl0mubgd74t7dadowjua296zh

SoW-Ecology (2012). *Preparing for a Changing Climate. Washington State's Integrated Climate Response Strategy. Document No. 12-01-004.* Prepared by Department of Ecology. Retrieved May 15, 2018, from https://fortress.wa.gov/ecy/publications/documents/1201004.pdf

SoW-Leading (2008). *Leading the Way on Climate Change: The Challenge of Our Time. Interim Report. Ecology Publication #08-01-008.* Prepared by Departments of Ecology and Community, Trade and Economic Development. Retrieved May 29, 2018, from https://fortress.wa.gov/ecy/publications/publications/0801008a.pdf

SoW-60th Legislature (2008). *Greenhouse Gas Emissions. Certification of Enrollment Engrossed Second Substitute House Bill 2815. Chapter 14, Laws of 2008.* Retrieved May 15, 2018, from http://lawfilesext.leg.wa.gov/biennium/2007-08/Pdf/Bills/Session%20Laws/House/2815-S2.SL.pdf

SoW-61st Legislature (2009). *State Agencies Emission Reduction. Certification of Enrollment Engrossed Second Substitute Senate Bill 5560 Chapter 519, Laws of 2009 (partial veto). Effective Date: 07/26/09.* Retrieved May 15, 2018, from http://lawfilesext.leg.wa.gov/biennium/2009-10/Pdf/Bills/Session%20Laws/Senate/5560-S2.SL.pdf?cite=2009%20c%20519%20%C2%A7%209

SRU (2017). *Umsteuern erforderlich: Klimaschutz im Verkehrssektor. Sondergutachten–November 2017 [Changes Needed: Climate Mitigation in the Transportation Sector. Special Report - November 2017].* Prepared by Sachverständigenrat für Umweltfragen [German Advisory Council on the Environment]. Retrieved June 18, 2018, from https://www.umweltrat.de/SharedDocs/Downloads/DE/02_Sondergutachten/2016_2020/2017_11_SG_Klimaschutz_im_Verkehrssektor.pdf?__blob=publicationFile&v=21

ST-Sound Transit

ST (2020). *Board of Directors.* Retrieved October 14, 2020, from https://www.soundtransit.org/get-to-know-us/board-directors

ST-Board Motion (2012). *Motion No. M2012-17 Identifying Lynnwood Link Extension Alternatives for Detailed Study in a Draft Environmental Impact Statement.* Retrieved on November 1, 2020, from https://www.soundtransit.org/st_sharepoint/download/sites/PRDA/FinalRecords/2012/Motion%20M2012-17.pdf

ST-EIS (2015). *Lynnwood Link Extension. Final Environmental Impact Statement.* Retrieved November 1, 2020, from https://www.soundtransit.org/sites/default/files/documents/pdf/projects/north_hct/lynnwoodeis/_frontmatter_summary.pdf

ST-Scope (2011). *North Corridor Transit Project Environmental Review and Potential Alternatives.* Retrieved on November 1, 2020, from https://www.soundtransit.org/sites/default/files/documents/pdf/projects/North_hct/Scoping_fs_web_v2.pdf

ST-Sound Move (1996). *The Ten-Year Regional Transit System Plan. Launching a Rapid Transit System for the Puget Sound Region.* Retrieved November 1, 2020, from https://www.soundtransit.org/sites/default/files/documents/199605-sound-move-ten-year-regional-transit-system-plan.pdf

ST3-Appendix D (2016). *Social, Economic and Environmental Impacts; Integration with Regional Land Use; Transit-Oriented Development.* Retrieved November 4, 2020, from https://st32.blob.core.windows.net/media/Default/Document%20Library%20Featured/8-22-16/ST3_Appendix-D_2016_web.pdf

ST3-Expansion (2018). *System Expansions.* Retrieved June 14, 2018, from https://systemexpansion.soundtransit.org/?_ga=2.143623984.422874784.1528705508-1233030921.1523278680

ST3-History (2018). *History: What Voters Approved.* Retrieved June 14, 2018, from https://www.soundtransit.org/Projects-and-Plans/Developing-Regional-Transit/History-what-voters-approved

ST3-Resolution R2012-24 (2012). Sound Transit-Transit-Oriented Development Policy. In *Transit-Oriented Development (TOD) Program Strategic Plan Update* (2014, pp. 33-38). Retrieved November 4, 2020, from https://www.soundtransit.org/sites/default/files/20140423_RPT_TOD.pdf

ST3-System Plan (2016). *The Regional Transit System Plan for Central Puget Sound.* Retrieved November 12, 2019, from https://st32.blob.core.windows.net/media/Default/Document%20Library%20Featured/8-22-16/ST3_System-Plan_2016_web.pdf

ST3-Tax (2018). *Regional Transit Taxes.* Retrieved June 14, 2018, from https://www.soundtransit.org/About-Sound-Transit/Taxing-district

ST3-TODP (2014). *Transit-Oriented Development (TOD) Program Strategic Plan Update. Resolution R2012-24.* Retrieved November 4, 2020, from https://www.soundtransit.org/sites/default/files/20140423_RPT_TOD.pdf

Stark, S. (2009). *Steuerung durch Regionalpläne–Anspruch und Wirklichkeit der Steuerungswirkung des Regionalplans am Beispiel der Wohnbauflächen in der Region Stuttgart [Steering with Regional Growth Strategies - Expectations and Reality of the Steering Capacity of the Regional Growth Strategy Looking at the Example of Housing Development in the Stuttgart Region].* In Forum Stadt und Regionalplanung e.V. (Ed.), Arbeitshefte des Instituts für Stadt- und Regionalplanung – TU Berlin. Heft 73.

Statistics Canada (2011). *Census Profile–Age and Sex for Census Metropolitan Areas and Census Agglomerations, 2011 Census.* Retrieved April 11, 2018, from http://www12.statcan.gc.ca/census-recensement/2011/dp-pd/tbt-tt/Rp-eng.cfm?TABID=2&LANG=E&A=R&APATH=3&DETAIL=0&DIM=0&FL=A&

FREE=0&GC=933&GL=-1&GID=1099089&GK=10&GRP=1&O=D&PID=103151&PRID=10&PTYPE=101955&S=0&SHOWALL=0&SUB=0&Temporal=2011&THEME=88&VID=0&VNAMEE=&VNAMEF=&D1=0&D2=0&D3=0&D4=0&D5=0&D6=0

Stead, D., & Nadin, V. (2009). Planning Cultures between Models of Society and Planning Systems. In J. Knieling & F. Othengrafen (Eds.), *Planning Cultures in Europe. Decoding Cultural Phenomena in Urban and Regional Planning* (pp. 283–300). Burlington: Ashgate Publishing.

Stephens, G.R., & Wikstrom, N. (2000). *Metropolitan Government and Governance. Theoretical Perspectives, Empirical Analysis, and the Future.* New York, Oxford: Oxford University Press.

Stevens, M.R. (2017). Does Compact Development Make People Drive Less? *Journal of the American Planning Association, 83*(1), 7–18.

Surrey, City of

Surrey CAP (2013). *City of Surrey Community Energy and Emissions Plan.* Retrieved May 10, 2019, from https://www.surrey.ca/files/CommunityEnergyEmissionsPlan.pdf

Surrey OCP (2013). *Plan Surrey 2013- Official Community Plan–Land Uses and Densities Section.* Retrieved September 18, 2020, from https://www.surrey.ca/sites/default/files/media/documents/OCP_Land_Uses_Densities.pdf

Surrey RTAA (2012). *Surrey Rapid Transit Alternative Analysis–Phase 2: Evaluation. Final Evaluation Report–Executive Summary.* Prepared by TransLink in Association with Hatch Mott Macdonald, Golder Associates, A. Steadman, and Coriolis. Retrieved October 2, 2019, from https://www.translink.ca/-/media/Documents/plans_and_projects/rapid_transit_projects/SRT/alternatives_evaluation/Surrey_Rapid_Transit_Study_Phase_2_Alternatives_Evaluation_Executive_Summary.pdf?la=en&hash=4F4E063880C6D7F01B23F015DC2B015E3FDE57CF

Surrey RTAA (2013). *Surrey* Rapid Transit Alternative Analysis–*Findings to Date.* Prepared by TransLink. Retrieved October 2, 2019, from https://www.translink.ca/-/media/Documents/plans_and_projects/rapid_transit_projects/SRT/alternatives_evaluation/Surrey_Rapid_Transit_Study_-Alternatives_Analysis_Findings.pdf

Termeer, C., Dewulf, A., &Breeman, G. (2013). Governance of Wicked Climate Adaptation Problems. In J. Knieling, & W. Leal Filho (Eds.), *Climate Change Governance: Series Climate Change Management* (pp. 32–43). Heidelberg: Springer.

Thiel, A. (2017). The Scope of Polycentric Governance and Resulting Challenges. *Journal of Self-Governance and Management Economics, 5*(3), 52–82. https://doi.org/10.22381/JSME5320173

TIGER (2020). *Build–TIGER Discretionary Grants.* Retrieved November 11, 2020, from https://ops.fhwa.dot.gov/freight/infrastructure/tiger/

TL-TransLink

TL (2018). *About Us.* Retrieved May 28, 2018, from https://www.translink.ca/About-Us.aspx

TL-Gov (2020). *TransLink Governance Model.* Retrieved March 04, 2020, from https://new.translink.ca/about-us/about-translink/governance-model

TL-Mayors Vision (2014). *Regional Transportation Investments–A Vision for Metro Vancouver.* Issued by Mayors Council on Regional Transportation. Retrieved October 2, 2019, from https://www.translink.ca/-/media/Documents/about_translink/governance_and_board/mayors_vision/mayors_council_vision_mar_2015.pdf

TL-Media Release (March 16, 2018). *Mayors Approve Largest Transit and Transportation Investment in Metro Vancouver History. Balanced Regional Plan to Fund Unprecedented Transportation Network Expansion.* Retrieved March 04, 2020, from https://www.scribd.com/document/374063651/Metro-Vancouver-transit-funding-annoucement#download&from_embed

TL-Memo (2017). *Memo to Mayors' Council on Regional Transportation. Meeting on September 27, 2017 about South of Fraser Rapid Transit–Surrey-Langley Technology Decision.* Retrieved September 18, 2020, from https://www.translink.ca/-/media/Documents/plans_and_projects/rapid_transit_projects/SRT/Surrey-Langley-LRT-Memo.pdf

TL-Phase 1 (2017). *Update to Phase One of the 10-Year Vision. 2017–2026 Investment Plan.* Approved by the TransLink Board of Directors–July 19, 2017 and the Mayors' Council on Regional Transportation–July 27, 2017. Retrieved October 30, 2020, from https://www.translink.ca/-/media/Documents/about_translink/governance_and_board/council_minutes_and_reports/2017/July/Item-31--Appendices-A-B-and-C--Mayors-Council-PUBLIC-MTG--Update-to-Phase-One-Plan.pdf

TL-RTS (2013). *Regional Transportation Strategy. Strategic Framework.* Retrieved May 28, 2018, from www.translink.ca/-/media/Documents/plans_and_projects/regional_transportation_strategy/rts_strategic_framework_07_31_2013.pdf?la=en&hash=0A459174FB44A8870D00EFCE54124A01078D0698

TL-Skytrain (2020). *Surrey Langley SkyTrain Project. Media Technical Briefing on January 24, 2020.* Retrieved September 18, 2020, from https://www.surreylangleyskytrain.ca/-/media/surreylangleyskytrain/documents/document-library/sls_business_case_media_tech_briefing.pdf

TL-SOFATP (2007). *South of Fraser Transit Plan. A Long Range Transit Plan and Vision for the South of Fraser.* Retrieved October 2, 2019, from https://www.translink.ca/-/media/Documents/plans_and_projects/area_transit_plans/south_of_fraser/South-of-Fraser-Area-Transit-Plan-Phase-1.pdf

TL-SOFATP–Phase 2 (2007). *Analysis of the Network for 2031/ 1 Million Residents.* Retrieved October 2, 2019, from https://www.translink.ca/-/media/Documents/plans_and_projects/area_transit_plans/south_of_fraser/South-of-Fraser-Area-Transit-Plan-Phase-2.pdf

Trebilcock, M. (2007). The Choice of Governing Instrument: A Retrospective. In P. Eliadis, M.M. Hill, & M. Howlett (Eds.), *Designing Government. From Instruments to Governance* (pp. 51–73). Montreal & Kingston, London, Ithaca, NY: McGill Queen's University Press.

TUK-Tukwila, City of

TUK-CNU 2017. *Tukwila International Boulevard–CNU Legacy Project. Implementing the Vision.* Prepared by Congress of New Urbanism together with the City of Tukwila. Retrieved on November 1, 2020, from https://indd.adobe.com/view/30a631e0-ee3c-45f4-8f76-a9c83850446a

TUK-Comp (2015). *Comprehensive Plan for the City of Tukwila.* Retrieved on May 14, 2018, from https://www.tukwilawa.gov/wp-content/uploads/DCD-Comprehensive-Plan.pdf

TUK-TIB (2020). *Tukwila International Boulevard Neighborhood Planning.* Retrieved on November 1, 2020, from tukwilawa.gov/departments/community-development/community-planning/tukwila-international-boulevard-neighborhood-planning/

Umweltbundesamt [German Environmental Agency] (2015). *Planungsebenen, Planungsräume– Stufen der räumlichen Planung [Levels of Planning, Scales of PlanningLevels of Spatial Planning].* Retrieved March 20, 2017, from http://www.umweltbundesamt.de/themen/nachhaltigkeit-strategien-internationales/planungsinstrumente/planungsebenen-planungsraeume-stufen-der

USC 23 Sec 134 – *United States Code 23 Section 134, Metropolitan Transportation Planning.* Retrieved May 5, 2018, from https://www.law.cornell.edu/uscode/text/23/134

US Census (2013). *Chapter 13 - Metropolitan Areas. Classification of Metropolitan Areas.* Retrieved February 07, 2020, from https://www2.census.gov/geo/pdfs/reference/GARM/Ch13GARM.pdf

US Census Quick Facts. Retrieved April 5, 2018, from https://www.census.gov/quickfacts/fact/table/minneapoliscityminnesota, denvercitycolorado, bostoncity-massachusetts, seattlecitywashington, US/PST040216#qf-flag-X

US Mayors Council (2019). *Mayors Climate Protection Center.* Retrieved November 21, 2019, from https://www.usmayors.org/mayors-climate-protection-center/

V–Z

Vancouver CAP (2015). *Greenest City 2020 Action Plan. Part 2: 2015–2020.* Prepared by City of Vancouver. Retrieved November 15, 2015, from http://vancouver.ca/files/cov/greenest-city-2020-action-plan-2015-2020.pdf

Van der Heijden, J. (2018a). City and Subnational Governance–High Ambitions, Innovative Instruments and Polycentric Collaboration? In A. Jordan, D. Huitema, H. van Hasselt, & J. Forster (Eds.), *Governing Climate Change. Polycentricity in Action?* (pp. 81–96). New York: Cambridge University Press. http://dx.doi.org/10.1017/9781108284646

Van der Heijden, J. (2018b). From Leaders to Majority: A Frontrunner Paradox in Built-Environment Climate Governance Experimentation. *Journal of Environmental Planning and Management, 61*(8), 1383–1401. http://dx.doi.org/10.1080/09640568.2017.1350147

Van der Heijden, J. (2019). Studying Urban Climate Governance: Where to Begin, What to Look for, and How to Make a Meaningful Contribution to Scholarship and Practice. *Earth System Governance, 1,* 1–10.

Van der Heijden, J., Patterson, J., Juhola, S., & Wolfram, M. (2019). Special Section: Advancing the Role of Cities in Climate Governance–Promise, Limits, Politics. *Journal of Environmental Planning and Management, 62*(3), 365–373. https://doi.org/10.1080/09640568.2018.1513832

van der Ven, H., Bernstein, S., & Hoffmann, M. (2017). Valuing the Contributions of Nonstate and Subnational Actors to Climate Governance. *Global Environmental Politics, 17*(1), 1–20. https://doi.org/10.1162/GLEP_a_00387

van Staden, M. & Musco, F. (2010). Introduction. In M. van Staden, & F. Musco (Eds.), *Local Governments and Climate Change Sustainable Energy Planning and Implementation in Small and Medium Sized Communities* (pp. 1–11). Dordrecht, Heidelberg, London, New York: Springer.

Verbücheln, M., & Dähner, S. (Eds., 2016). *Klimaschutz in der Stadt- und Regionalplanung - Erneuerbare Energien und Energieeffizienz in der kommunalen Planungspraxis.* Part of the EU-funded project SPECIAL - Spatial Planning and Energy for Communities in all Landscapes. Retrieved April 10, 2019, from http://www.difu.de/publikationen/2016/klimaschutz-in-der-stadt-und-regionalplanung.html

von Hinüber, H. (2005). Geschichte der überörtlichen Raumplanung [History of Planning Beyond Local Boundaries]. In ARL-Akademie für Raumforschung und Landesplanung (Ed.), *Handwörterbuch der Raumplanung [Dictionary of Spatial Planning]* (pp. 384–393). Hannover: VSB Verlagsservice Braunschweig.

VRS-Verband Region Stuttgart

VRS (2009). *Region tritt EU-Konvent für Klimaschutz bei. Pressemitteilung vom 29.01.2009 [Region Joints the EU-Covenant for Climate Mitigation. Press Release on January 29, 2009]*. Retrieved March 15, 2018, from https://www.region-stuttgart.org/nc/presse/artikel/aktuell/region-tritt-eu-konvent-fuer-klimaschutz-bei/?tx_news_pi1%5Bcontroller%5D=News&tx_news_pi1%5Baction%5D=detail&cHash=c176a8e3da0e731ab01aa1aab3fad54d

VRS-Klima (2016). *Klima–Stadt–Wandel. Strategien und Projekte für die Klimaanpassung in der Region Stuttgart [Climate-City-Change–Strategies and Projects for Climate Adaptation in the Stuttgart Region]*. Schriftenreihe Verband Region Stuttgart Dezember 2016 / Nummer 32. Retrieved June 5, 2018, from https://www.region-stuttgart.org/index.php?eID=dumpFile&t=f&f=5806&token=1dddabcc77765b8c82b4a4e2fac9491b6951e1bc

VRS-Klimaatlas (2008). *Klimaatlas Region Stuttgart [Maps for the Climate in the Stuttgart Region]*. Retrieved June 19, 2018, from https://www.region-stuttgart.org/index.php?eID=dumpFile&t=f&f=1957&token=4d8347ada273d2478550cec0cacdf602dfb15412

VRS-Regionalplan (2009). *Region Stuttgart–Regionalplan [Regional Growth Strategy for the Stuttgart Region]*. Retrieved June 19, 2018, from https://www.region-stuttgart.org/index.php?eID=dumpFile&t=f&f=682&token=5d584afc521d2491a202126da5d2d600e8192c77

VRS-RTP (2018). *Regionalverkehrsplan Region Stuttgart Beschluss der Regionalversammlung vom 18.07.2018 [Regional Transportation Plan for the Stuttgart Region, Adopted on July 18, 2018]*. Retrieved April 25, 2020, from https://www.region-stuttgart.org/index.php?eID=dumpFile&t=f&f=8411&token=c05a0f77c98c81a92d3221395719655316e4cf84

VRS-RTP Entwurf (2016). *Regionalverkehrsplan Region Stuttgart–Entwurf vom 21.12.2016 [Draft of the Regional Transportation Plan for the Stuttgart Region Issued on December 21, 2016]*. Retrieved June 5, 2018, from https://www.region-stuttgart.org/video/20161221_Entwurf_Regionalverkehrsplan.pdf

VRS-S4 (2012). *S4: Verlängerung Marbach (Neckar)–Backnang Wir bringen die S-Bahn ins Murrtal [Rapid Transit Line S4- Extension Marbach (Neckar) to Backnang. We deliver the rapid transit to the Murrtal]*. Published in collaboration with Deutsche Bahn. Retrieved September 27, 2020, from https://www.region-stuttgart.org/index.php?eID=dumpFile&t=f&f=2491&token=d163ea33c243c3f396df82579bf8fc126f1cf1f8

VRS-WIV 11617 – (2017). *Sitzungsvorlage Nr. 116/2017- Ausschuss für Wirtschaft, Infrastruktur und Verwaltung am 08.03.2017 zur Beschlussfassung 10.02.2017- Öffentliche Sitzung -116- WIV-Ö -257/2016 [Memo Number 116/2017 for the Committee on the Economy, Infrastructure and Administration Meeting on March 08, 2017]*. Retrieved June 19, 2018, from https://gecms.region-stuttgart.org/gdmo/Download.aspx?id=62964

WAC-*Washington Administrative Code*, Title 468 (Department of Transportation - Certification). Retrieved September 12, 2019, from https://apps.leg.wa.gov/wac/default.aspx?cite=468-86-150

Wachs, M., & Dill, J. (1999). Regionalism in Transportation and Air Quality: History, Interpretation, and Insights for Regional Governance. In A. Altshuler, W. Morrill, H. Wolman, & F. Mitchell (Eds.), *Governance and Opportunity in Metropolitan America* (pp. 296–323). Washington, D.C.: National Academy Press.

Ward, D. (2015). *Secrets of Failure: Why the Transit Referendum Crashed. Experts Say It was Doomed by Design, and a Politically Crafty Premier.* Retrieved March 04, 2020, from https://thetyee.ca/News/2015/07/06/Crashed-Van-Transit-Referendum/

Wei, T. & Tang, Z. (2014). Building Low-Carbon Cities. Assessing the Fast Growing U.S. Cities' Land Use Comprehensive Plans. *Journal of Environmental Assessment Policy and Management, 16*(1), 1–28.

Weitz, J. (2012). Growth Management in the United States 2000–2010: A Decennial Review and Synthesis. *Journal of Planning Literature, 27*(4), 394–433.

Wheeler, S. (2002). The New Regionalism: Key Characteristics of an Emerging Movement. *Journal of the American Planning Association, 68*(3), 267–278. http://dx.doi.org/10.1080/01944360208976272

Wheeler, S. (2008). State and Municipal Climate Change Plans: The First Generation. *Journal of the American Planning Association, 74*(4), 481–496.

Wheeler, S. (2009). California's Climate Change Planning: Policy Innovation and Structural Hurdles. In S. Davoudi, J. Crawford, & A. Mehmood (Eds.), *Planning for Climate Change–Strategies for Mitigation and Adaptation for Spatial Planners* (pp. 125–135). London and Sterling, VA: Earthscan.

Whittemore, A. H. (2012). How the Federal Government Zoned America: The Federal Housing Administration and Zoning. *Journal of Urban History, 39*(4), 620–642.

Wichern, P. (2004). Metropolitan Governance in Canada: The 1990s. In D. Phares (Ed.), *Metropolitan Governance without Metropolitan Government?* (pp. 34–54). Wiltshire: Ashgate.

Williamson, T. (2010). *Sprawl, Justice, and Citizenship: The Civic Costs of the American Way of Life* (1st ed., Kindle). Oxford, New York, Auckland: Oxford University Press.

Wilson, E., & Piper, J. (2010). *Spatial Planning and Climate Change.* New York: Routledge.

WS-DoC (no date). *Climate Change. Website by the Washington State Department of Commerce.* Retrieved November 12, 2019, from https://www.commerce.wa.gov/serving-communities/growth-management/growth-management-topics/climate-change/

WSDOT-Washington State Department of Transportation

WSDOT (2013). *Tools for Estimating VMT Reductions from Build Environment Changes. WA-RD 806.3.* Prepared by Anne Vernez Moudon and Orion Stewart (Office of Research and Library Services). Retrieved November 12, 2020, from https://www.wsdot.wa.gov/research/reports/fullreports/806.3.pdf

WSDOT-Budget (2017). *Supplemental Budget for 2015-17 and 2017-19 Enacted Budget.* Retrieved May 31, 2018, from https://www.wsdot.wa.gov/sites/default/files/2018/01/12/Budget-Enacted2017-19-BudgetBook_0.pdf

WSDOT-PTP (2016). *Washington State Public Transportation Plan.* Retrieved November 12, 2019, from https://www.wsdot.wa.gov/sites/default/files/2017/05/02/WashingtonStatePublicTransportationPlan-2016.pdf

WSDOT-RMG (2018). *Regional Mobility Grant Program.* Retrieved on May 30, 2018 from https://www.wsdot.wa.gov/Transit/Grants/mobility.htm

WSDOT-Sustainability (2016). *Sustainable Transportation Action Plan 2015–2019.* Retrieved on May 30, 2018 from http://www.wsdot.wa.gov/sites/default/files/2017/05/02/SustainableTransportationActionPlan2015-2017.pdf

WSDOT-Sustainable Report (2010). *Sustainable Transportation Report*. Retrieved on May 30, 2018 from https://www.wsdot.wa.gov/NR/rdonlyres/2043E93C-6DC4-4C81-8534-1FADE6475E8F/0/02Report.pdf

WSDOT-VMT Report (2010). *Impacts of VMT Reduction Strategies on Selected Areas and Groups. WA-RD 751.1*. Prepared by Daniel Carlson and Zachary Howard. Retrieved June 3, 2020, from https://www.wsdot.wa.gov/research/reports/fullreports/751.1.pdf

WSDOT-VMT-MPO Report (2011). *Governor's Executive Order 09-05 Washington's Leadership on Climate Change–Report on Section 2(b) Regional Greenhouse Gas and Vehicle Miles Traveled Reduction Strategies*. Retrieved May 29, 2018, from https://www.wsdot.wa.gov/NR/rdonlyres/F06E9BFD-36FB-4D5A-B5EE-C4F42BF9DFB0/0/FinalExecutiveOrder09052bReport.pdf

WSDOT-WTP (2040; 2018). *Washington Transportation Plan Phase 2–Implementation 2017–2040*. Retrieved May 30, 2018, from https://washtransplan.com/wp-content/uploads/2018/05/WTPPhase2-2017-web-Plan-1.pdf

WSDOT-WTP (2035; 2015). *Washington Transportation Plan–Connecting Washington Communities for a Healthy and Prosperous Future*. Retrieved May 30, 2018, from https://washtransplandotcom.files.wordpress.com/2017/05/wtp2035_final_21-jan-2015.pdf

Yin, R.K. (1994). *Case Study Research–Design and Methods* (2nd ed.). Newbury Park, CA: Sage Publications.

Zeemering, E. (2012). Recognising Interdependence and Defining Multi-Level Governance in City Sustainability Plans. *Local Environment*, *17*(4), 409–424. https://doi.org/10.1080/13549839.2012.678315

Zimmermann, M., Van Begin, G., & Vergara Cristóbal, I. (2010). The International Local Government Climate Roadmap. In M. van Staden, & F. Musco (Eds.), *Local Governments and Climate Change Sustainable Energy Planning and Implementation in Small and Medium Sized Communities* (pp. 78–107). Dordrecht, Heidelberg, London, New York: Springer.

Zingale, N., & Riemann, D. (2013). Coping with Shrinkage in Germany and the U.S.: A Cross-Cultural Comparative Approach toward Sustainable Cities. *Urban Design International, 18*(1), 90–98.

Glossary

German-English Translations

German	English
Abstimmen	to align
Abstimmung	alignment, coordination
Abwägen	to balance
Achsenzwischenräume	areas in between primary development corridors
Aufgaben and Kompetenzen	statutory responsibilities
Ausweisen	to designate
Baugesetzbuch	federal zoning law
Bebauungsplan	Local zoning map
Bruttowohndichte	density of housing
Bundesverkehrswegeplan	National Transportation Program
Coercion	Zwang
dauerhaften, großräumig ausgewogenen Ordnung	well-balanced development patterns
Dezentrale Konzentration	polynodal development
Dörfer	rural villages
Ebenen der Planung	scales or levels of government
Entwicklungsachsen	primary development corridors
Fachplanungen	sectors of government, sectoral planning
fachübergreifend	sectorally integrated
Festlegung von Entwicklungsachsen	designation of priority development corridors
Flächeninanspruchnahme	sprawl
Flächennutzungsplan	land use designations map

Formelle Pläne	legislatively-binding plans
Freiraumstruktur	open spaces
Gegenstromprinzip	principle of reciprocity
Gemeinden beschränkt auf Eigenentwicklung	low-growth communities
Gemeindeverkehrsfinanzierungsgesetz	Municipal Transportation Financing Act
Generalverkehrsplan	statewide transportation plan
Gewerbeschwerpunkten	preferred locations for retail development
gleichwertigen Lebensverhältnissen in den Teilräumen	equal living conditions in all part of Germany
Grundsatz	guiding policies
Grünzüge	protected open spaces
Informelle Pläne	plans with a guiding character
Integraler Taktfahrplan	transit system integration
Integrierte Stadtentwicklung	integrated urban development
Interdependenzbewältigung	how interdependencies are managed
Issue	Forschungsgegenstand
klimafreundliche Siedlungsstruktur	low-carbon development patterns
Klimaschutzkonzept	climate action plan
Klimaschutzpakt	climate mitigation compact
Landesebene	state government
Landesentwicklungsplan	statewide development plan
Landesgemeindeverkehrsfinanzierungsgesetz	State Municipal Transportation Financing Act
Ländlicher Raum	rural area
Landschaftsrahmenplan	open space plan
Leistungsfähige Bandinfrastruktur	infrastructure along primary development corridors
Leitbilder	spatial vision
Mehrwert	win-win-situation
Ministerium	the state department
Mittelzentren	2nd tier communities
Nachrichtliche Übernahme	statewide policies included in RGS as information
Nachverdichtung (städtebaulich)	infill development

Nachverdichtung in Gemeinden (regionalplanerisch)	compact communities
Nachverdichtung und Nutzungmischung in Gemeinden entlang der ÖPNV-Achsen	compact and complete communities along transit corridors
Nahverkehrsplan	countywide transportation plan
negativ Koordination	passive coordination
Nutzungsmischung (städtebaulich)	mix of uses
Nutzungsmischung in Gemeinden (regionalplanerisch)	complete communities
Oberzentren	1st tier communities
Öffentlicher Personennahverkehr	Transit
Örtliche Aufgaben	local responsibility
Politikverflechtungen	interdependent policy problem
raumbedeutsamer Planungen und Maßnahmen	spatially-impactful plans and projects
Raumnutzungskarte	regional land use designation map
Raumordnungsgesetz	federal spatial planning law
Raumordnungsverfahren	spatial compatibility assessment
Raumplanung	spatial planning
Recht auf lokale Selbstverwaltung	right to local self-administration
rechtlich bindend	legislatively binding
rechtskräftiger Plan	adopted planning document
Rechtswirksamkeit von Plänen	legal status of planning documents
Regeln	rules-in-use
Regionale Planungsverbände	regional planning organizations, metropolitan planning organization
Regionalisierungsmittel	regional funds
Regionalplan	Regional Growth Strategy (RGS)
Regionalverkehrsplan	regional transportation plan
Richtwerte für Siedlungsdichte	density requirements/ guidelines
Schwerpunkte des Wohnungsbaus	preferred locations for higher-density housing
Selbstregelung zwischen den Akteuren, selbstregulierte Ansätze	self-regulated

sich verlassen	to trust
Siedlungs- und Versorgungskern	designated urban center
Siedlungsbereich	urban growth area
Siedlungsentwicklung	spatial development
Siedlungsstruktur	development patterns
Stadt der kurzen Wege	city of short distances
Städtebau	urban design
städtebauliche Maßnahmen	development efforts at the local level/ urban design actions at the neighborhood level
städtebauliche Verträge	contracts between developers and cities
Steuerung, planungsrechtliche Regeln	state-regulated
Strukturkarte	development pattern map
System der Zentrale Orte	classification of communities
Teilräume	parts of the territory
überörtliche Aufgaben	responsibilities larger than local concerns
Umlegungsverfahren	land-reassembly-process
Unterzentren	3rd tier communities
Verbindlichkeit für eine Entscheidung	bearing on a decision; legal status of a planning document
verdichteter Raum; Verdichtungsräume	urbanized area
verfassungsmäßig festgelegten Machtverteilung	constitutionally preserved power structures
Verkehr vermeiden, verlagern, und verträglicher abwickeln	avoid traffic, shift traffic and improve traffic
verkehrsvermeidende Siedlungs- und Verkehrsplanung	development patterns that avoid increasing transportation demand
Versorgungssicherheit	sufficient services
Verwaltungsfachgesetz	administrative law
Vorbildfunktion der Kommunalverwaltung	municipal corporate climate actions
Vorranggebiet	preferred locations
Vorschlag im Regionalplan	suggested policies

Zielabweichungsverfahren	permission-to-deviate-from-requirements
Ziele	requirements
zusammenfassende Planung	comprehensive planning

English-German Translations

English	Deutsch
1st tier communities	Oberzentren
2nd tier communities	Mittelzentren
3rd tier communities	Unterzentren
administrative law	Verwaltungsfachgesetz
adopted planning document	rechtskräftiger Plan
alignment, coordination	Abstimmung
areas in between primary development corridors	Achsenzwischenräume
avoid traffic, shift traffic and improve traffic	Verkehr vermeiden, verlagern, und verträglicher abwickeln
bearing on a decision; legal status of a planning document	Verbindlichkeit für eine Entscheidung
city of short distances	Stadt der kurzen Wege
classification of communities	System der Zentrale Orte
climate action plan	Klimaschutzkonzept
climate mitigation compact	Klimaschutzpakt
compact and complete communities along transit corridors	Nachverdichtung und Nutzungmischung in Gemeinden entlang der ÖPNV-Achsen
compact communities	Nachverdichtung in Gemeinden (regionalplanerisch)
complete communities	Nutzungsmischung in Gemeinden (regionalplanerisch)
comprehensive planning	zusammenfassende Planung
compulsory coordination	Zwangsverhandlung
constitutionally preserved power structures	verfassungsmäßig festgelegten Machtverteilung
contracts between developers and cities	städtebauliche Verträge
countywide transportation plan	Nahverkehrsplan

density requirements/ guidelines	Richtwerte für Siedlungsdichte
designated urban center	Siedlungs- und Versorgungskern
designation of priority development corridors	Festlegung von Entwicklungsachsen
development efforts at the local level	städtebauliche Maßnahmen
development pattern map	Strukturkarte
development patterns	Siedlungsstruktur
development patterns that avoid increasing transportation demand	verkehrsvermeidende Siedlungs- und Verkehrsplanung;
equal living conditions in all part of Germany	gleichwertigen Lebensverhältnissen in den Teilräumen
federal spatial planning law	Raumordnungsgesetz
federal zoning law	Baugesetzbuch
guiding policies	Grundsatz
density of housing	Bruttowohndichte
how interdependencies are managed	Interdependenzbewältigung
infill development	Nachverdichtung (städtebaulich)
infrastructure along primary development corridors	Leistungsfähige Bandinfrastruktur
Issue	**Forschungsgegenstand**
integrated urban development	Integrierte Stadtentwicklung
interdependent policy problem	Politikverflechtungen
land use designations map	Flächennutzungsplan
land-reassembly-process	Umlegungsverfahren
legal status of planning documents	Rechtswirksamkeit von Plänen
legislatively binding	rechtlich bindend
legislatively-binding plans	Formelle Pläne
local responsibility	Örtliche Aufgaben
low-carbon development patterns	klimafreundliche Siedlungsstruktur
low-growth communities	Gemeinden beschränkt auf Eigenentwicklung
mix of uses	Nutzungsmischung (städtebaulich)

municipal corporate climate actions	Vorbildfunktion der Kommunalverwaltung (bspw. Sanierung von kommunalen Gebäuden)
Municipal Transportation Financing Act	Gemeindeverkehrsfinanzierungsgesetz
National Transportation Program	Bundesverkehrswegeplan
open space plan	Landschaftsrahmenplan
open spaces	Freiraumstruktur
parts of the territory	Teilräume
passive coordination	negativ Koordination
permission-to-deviate-from-requirements	Zielabweichungsverfahren
plans with a guiding character	Informelle Pläne
polynodal development	Dezentrale Konzentration
preferred locations	Vorranggebiet
preferred locations for higher-density housing	Schwerpunkte des Wohnungsbaus
preferred locations for retail development	Gewerbeschwerpunkten
primary development corridors	Entwicklungsachsen
principle of reciprocity	Gegenstromprinzip
protected open spaces	Grünzüge
regional funds	Regionalisierungsmittel
Regional Growth Strategy (RGS)	Regionalplan
regional land use designation map	Raumnutzungskarte
regional planning organizations, metropolitan planning organization	Regionale Planungsverbände
regional transportation plan	Regionalverkehrsplan
requirements	Ziele
responsibilities larger than local concerns	überörtliche Aufgaben
right to local self-administration	Recht auf lokale Selbstverwaltung
rules-in-use	Regeln

rural area	Ländlicher Raum
rural villages	Dörfer
scales or levels of government	Ebenen der Planung
sectorally integrated	fachübergreifend
sectors of government, sectoral planning	Fachplanungen
self-regulated	Selbstregelung zwischen den Akteuren, selbstregulierte Ansätze
spatial compatibility assessment	Raumordnungsverfahren
spatial development	Siedlungsentwicklung
spatial planning	Raumplanung
spatial vision	Leitbilder
spatially-impactful plans and projects	raumbedeutsamer Planungen und Maßnahmen
sprawl	Flächeninanspruchnahme
state government	Landesebene
State Municipal Transportation Financing Act	Landesgemeindeverkehrsfinanzierungsgesetz
state-regulated	Steuerung, planungsrechtliche Regeln
statewide development plan	Landesentwicklungsplan
statewide policies included in RGS as information	Nachrichtliche Übernahme
statewide transportation plan	Generalverkehrsplan
statutory responsibilities	Aufgaben and Kompetenzen
sufficient services	Versorgungssicherheit
suggested policies	Vorschlag im Regionalplan
the state department	Ministerium
to align	abstimmen
to balance	abwägen
to designate	ausweisen
to trust	sich verlassen
Transit	Öffentlicher Personennahverkehr
transit system integration	Integraler Taktfahrplan
urban design	Städtebau
urban growth area	Siedlungsbereich
urbanized area	verdichteter Raum; Verdichtungsräume
well-balanced development patterns	dauerhaften, großräumig ausgewogenen Ordnung
zoning map	Bebauungsplan

Index

accessibility 9–11
accountability 28, 52, 158, 160–168, 173, 182
activity units per acre 88
actor-centered institutionalism 30
agricultural uses 12, 19, 23, 44–49, 81, 129, 138, 140, 144, 150, 152
alignment 21–22, 107, 154, 174; *see also* corridor alignment
alignment mechanisms 42–43, 51, 151, 156, 158–159, 162–165, 174–176, 179, 182–183; *see also* integrating procedures (alignment of goals and actions)
application mechanisms 88, 156, 158, 174; *see also* integrating procedures

Baden-Württemberg 3, 6, 32–35, 105–145, 163–164, 179–183
balanced growth *see* smart growth
balance interests 119
ballot 90
Baugesetzbuch *see* federal zoning law
British Columbia 3, 5, 32–35, 36–69, 146, 151, 156–160, 163–164, 179–183
building boom 57–58, 170
Burquitlam-Lougheed station 59 62

Canada 14, 36–69
Christaller's theory of central places 123
"cities as saviors" narrative 13–14, 180
City of: Coquitlam (British Columbia, Canada) 57–62, 166; Schorndorf (Baden-Württemberg, Germany) 140–143; Shoreline (Washington State, USA) 91–94, 100–104, 169; Sindelfingen/Maichingen (Baden-Württemberg, Germany) 138–141; Surrey (British Columbia, Canada) 55–57, 63–69; Tukwila (Washington State, USA) 91, 93–100, 166
climate actions: climate action plans 3, 8–9, 110–111, 145, 179–184; energy-sector focus 110; land use actions (*see* low-carbon development patterns); local climate actions (*see* "Cities as saviors" narrative); scale of (*see* levels of government); state and federal level action 13, 22–23, 36–40, 56, 72–74, 109–111
climate compact: British Columbia Climate Action Charter 36–38; Klimaschutzpakt Baden-Württemberg 110
climate governance 3, 13–15, 21–23, 72, 172–174, 179–186
climate manager 110
coarser view of the regional level on land uses 113
collaboration 17, 36, 56, 64, 70, 75, 91, 115, 119, 142
collective action 15, 22–23, 53, 74, 173; *see also* common goal
common goal 12, 15, 25, 72, 117, 174; *see also* spatial policies
community classification 146, 150, 177; in Stuttgart region 122–124, 133; *see also* regional geographies
commuting patterns 13
compact and complete communities along transit corridors 10–12, 38, 44, 85, 111–112, 120, 145–146, 159
comprehensive planning 8, 27, 73–81, 84–85, 106–107, 118, 145, 157–161, 180
conflict 15, 31, 109, 119, 174, 175; balancing conflicting goals 138–140; *see* integrating procedures

conflict resolution mechanisms 156, 160, 176; *see also* integrating procedures
congestion 14, 19, 133, 135, 176
connectivity 9–11, 91
consistency requirements 29, 43, 70, 74–79, 152, 155–157, 172, 177
constitution 4, 13, 25, 33, 38, 108–109, 120, 146, 152, 178
contracts 36, 39, 42–43, 142, 157, 160–163, 167–168, 175, 179, 183
coordination 13, 53, 70, 109, 183, 184; across level (vertical) 28–30, 131; across sectors (horizontal) 28–30; passive coordination 117; proactive coordination 117
corridor alignment (transit) 2, 6, 55–58, 63–64, 89, 91–95, 100, 164–168
countywide planning policies 75–76
courts 108, 119, 159
cross-country comparative research 14
councils of government 72, 107
cultural rules/values/preferences 3, 15, 24, 34, 152, 173, 174

decision-making 1–12, 155–165, 170–171; cost-driven transit decision 174–175; decision-making centers 15–20, 21–35, 40, 57; integrated decision-making 33, 74, 155–171, 172–175, 178–180, 183–185; local decision-making 57–69, 77, 94–104, 137–144; spatially-driven transit decision 174–175; transit decision-making 32, 51–56, 89–93, 131–136; *see also* integrating mechanisms
degree of dependency 15–17, 21–23, 25–30, 33–34, 147, 154–171, 182, 184; interdependencies in planning systems 28–30 (*see also* power sharing); in Metro Vancouver region 37, 43, 53, 57; in Puget Sound region 72, 89–92, 95, 99; in Stuttgart region 114
density 9–11, 18–19, 31–33, 49–52, 60–61, 97, 85, 138–140; density requirements 123, 125–128, 146, 149, 150–151, 177; *see* minimum density for transit
development patterns *see* low-carbon development patterns; market-led dispersal/development patterns; polycentric development patterns; transit-connected communities; transit-oriented development

discretion 24, 116, 121, 126, 130
due process 106, 137–138

economic activity 78, 106
ecosystem 23, 121, 147
Eigenentwicklung (low-growth communities) 125
election 64, 91, 103, 128
enforcement/approval mechanisms 77–78, 85, 119, 143, 157–160, 174; *see also* integrating procedures
environmental protection 106, 117, 121, 178
European Energy Award 110, 179, 183

federal funding 57, 136–137, 183
federal level 38, 56, 64, 71–72, 90, 121, 136–137, 151, 178, 181
federal spatial planning law (Raumordnungsgesetz) 106–107, 114–115
federal zoning law (BauGB) 106–108, 111, 119–120, 137
forests 81, 129, 147, 150
frequent transit development areas 45–46, 49–51, 53, 177
functionally separated powers 32, 66, 69, 87, 106; coordinating role 175; implementing role 143, 175; regulatory role 143, 175

game theory 31
Germany 29, 33, 105–145, 146–147, 156–158, 164, 178, 180
GHG emissions 3, 9, 23, 37–45, 64, 79, 81, 112, 145, 177, 179, 181; GHG targets 37–38, 52, 73, 179
governance: arrangements 15, 17, 21–30, 161, 173–174, 178, 184–186; 5 dimensions of 15–17; *see also* climate governance; land use governance; metropolitan governance; multi-level governance; polycentric governance; transportation governance
ground rules of the game 2, 107, 151, 175, 179, 183, 185
growth boundary *see* urban containment boundary
growth centers *see* urban centers
growth management 4, 18–20, 70–79, 148, 162, 173–174, 178, 180
growth percentages 124–126, 149–151

growth projections 27, 43, 50–51, 84–85, 100, 147–150
growth targets 49–50, 82–85, 125–126, 143, 146, 148–151, 177

hierarchy of plans 105, 115
home-rule 33, 71–72, 82, 146, 157, 159
housing affordability 19, 54, 60, 177
housing market 151
housing quotas 148

implementation problem 182
implementing entities 4, 28–30, 36, 57, 146, 153–155, 167–168, 175, 178–179, 182–185
incrementalism 109, 176
infill development 67, 111–112, 126, 129, 140–142, 177
instrument choice 23
integrating land use and transit decisions 154–171, 171–173
integrating mechanisms 4, 28–30, 39, 146, 152–153, 154–171, 172–175, 182–186; self-regulated 34, 74–77, 79–80, 154–155, 183; legislatively defined 40–50, 57, 95, 114–118, 138, 154
integrating procedures 30–31, 85, 124, 147, 150–152, 155–161; *see also* alignment mechanisms; application mechanisms; conflict resolution mechanisms; enforcement/approval mechanisms; intergovernmental participation requirements; plan adoption mechanisms; review process
integration requirements 29, 72, 74, 152, 154–159, 163, 180; *see also* consistency requirement
interactions 15–17, 22, 25–26, 30–40, 156–160, 175; *see also* conflict; coordination; negotiations
interactive planning system 36–44, 156
interdependencies *see* degree of dependency
intergovernmental 25, 74, 150, 158, 160
intergovernmental participation requirements 156, 160; *see also* integrating mechanisms
issues 15–19, 31, 109, 146; as interdependent policy problem 15–19; of statewide significance 76, 146; of regional significance 33, 39–40, 42–44, 73, 146, 161; of local significance 73, 76, 108, 146, 161; *see also* responsibilities

job agglomeration 10, 113, 123
job-housing balance 10

King County 74, 77, 79–90, 80, 97, 147, 152, 162, 180, 182

Landesentwicklungsplan *see* statewide development plan
land re-designation process 48, 55, 58, 59–60
land use development 65, 107
land use designation map 45–47, 108–109, 118–120; local (Flächennutzungsplan) 108, 119, 138, 150, 160, 162, 163; regional 45–47
land use governance 41, 72, 105
land use mix *see* mix-of-uses
large lot zoning 146–147
leadership 14, 64–65, 76, 101, 169–170, 180, 182, 184–185
legal framework 4, 25, 39, 71, 76, 143; coherent 106
legal status of planning documents 29, 157, 160; contractually-binding 39, 152, 157, 160–163, 183; guiding/self-regulated/non-binding plans 6, 8, 29, 74, 117, 152, 157, 160, 182; legislatively-binding plans 29, 113, 116–120, 123, 132, 143, 163, 168, 183
legislative rules/legal rules 15, 24, 33–35, 71, 146, 154–171; *see also* constitution; legal framework; legal status of planning document; state-regulated; planning enabling legislation
level of detail 33, 146, 174
level of government 6, 13, 16, 18, 27–28, 33, 70, 87, 105–106, 109, 115, 146, 160, 170, 176, 178, 184; *see also* federal level; local level; regional level; state level/Bundesland/province
Local Government Act–British Columbia 5, 32, 36–40
local level 13–14, 19–20, 30–33, 57–69, 95–104, 137–144, 145–147, 151–153, 161–163, 168–171, 175–178
low-carbon development patterns 8–12, 36–39, 70–73, 109–113, 145–153, 172–184; as interdependent policy problem 15–16; actors involved in creating 17–19; challenges with

implementation of 30–31, 85, 91, 182; implementation of 168–171, 172–184
Lynwood Link Extension 100

map *see* land use designation map; zoning map
mapping of policies 130–131, 146, 150; *see also* land use designation map
market-led development 18–19
market-led planning system 19, 24, 28, 131, 143, 145, 168, 172
Mayors Council 41, 56, 64, 69, 164
metropolitan governance 1–2, 11, 13–20, 38, 72, 154, 173, 184–186
metropolitan planning organization 72, 78; *see also* regional planning organization
metropolitan region 2–3, 10–11, 13–20, 21, 31–35, 72, 99, 108, 111, 114, 145, 164, 173–174, 185
Metro Vancouver 5, 32, 36, 39–69
minimum density for transit 67, 117, 126–127, 139, 151
mix of uses 10–11, 18, 32, 70, 86, 88, 100, 108, 113, 146, 149, 169
modal choice 10
multi-county planning policies 77–78, 157, 159, 161
multi-level governance 14–15, 22, 35, 184
multiple accounts evaluation 55–56, 63–64, 168
mutually agreeable solutions 31, 94, 142, 174, 176

negotiations 43–44; between cities and county 84; between city and developers 61; between local and regional level 105, 116, 119; between transit provider and local governments 2, 5–6, 20, 31, 89, 93, 95–97, 100–101; role of regional level and RGS in shaping 165–166, 174–176
neighborhood engagement 60
neighborhood opposition 18, 101, 103, 168
neighborhood plan 55, 57–58, 60–61, 97, 101–103, 162, 169
Newton-Guildford Line 63–69

official community plan (OCP) 38, 40–43, 51, 55, 57–58, 65, 155, 180, 183
open spaces 112–117, 130, 140, 147–150; spatial policies to protect 129–131, 150
orchestration 176
Ostrom, Elinor 21–22, 29

paradox of climate mitigation 103
parcel-specific or parcel-based 47, 118, 121, 128–130, 143, 146, 150–151
park and ride 133–136
participation 69, 108–109, 171
participation mechanism 157–160, 182–183
permitting process 51, 65, 106, 108
plan adoption mechanisms 156, 158; *see also* integrating mechanisms
planning documents 28
planning enabling legislation 2, 4, 21, 24–25, 27–29, 36, 40, 72, 111, 155, 161, 163, 173, 180
planning system 4, 17, 21–35; aligned planning system 32–33, 38–44, 162 (*see also* interactive planning system); as source of rules-in-use 23–34; nested planning system 32–33, 105–145, 151 (*see also* spatial planning); overlapping planning system 32–33, 70–104 (*see also* growth management in Washington State); scale and scope of planning 27–28
policy: interdependent policy problem 15, 172–173, 185; making 79, 105, 173; objectives 5, 10–11, 23, 28, 105, 130, 163; sectors 4, 8, 14, 184; transfer 178, 184–185; types of 32, 116; *see also* spatial policies
polycentric development patterns 114, 121–122
polycentric governance 3, 13, 15, 22, 72, 184
population forecasts/projections 45, 84–85; *see also* growth targets
power relationships 16, 66, 152, 171, 184–186; *see also* functionally separated powers
power sharing 3, 13, 28–30, 33, 185
power struggles 4, 34, 86, 92, 99, 151, 175
preferred locations for housing and retail 113, 127–129, 139, 147, 149
principle of reciprocity (Gegenstromprinzip) 109, 156
principle of subsidiarity 105, 108
priority/primary development corridors 6, 107, 112–113, 121–125, 129–133, 136, 166

property owners 24, 27, 60, 65, 67, 81, 106–107, 116–117, 137–138, 152, 162, 169, 178
property rights 4, 24–25, 152, 178
Puget Sound Region 6, 70–104, 148–150, 157–170, 174–177, 180, 182
Puget Sound Regional council 74–79, 80–90, 93–94, 150, 152, 158, 162

rapid transit network 51–57, 89–93, 113, 124, 125, 131–136, 153, 164–168, 170, 177
real estate developers 18, 178
real estate market 57–59
regional context statement (RCS) 39–40, 42–43, 47–51, 151, 158, 160, 162, 176–177
regional geographies: as a spatial policy in Puget Sound Region 82–85, 87, 149–150; *see also* community classification
regional growth strategy (RGS) 2, 11, 18, 21, 28, 40–50, 74–88, 114–130, 145, 154, 160–167, 173; *see also* legal status of planning document
regional level 2, 13, 19–20, 32–35, 40–48, 74–90, 107–109, 114–120, 121–133, 145–153, 157–158, 175–179
regional planning organization 3–5, 13, 19, 32, 95, 106–107, 111, 116–119, 132, 146, 152–153, 170; *see also* metropolitan planning organization
regional transportation strategy (RTS) 164–168; in Metro Vancouver region 41, 51–54; in Puget Sound region 89–93; in Stuttgart region 131–136
region of short distances 111, 114
resource lands 80–81, 152
review process 39, 74, 77, 78, 119; *see also* integrating mechanisms
rezoning 18, 19, 50, 54, 58, 65, 81, 88, 94, 100–103, 168–171
rules-in-use 3, 15–17, 21–34, 145–153, 154–171, 172–173; *see also* cultural values; legislative rules; self-regulation; state regulation
rural areas/lands 37, 45–50, 67, 80–81, 107, 123, 125, 129, 148

Scharpf 30–31, 176
sectoral agencies 25, 107, 116, 120, 159, 176
self-governance 72
self-regulation 15, 33–35, 70, 72, 74–79, 88, 146, 154–171
single-family neighborhood 58, 67, 94, 100–103, 114, 142, 169, 178
smart growth 1, 10, 71
sound transit 70, 74, 89–101, 164–171
spatially-significant actions 120, 156, 163–164
spatial match 89, 167, 172
spatial mismatch 1–2, 175
spatial planning 4, 10, 105, 114–131, 136–137, 148–150, 173, 183
spatial plans 106, 115–116, 121, 132, 156, 173
spatial policies 4, 27, 28, 32, 78, 105, 122, 137, 145–153, 162–164, 178; as common goals and shared vision 15, 27, 66; growth affirming 146–148; growth limiting 146–148; in Metro Vancouver region 44–50; mix of spatial policies 146, 176; in Puget Sound region 80–89; responsibility for 146; in Stuttgart region 120–131, 136; types of spatial policies 146–147
spatial vision 3–4, 11, 30, 45, 69, 89, 121, 165–166
sprawl 10, 18, 37, 45, 76, 86, 121, 125
state level/Bundesland/province/senior level 13–14, 22, 34, 36–40, 72–74, 76, 106–107, 109–111, 145–146, 179–184
state-regulation 21, 24, 33–35, 146, 152, 160–161, 173, 183–185; as ground rules of the game 2, 107, 151, 175, 179, 183–185
statewide development plan 107, 112, 115, 156
statewide transportation plan 131
stewardship 109, 112
Stuttgart region 6, 105–144, 149–150, 157–165, 174–177, 181
substantive and procedural standards 22, 32, 107, 114, 145
suburban development 65–66, 71, 86, 123, 148

top-down 7, 28, 109, 143, 173
townhome development 65–66
transit: low-transit ridership 14, 154; funding for 23, 41, 56, 61, 90, 95, 136–137, 164; planning 132; provider 30–31, 153, 168–171; *see also* corridor alignment; rapid transit station
transit-connected-communities/centers 1–3, 8–12, 14, 44–45, 51–53, 89, 114, 120, 152, 165–168, 173

transit-oriented-development 10, 49, 59–60, 91–94, 99, 147
TransLink 36, 40–42, 47, 49, 51–57, 63–64, 91, 156, 159, 164–171, 175–176
transportation; emissions 9–12, 79, 85, 110, 145, 154; influence on land use 11; *see also* commuting patterns
trust 47, 151, 175, 182–185

unilateral actions 26, 31, 89, 166, 168, 174
United States of America 70–104
urban centers 8, 17, 27, 32, 146–151, 158, 160, 162, 164–168, 168–171, 175–177; locally-designated in Metro Vancouver region 45, 48–49, 148; preferred locations for higher-density housing in Stuttgart region 127–128; regionally-designated in Puget Sound region as growth centers 86–89
urban containment boundary 145–150, 150–151, 177–178; in Metro Vancouver region 45, 46–48, 57–58; in Puget Sound region 80–82
urban growth area (Siedlungsbereich) 76, 80–82
urbanized area 1–7, 10–13, 18–19, 32, 45, 70–76, 107, 112–115, 122–123, 130, 146–147, 150–151, 177; define urbanized area 149
urban planning 8, 108, 126, 173, 179

variances 120
vehicle miles traveled 85, 135; reduced VMT 8, 11, 19, 73, 81, 110–114, 128, 133, 177
Verband Region Stuttgart (VRS) 33, 107, 111–115, 120, 132, 150, 164
voters 89–91, 93, 100, 107, 164, 168

walk-shed 101
Washington State 3, 6, 32–35, 70–104, 146, 152, 155–160, 163–166, 179–183
win-win solutions 7, 19, 94, 101, 117, 119, 165, 175; *see also* mutually agreeable solutions
working groups 73, 179, 182–183

zoning 2–7, 17–19, 23–24, 22, 168–171, 178; code 97, 119–120, 145; maps 107–108, 116, 119–120, 130, 162; Standard Zoning Enabling Act (USA) 71; *see also* city of; federal zoning law; land use designation map; rezoning